CW01184051

FURRY PLANET

FURRY PLANET

A WORLD GONE WILD

JOE STRIKE

APOLLO
PUBLISHERS

Furry Planet: A World Gone Wild
Copyright © 2023 by Very Atomic Entertainment LLC

All rights reserved. No part of this book may be used or reproduced in any manner whatsoever without the written permission of the publisher, except in the case of brief excerpts in critical reviews or articles. All inquiries should be sent by email to Apollo Publishers at info@apollopublishers.com. Apollo Publishers books may be purchased for educational, business, or sales promotional use. Special editions may be made available upon request. For details, contact Apollo Publishers at info@apollopublishers.com.

Visit our website at www.apollopublishers.com.

Published in compliance with California's Proposition 65.

Interior design by Maeve Norton.
Front cover illustration by Kacey Miyagami.
Front cover photograph courtesy of Alamy.

Library of Congress Control Number: 2022945361

Print ISBN: 978-1-954641-10-5
Ebook ISBN: 978-1-954641-11-2

Printed in the United States of America.

This book is dedicated to the memory of Fred Patten, in honor of his unsurpassed devotion and service to the furry community.

CONTENTS

INTRODUCTION: WHAT, ME FURRY?	1
1: IT'S A FURRY WORLD	7
2: MAINSTREAM ANTHROPOMORPHIC MOVIES AND TELEVISION	35
3: MEETINGS WITH REMARKABLE FURS	61
4: MAINSTREAM ANTHROPOMORPHIC LITERATURE	91
5: SUITS ME JUST FINE	117
6: MAINSTREAM ANTHROPOMORPHIC THEATER	129
7: AUTHOR! AUTHOR!	139
8: MAINSTREAM ANTHROPOMORPHIC SCULPTURE	151
9: I DIG A BRONY	159
10: MAINSTREAM ANTHROPOMORPHIC ART	181
11: PRETTY AS A PICTURE (FURRY ART)	195
12: FURRY AFTER DARK	199
13: MAINSTREAM ANTHROPOMORPHIC PERFORMANCE ART	211
14: IS EVERYBODY HAPPY? (WELL, NOT QUITE)	237
15: MUSIC TO MY FURRY EARS (AND EYES)	249
16: MAINSTREAM, HERE WE COME (MAYBE)	261
17: THE FURRY FUTURE	273
AFTERWORD	281
ACKNOWLEDGMENTS	283
NOTES	287

INTRODUCTION: WHAT, ME FURRY?

Greetings, reader. You are about to enter the world of furry fandom. But what exactly *is* a furry you may ask, and what are they fans of?

Put simply, a furry—like myself—is a fan of, or fascinated by, anthropomorphic animals, animals with human qualities: speech, intelligence, and perhaps a semi-human body. Furries may share our human world or they may live in an alternate, all-animal universe. They may be cartoon animals, imaginary ones like dragons and griffins, storybook animals like Peter Rabbit, or furries' own imagined animal selves: their fursonas.

Furry fandom is a relatively recent addition to the pop culture firmament. We've only been around since the mid-1980s, but in the intervening years we've grown from a handful of folks to tens of thousands of people across the globe. Almost every one of us has been into anthropomorphic ("anthro") animals, keeping what we thought was our unusual, even weird interest to ourselves—until we discovered we were part of a worldwide community. Furry conventions now take place on every continent and it's a safe bet that even the smallest countries are home to more than a few furs.[1]

I wasn't there the day furry fandom was born. I like to say I discovered it, metaphorically speaking, on day three—not when it took its first breath, but early enough to meet the people who birthed our community.[2] I told their story in my previous book, *Furry Nation*, and in the years since *Furry Nation* was published, the furry community has grown far beyond anything its founders and earliest members would have dared imagine.

Furry Nation was subtitled *The True Story of America's Most Misunderstood Subculture* and furry was born in the good old U.S. of A. But like all ideas whose time has come, nothing could stop its spread, and several non-North American furs objected to the book's American focus. Perhaps this volume should be subtitled *The World's Most Misunderstood Subculture*, except that misunderstanding, while still sizeable, is slowly ebbing as we become better known.

Furry Planet: A World Gone Wild remedies *Nation*'s oversight of the global furry community and in the following pages you'll meet furs based worldwide who have been inspired by our misunderstood subculture and now have their own homegrown conventions. You'll also meet furry authors and other unique members of our community (including "bronies" and the overlapping *My Little Pony: Friendship is Magic* fandom), as well as non-furry mainstream creators of anthropomorphic characters. These are artists, authors, and filmmakers who have developed or employed intelligent animals as their subject matter. Their works and those of furry artists, authors, and filmmakers are simply different points on a single continuum.

Finally, we'll also cover the question that has haunted furs since the media moved beyond an automatic, "Ew, furries—*gross!*" into a more nuanced and understanding view of us: Will furry go mainstream? Here we'll dive into the questions of whether furry culture will be seen simply as another silly pop culture manifestation on the order of *Star Trek* or *Harry Potter*, another market to be monetized and catered to, or whether it's much more profound, with furs tapping into something important yet forgotten in our modern world, something hardwired into our minds. This would call out the common desire to imagine nonhuman animals on a more equal footing with us supposedly civilized beings. For most people this anthropomorphizing takes form in how we view or develop animal characters used in advertising or through sports mascots, cartoon characters, a fondly remembered childhood stuffed animal, or childhood companion animals.[3]

But furry fandom is about the *idea* of animals, not their actuality, and furs *viscerally* feel a connection and attachment to what these characters represent in our minds and hearts. An extension of this is that we also personally assume animal identities and *become* the animals of our imagination. Animals speak to us furs and take us to lands unreachable through our human legs. Since you're reading this book, you may already be on a furry journey—or perhaps you're about to embark on one.

FURRY PIONEERS

While countless people have contributed to the creation and growth of the furry community, four people stand out:

• Fred Patten (1940–2018), father of American anime fandom, author of hundreds of reviews and news articles about furry creativity, editor of numerous anthologies of furry short stories, and for seventeen years editor of *Rowrbrazzle*, a seminal amateur press association/fanzine of furry art and literature.

• Life partners Rod O'Riley and Mark Merlino, who together organized ConFurence Zero, the very first furry convention, which took place in 1989.

• Steve Gallacci, who at early- and mid-1980s sci-fi convention hotel room parties fascinated guests with art and concepts for a science fiction epic starring intelligent, human-like animals that was ultimately published as the comic book *Albedo Anthropomorphics*. This type of hotel room gathering came to be known as a "Gallacci group," and inspired others to bring their own art and stories to share with like-minded people. As these get-togethers became more popular, they took on a new name: "furry parties."

HOW HAS FURRY FANDOM CHANGED? INTERVIEWS WITH PIONEERS

STEVE GALLACCI:

Early on it consisted of fans of old-school "funny animal" comics, anthropomorphic characters, underground and alternative press publications, as well as animation of all kinds. It wasn't long before many fans became content providers, artists. Later, furry accessories (tails and ears) and then fursuits became increasingly popular. The newer fans were keen on having their own furry identities. Like any fandom, the "one of us" inclusive social aspect is always a thing; furry fandom has gone in that direction more than most other fandoms.

As an old fart/early player in the fandom, it's fun to see the brilliant artists and crafters who have come in, especially the many women in a genre that was very much a boys' game early on. At the same time, however, newer fans tend to view the fandom only as it is now. The older generation and their works can get sidelined due to the changing emphasis of the fandom away from some of its roots.

MARK MERLINO:

It just seems like certain people, no matter where they live, find animal characters attractive, but Rod and I had no way to know how many were afflicted with the "furry disease" back then [in the early 1980s]. Together with our friends we tried to find others like us on purpose. Being involved in early anime fandom we discovered anime fans all over the world, including in the US. But unlike in the rest of the world, the only anime we saw here were dubbed versions of shows like *Astro Boy* or *Kimba the White Lion*, shown here in the 1960s. If you wanted to see more recent anime you had to find fans who traded [imported] tapes and held screenings.

[Many anime fans—particularly *Kimba* enthusiasts—were also into anthropomorphic animals. Clusters of them met at those screenings, the nuclei of the future furry community; and, in Mark's words,] as it turned out, there were quite a lot!

ROD O'RILEY:

I'll say this and stand by it: in every nation on Earth you will find a furry community. Not just furry fans living there, but a furry community.

When we started, we largely assumed that our fandom already was global because we'd already seen anthropomorphic cartoons, advertising, educational materials, etc., from all over the world. Furry fandom was there all along; all we did was get people talking to each other.

A REMINISCENCE OF FRED PATTEN BY HIS SISTER SHERRY:

Perhaps the most apt quote from Fred is his dedication in his last book, *Furry Tales,* published posthumously: "To the pioneers (or maybe just the weirdos) who created furry fandom."

I bet this sums up exactly how Fred would describe himself:

- The "weird friendless kid" who eventually found friends who shared his love of sci-fi when he attended his first Los Angeles sci-fi club meetings in 1960.
- The "far-sighted fan" who recognized the worldwide popularity of Japanese anime and manga (comic books) he "introduced" to America in the late 1970s.
- As a senior, the founder of furry fiction and fandom. It thrilled him to see it spread like wildfire into so many countries in the twenty-first century.

＃ 1

IT'S A FURRY WORLD

Believe it or not, once upon a time furry fandom simply didn't exist. There were fans of animation, anime, "funny animal" comic books, and science fiction, and it seemed they had little in common. Yet when they started running into each other at end-of-day sci-fi convention hotel room parties, they discovered they did indeed have something in common: a fondness for anthropomorphic animal characters. From there, a shared spark was all it took. It wasn't long before there were furry hotel room parties where animation was devoured, sketchbooks were shared, and debates over the relative merits of various cartoon characters were held.

With time the parties grew larger, but the rooms didn't—until the right time finally arrived. On January 21, 1989, furry fandom was semi-officially born when ConFurence Zero, the first furry convention, was held at a Southern California Holiday Inn. A mere sixty-five anthropomorphics enthusiasts convened for a weekend of workshops (such as "A Furry Starter Kit" or "Furry

Costuming"), film screenings (*Animalympics* is always a furry favorite), art auctions, and plain old hanging around with like-minded folks.

Thirty-four years later, on December 1, 2022, 13,641 furs gathered in Chicago for the twenty-second Midwest FurFest. The attendance rate marked a whopping 21,000 percent increase over ConFurence's original sixty-five attendees. During the three decades between the two events, furry conventions large and small had sprung up across America and around the world, and interest in attending, as well the ability to publicize a festival, had soared.[4]

THE UNITED KINGDOM . . . OF FUR

In a country teeming with no small number of beloved rabbits (Beatrix Potter's Peter and friends, Alice's late-for-a-date bunny, *Watership Down*'s Hazel and company, to name a few), bears (such as Winnie the Pooh, Paddington, and Rupert), a detective mouse (*Basil of Baker Street*), and an animal community living more or less peacefully among humans (*The Wind in the Willows*), it might come as a surprise to learn that furry fandom didn't exactly take England by storm, even with help from a pair of visiting Americans.

But the United Kingdom did get there eventually, by way of the World Science Fiction Convention. Worldcon, as it is called, has been held in a different city every year since 1939 (with a few years off to fight Hitler). Host cities are selected as local sci-fi groups around the globe campaign to host it, and the winning cities often merge their Worldcon with their city's native sci-fi convention. The 1987 Worldcon (a.k.a. Conspiracy '87) was held in the UK seaside town of Brighton, and Californians Mark Merlino and Rod O'Riley were among the attendees. Two years later Mark and Rod would create ConFurence, the world's first furry convention, based on their experience hosting many hotel room furry parties, but back in 1987 they hoped their presence at Worldcon would help jumpstart a British furry scene.[5]

In British fur Tim Stoddard's book, *Furtannia: The History of the Furry Fandom in the United Kingdom*, he described the strategy Mark and Rod used to bring guests to their hotel room furry party in Brighton:

> . . . attendees reading the convention's daily newsletter, The Plot, would have spotted a peculiar event in the announcements section for that day: "FURRY Party, 9pm Saturday night for fans of Anthropomorphic Art, Comics, Lit. and Animation. Downlands Hotel, 19 Charlotte St., Room 6."
>
> Mark Merlino travelled to the convention with his partner Rod O'Riley and they were planning a furry party just like the ones they ran in the States. If the announcement in the newsletter was not going to gain interest, their own fliers probably would. They featured an anthropomorphic female fox drawn by Merlino stretching on top of a stone wall, with seldom of any clothing. The flier added some British-friendly humour by proclaiming "Those Yanks are having a FURRY PARTY!"[6]

Mark and Rod's furry party was held at a local bed-and-breakfast a good mile away from the convention itself. A helpful map below the fox's tail gave directions to the B&B, but once at the lodging, it was no simple matter to gain entry: one needed to tug a string attached to a copy of the flyer by the building's entrance. The string ran into the building and up to the pair's room, and the tug, a signal that curious con-goers were waiting outside the building, would send Mark or Rod downstairs to let them in.

Mark and Rod had brought an assortment of furry art to show, along with several videos, including the furry favorite *Animalympics*. Only about twenty curious people made the trek from the convention, several of whom had no idea what a "furry" was. There was more interest in a recent anime film, *Royal Space Force: The Wings of Honnêamise*, that several fans of the genre were eager to see, even on Mark's tiny seven-inch screen, with Rod explaining it since it was not subtitled.

Despite the party and efforts by Mark and Rod, British furry didn't exactly take off like a rocket as a result; instead, it was a slow build-up of "housecons," where a handful of furs and fur-curious folks gathered at someone's home to share furry art and watch animation and anime videos. (One housecon impressed two visiting German furs so much that they returned home and launched what would eventually become Eurofurence, Europe's largest, and the world's longest continually running, furry convention.) As for a larger event, several unsuccessful attempts were made at launching a British furry convention; among them, BritFur, FurCon UK, and BritFur 2005. It became a running joke in the British furry community that they would never enjoy a convention of their own.

Actually, it was just a matter of time. Just as Steve Gallacci's *Albedo Anthropomorphics* galvanized America's earliest furries, the comic had a similar effect on Britons unaware they were carrying the furry gene. Stoddard's *Furtannia* tells the story of Simon Barber, a young man who'd been writing and illustrating his own furry comics, unaware that a fandom of like-minded people was developing in the United States. One day he came across a copy of *Albedo* in an Oxford comics shop and experienced an "I'm not the only one!" moment. Barber then began corresponding with American furs and contributing to US furry publications, and became one of the earliest members of the developing network of British furries and their associated housecons.

In early 1992, a handful of American furs on their way back from the French Angoulême International Comics Festival visited a housecon (jokingly called "the First British Furry Micro-ConFurence" by its organizer, Ian Curtis[7]) in Yateley, a small village west of London.[8] This led to a cross-pollination of American and British furry fans that helped set the stage for the UK furry scene. The first step was the Yateley housecon becoming an ongoing event, and in time England would have its own furry convention.

Also boosting England toward its own furry convention was the beginning of online gathering spots known as MUDs (Multi-User Dungeons) and "mucks" (a play on MUDs). FurryMUCK, created in 1990, became the best-known virtual furry world. Now furries great distances apart (such as in the United States and United Kingdom) could communicate far more easily, and in real time. FurryMUCK attracted no small number of British furries, including Ian Stradling and Tiffany "Foxy" Fox, who organized a housecon so that they and other local furries could meet in person.

While an actual homegrown British furry convention would take several years to come together, housecons and other temporary gatherings sufficed for many years. Then in 1998, a pair of university students launched a meetup that continues to this day. The LondonFurs, as the meetup's attendees would become known, have consistently gathered at a pub on the third Saturday of every month (over 350 times since 1998!) to see friends, catch up on news, and hoist a few mugs of beer. The meetups are free to attend and fursuits are welcome—there's even changing space in the pub to facilitate fursuiting. And as the meetups have increased in popularity throughout the years (currently averaging about 150 furs per meetup), the group has moved to ever larger venues. The spacious Tank & Paddle pub in Minster Court (where they invite guests to sample their gin of the month) has been hosting the event since 2020.

Finally, it was time for the first British furry convention—an event so long promised but never delivered that many furs assumed this one was doomed to failure as well. To make it happen, a team of BritFurs experienced in organizing furmeets (with input from European and American furs already familiar with hosting conventions) combined their expertise and in 2005 started planning a convention that wouldn't take place until 2008, thus giving them plenty of time to work out any bugs beforehand.

On June 20, 2008, the premiere iteration of ConFuzzled (memories are hazy as to who was responsible for the name) took place at a Manchester youth hostel.[9] Its attendance of 136 furs may sound meager by today's standards, but it was enough to get things rolling, and almost half the attendees were fursuited, a percentage rarely approached at larger conventions. By the end of the convention, £1,610 was raised for the convention's charity, the Badger Trust, an amount derived from an average donation of £12 per attendee.[10]

Now based in Birmingham (eighty-six miles closer to London for the convenience of that city's furry community), ConFuzzled's attendance has increased more than tenfold, from the original 136 to the 2,100 furs at ConFuzzled 2022, an increase of 1,444 percent in just fourteen years. The recent attendance rates have made ConFuzzled the second largest non-North American fur convention, trailing only Germany's Eurofurence. And it's no longer the United Kingdom's sole furcon, as it has convention company in Bristol, Cornwall, Northumberland, and Glasgow, among other UK cities.

"WHERE THE ELBE RIVER FLOWS INTO THE NORTH SEA": THE BIRTH OF EUROFURENCE

Given the passion for furry fandom in the United States, one might assume that the longest continually running furry convention would be an American institution—but one would be wrong to do so. While ConFurence, the very first furry convention, was held in California in 1989, after setting the stage for all future furry cons to follow, ConFurence lost its mojo and breathed its last breath in 2003.

In the decades since ConFurence's last convention, dozens of furcons have become furry fixtures in cities around the US, attracting attendees ranging in number from a few hundred to several thousand. Anthrocon, born in 1997 as Albany Anthrocon and operating every year since, almost snags the title of the longest continually held furry convention—but Eurofurence, launched in 1995 as the first furry convention outside the US, has it beat by two years. Attendance at the first Eurofurence, by the way? A grand total of nineteen—a number you could count on your fingers and toes and still have a pinky or two left over.

That first Eurofurence was the doing of two young Germans known by the names Unci Narynin and Tes-Tui-H'ar, who in May 1995 attended UK Fur CON 2 in Oxford, one of the British housecons that preceded the birth of an actual, not-in-anyone's-living-room British fur convention.

In my personal correspondence with the two, I learned that Unci (also known as Tobias Kohler) always had a thing for felines, a preference he attributes to his family having had a black cat during his childhood and his longtime fondness for snow leopards. (His fursona name is a combination of the snow leopard's Latin name, *Panthera uncia*, and a region in Kyrgyzstan where they're often found.) Tes-Tui-H'ar is not of this Earth, but an alien from another galaxy stranded here when his spaceship's linear drive quit working—at least according to his creator, Gerrit Heitsch, who is definitely of this planet.[11]

Both men had access to the internet at the universities where they studied, both were fascinated by anthropomorphic characters, and both found their way to the alt.fan.furry message board where they discovered the furry community and each other. Kohler had been in touch with Silvermane, an organizer of UK Fur Con 1, one of the housecons small groups of British furries held in lieu of actual conventions, and when he learned Tes had been to the first one, they both decided to attend the second UK Fur Con in 1995.

"It was a small meeting of like-minded people," Heitsch told me, as he described that second furcon. "I got exposed to all kinds of furry comics, *Albedo* among them, and I was even able to find some at the local comics store. So we thought we should do something like this in Germany."

"Tes's parents owned a farm building in rural northern Germany," Kohler explained.[12] "That seemed like a good place to invite furries from various places in Europe. A good number of them came from Scandinavia, so a place in northern Germany was more convenient than anything farther south. Inspired by ConFurence, I named the event EuroFurence. We made a website, printed maps and signs, planned some events, and in July 1995 had a few nice days connecting to other furries. I even designed a typeface for the convention, which I would later release under the name Eurofurence."

Eurofurence 1 was a success, and a splendid time was enjoyed by all. The majority of attendees were German, but also included were five Britons and one attendee each from Denmark, Sweden, and Finland, together representing Scandinavia.

"Everyone was well behaved," Heitsch recalled, probably in relief that his parents' farmhouse was still intact after the event. "There was no damage except a broken glass lampshade when someone tripped over the lamp's power cord."

Eurofurence 2 was held in Sweden and organized by new people. "The idea of the con was to have a different team hold it in a different location every year. That way it would have a different flavor every time, and nobody would wear themselves out doing the same thing every year," Heitsch continued. "The idea was also that there shouldn't be an elite dominating the community by defining what it's all about." As things played out, after creating, naming, and holding the event that would eventually become the world's longest continually held furry convention, Unci and Tes passed Eurofurence onto other paws. For most years since 1997 it has been organized by a German electronic musician, Sven "Cheetah" Tegethoff—who evidently doesn't mind wearing himself out as Eurofurence's head honcho.

Year by year the convention's attendance increased: it broke into three digits in 1999, four digits in 2011, and in 2022, 3,453 furs attended the convention.[13] Other than 1998's Eurofurence 4, which was held in the Netherlands, and 2003's Eurofurence 9, which was held in the Czech Republic, Eurofurence has always been held in various German cities. Since 2014, it has been held in Berlin's Estrel Hotel, the largest convention, entertainment, and hotel complex in Europe. Not too shabby for an event that began with nineteen furs in a rural German farmhouse.

FROM RUSSIA, WITH FUR

The Soviet Union wasn't known for its sense of humor. In the legendary words of Russian émigré comic Yakov Smirnoff, "In America you can always find a party. In Russia, Party always finds you."

Even so, the USSR allowed numerous, government-approved humor magazines that did little more than poke fun at bureaucrats or minor social problems. The best-known of these magazines might be Крокодил (*Crocodile*), which was named for the toothy animal's sardonic smile. And yes, "government-approved humor" is probably the ultimate oxymoron.

In this post-Soviet age, things have definitely lightened up behind that long-gone "iron curtain"—so much so that Russia now has its own vital and growing furry community. The roots of Rusfurence, the country's largest furry convention, date back to the 1999 birthday party of Ukiwa, a Moscow cheetah—the only one of his furry circle to have their own apartment. The gathering was nicknamed RusCon, and it became an annual event. Its six attendees became eight the next year, and in 2001 the get-together broke into the double digits when twenty-three Russian furs assembled. Soon, as with furcons everywhere, attendance was doubling and redoubling, causing the gathering (now renamed Rusfurence) to move to ever-larger venues. In 2019, its final pre-COVID gathering brought 135 furs (not a bad number considering the country's vast expanse) to a four-star hotel in a Moscow suburb.

"There are definitely more than I can count," Taffka, a Moscow unicorn active in the local furry scene, shared with me to describe the number of furs in Russia. "Ten years ago I would say about three or four thousand. I'm not so sure now, probably one or two thousand in Moscow alone. There are furry groups on Russian social networks with forty or fifty thousand members. And of course, I have [furry] friends in adjoining countries—Ukraine, Belarus, Moldova, and elsewhere. I think it's good that furry fandom does not notice borders between countries."[14]

Taffka's journey toward furry fandom began as it has for so many others around the globe: watching cartoons. "*Robin Hood, Tom and Jerry, Bambi, The Lion King* . . . most of all, *Spirit: Stallion of the Cimarron*. It was one of my first furry interests," she tells me, "I probably watched my VHS tape of it at least a hundred times. One day, my younger brother told me he found an interesting forum with animal and human characters, named furries. After a long night exploring the forum, I decided to make my own profile. I loved unicorns and decided to make one my fursona."

Taffka is an active participant in the Moscow furry scene and even briefly served as Rusfurence's chairperson. She met her mate, Llanowar, a gold dragon, at Rusfurence 2011, and he proposed to her at the 2014 convention's closing ceremonies. In 2014 they launched their own convention, SillyCon ("for silly furs"), or using the Russian word for "silly," TupiCon (ТупиКон).

According to Taffka, the Russian furry community has grown significantly and today is divided into groups by age, interests, and more. As she says, "Everyone wants something of their own. There aren't a lot of large conventions in Russia, but there are more and more small ones, with maybe fifty or sixty furries attending each. Furry teens also tend to gather separately from older ones. This is great because everyone can find a furry gathering they feel at home in."[15]

When I ask Taffka how the public responded to fursuiters, she says it wasn't easy at first, but that progress has been made. "Our suits seemed unusual to ordinary people. Some perceived it as pampering and stupid entertainment. Kids and adults tried to pull our tails. It was especially dangerous to run into drunk people. Now everything is much simpler. People accept the unfamiliar more easily, and information can be found faster on the internet. In addition, many different subcultures have appeared, so furries no longer stand out as freaks. There are lots of teens who explain furry to their parents while they build their own fursuits. For Russia, it has become a popular subculture."

Unfortunately, not everyone in Russia is accepting of furries. The country has one prominent anti-furry crusader, Andrew Tsyganov, who is chairman of the totally unofficial but official-sounding Commission for the Protection of Children from Destructive Content. According to the Russian news agency TASS, Tsyganov claimed, "LGBT+ ideology, radical feminism, all these furries, child-free—they, of course, should be recognized at least as extremism, extremist ideology."[16]

And Tsyganov didn't stop at his chest-pounding bombast. He took things to the next level when he and his allies harassed attendees of an August 2021 fursuit walk[17] in Moscow's Kolomenskoye Park, where he accused the furs of pedophilia, among other things. According to an extensive article on Dogpatch Press, one of the furry community's top news websites, Tsyganov confronted the marchers and falsely claimed, "You were banned! Why are you still going out? You are LGBT propaganda! I have children, I do not want people like you to pose a threat to them and society."[18]

In response, the fursuiters stood up to Tsyganov and called his bluff on his threats to send the police, who were already familiar with the 'suiters. One of the furs told him, "OK, you can call, but you will be fined for knowingly making a false call. And your personal opinion is not interesting to anyone." Finally Tsyganov retreated.

Following the episode, Matvey Mukhin, one of the furs at the walk, contacted Sergey Mironov, a sympathetic politician. Mironov let Mukhin know Tsyganov was "a member of the public chamber and not a Roskomnadzor [the Russian body regulating communications] official [and thus] only an opposition activist who belongs to the radical Christian anti-vax movement ROS."

According to Skip Doggy, another Russian fursuiter, public opinion has turned against Tsyganov. "Bloggers began to defend the furries. People said Tsyganov was simply sick or incompetent."[19] At least for the time being, Moscow's furs are free to walk and meet in the city's public parks.

THE LITTLE RED (FURRY) DOT

One might not expect a newsgathering organization covering the worldwide furry scene to be based in Singapore, but that's where you'll find Global Furry Television (GFTV).

In March 2022 GFTV's YouTube channel posted a half-hour phone interview with a Ukrainian fur living in Poland as a refugee, and in it he shared his experiences as Russia's invasion of his country was underway. (The possibility that Russian and Ukrainian furs under different circumstances might be mingling at a furry convention, instead of trying to kill each other in service of their countries, was not far from his mind.) Other stories around that time on GFTV's NewsHub included a report that the Polish furry convention Gdakon would offer Ukrainian attendees ticket and hotel refunds, another on possible financial improprieties by a convention organizer, one on changes to the Florida furry convention Megaplex's board of directors, an article on how Eurofurence was facing spiraling hotel room rates, and a look back at "2021: The Year in Furry"—all written by GFTV's founder and project head, Pawsry Hamktxchuzhni.[20] Pawsry's journey to the heart of furrydom began with an interest in sports mascots and culminated in a crush on Zabivaka, the 2018 FIFA World Cup's Eurasian wolf mascot. Searching for more art of the endearing canine, Pawsry quickly came across furry postings, videos, and websites.

"Well, I'm not the kind who went super crazy over furry fandom 'classics' like *The Lion King*, *Zootopia*, and *Robin Hood*." Pawsry explained to me. "It [was] mascot fandom. The global mascot community is chock full of anthropomorphic animals!"[21]

Pawsry describes himself as a media production design student and an "unofficial furry fandom journalist," which explains his eager reportage on breaking furry news. Journalism was already dear to his heart when he started working for GFTV—his interest having formed in childhood when he drew and wrote his own newspapers. In 2018 he launched GFTV, and today he heads up its fourteen-person staff, who are gathered from around the world.

Like many furs who felt like outsiders before discovering the community, Pawsry was, in his own words, "relentlessly abused, ostracized, and bullied" as a kid. But furry fandom excited him, perhaps even saved him. As he told me, "Furry fandom presented itself as a bright land of opportunity, color, and hope. I was finally pulled in, embraced, and accepted for who I am. I'm improving a lot emotionally and psychologically through this community."

Freedom House, an organization that rates countries' degrees of internal liberty, rates Singapore as "partly free,"—but, thankfully, that includes the freedom to be furry.[22] According to Pawsry, "the little red dot's" [the nation's proud nickname for itself] furry community may be infinitesimal compared to the furry capital nation called the United States of America, but here furries are still able to do what we do best: art, fursuiting, and having fun together."[23] That fun includes Singapore's Alter Ego Cosplay, a multiday furry convention that was held at the Jewel Changi Airport, a nature-themed shopping and entertainment complex near Singapore's Changi Airport. When the fursuiters gathered there, in the public's eye, shoppers were entertained by the sudden profusion of colorful animals in their midst. They've also delighted locals who've stumbled upon them while they've gathered together for public walks, photoshoots, and other activities.

GFTV, which offers news articles, video clips, and more, evolved out of several earlier versions of the service, including one devoted to sports mascot fandom. According to Pawsry, the channel's audience skyrocketed as more people started to take notice and several joined the channel's staff. ("There are furries from seven countries under our wing.") GFTV now includes a newshub, YouTube channel, Facebook page, and other social media outlets; their videos are even carried on China's Bilibili, a hugely popular Chinese streaming service similar to YouTube that also functions as a gaming platform. The channel has evolved from what Pawsry calls "informal YouTuber commentary" into one attempting to cover the furry scene "neutrally and objectively," a challenging goal in this polarized age, especially when some might see impartial coverage as inherently biased.

I'm told that GFTV's international audience includes thousands of Chinese furs, who, like the rest of their worldwide audience, appreciate its in-depth coverage of the worldwide furry scene and how the COVID-19 pandemic has postponed or ended many conventions, or at the very least decimated their attendance.

The Little Red Dot might even be considered a hub of world furry culture. As Pawsry says, "Given our location in Asia, Singaporean furries can hit two birds with one stone: experiencing both the Western and Eastern furry cultures."

MADE IN FURRY CHINA

As the lure of furry knows no borders or boundaries, it was inevitable that it would take root in China, the planet's most populous country, where thousands of young people, many of them already anthropomorphically inclined, have discovered the worldwide furry community. As just one example of this, the Furry Forum on China's Baidu Tieba social media site numbered over twenty-five thousand followers as of a 2021 count, and likely boasts many more today.[24]

Among China's furry fans are Man Ying-laam, a twenty-two-year-old Hong Kong furry, who shared in a media interview that he has "always had an obsession with hyenas," has been drawing them since grade school, and in recent years, thanks to furry fandom, has become one through his *Hyaenidae* fursona, Essex.[25] There's also the furry who goes by the name Kush, who came across furry fandom on the internet and immediately realized he was a fur. In an interview with a local reporter, he shared, "I remember thinking, *That is exactly me*." And there's Dingz, who "found himself" after a stint suited as Toys "R" Us's giraffe mascot, and not long afterward discovered the furry community online. In 2017 he constructed his first fursuit (an antlered animal he calls a "Druid bird" that is named Yoeleaf) and today he builds suits for local furs.[26] Then there's Lin Yuntao, a.k.a. Robert Lynn, a.k.a. the "blue fox," who, in my humble opinion, is China's number-one *Furry Nation* fan. Like so many furs, Robert's first exposure to talking animals was courtesy of Walt Disney. "I was a huge fan of Mickey Mouse comics," Lynn explained to me in an email. "I bought every issue as soon as it appeared at the local newsstand."

"*Ratatouille* was one of the very first movies I fell in love with," he went on, explaining that his love for anthropomorphic animals deepened with the animated DVDs his dad brought home. "While other kids spent their weekends taking math or music classes, I was watching Disney films like *One Hundred and One Dalmatians* and *Lady and the Tramp*." He also soaked up non-Disney TV shows like *Backkom*, a South Korean series starring an accident-prone polar bear. With this passion, it was only a matter of time before Lynn discovered furry fandom, courtesy of Bilibili. What sets Bilibili apart from its rivals is the viewers' ability to comment in real time on the current video, creating an endless progression of messages traveling right-to-left across the screen (often to the point of obscuring the video itself).

Changed is one of the many playable games on Bilibili, and one that Lynn found particularly intriguing. The gamer plays as the game's protagonist, Colin, who wakes up in a strange laboratory building and then must face various monstrous creatures as they attempt to capture and "transfur" him into one of their kind—very often an animal. This led to people commenting on furries. As Lynn shares, "In the videos people posted about the game, one word kept showing up: 'furry.' I wondered, what on Earth is a furry?" So he took to the internet and found out, describing his findings and revelations to me by sharing: "Furries are people who love something fluffy, but they're not dog or cat lovers. . . . One day a thought occurred to me: *How did such a huge subculture come into existence without anything written about its origins, about what it really is?*"

A relentless internet search eventually led Lynn to my book *Furry Nation* and an understanding of the enjoyment of the fandom. He shares, "I finally understood why we're furries: to express ourselves, to rest a little in this cruel mortal world, to release our beast inside."

Xiao Yao would agree. Described by China's online publication Sixth Tone as "a husband and father from the eastern Fujian province [who] likes to put on his fursuit after he gets home from work," Yao shared with a reporter that "this act helps him release the childlike part of himself that he has to suppress to survive in a cutthroat business world." According to Yao, "It allows me to escape the routine of everyday life. . . . Furry fandom is a place where I can stop thinking about my mortgage, work, and kid for a moment."[27]

A video accompanying the article shows Yao in his blue dragon fursuit playing with his toddler son (who seems unimpressed with his father's fursona). After the child is put to bed, Yao sits on the edge of his own bed and just minutes before midnight is clicking away on his laptop, trying to keep up with his real-life responsibilities as a data analyst. He explains to the camera that he is very happy being a furry and that his fursona is just another version of himself, but with parts of his personality he can't show in real life: happy, cheerful, very silly, and a bit dumb.

Hong Kong's Man Ying-laam calls Taiwan and Singapore Asia's "emerging [furry] cities" and shared in a media interview, "I think Taiwan has about one thousand furries and Singapore more than two hundred." Kush, meanwhile, counts himself as one of Hong Kong's estimated fifty furries and added, "Almost all of the local furries first met on now-defunct old school forums. I'm glad we now have social media, which really helps us find each other."[28] An accurate estimate of the gender composition of any genre is more often a matter of opinion than statistics, and furry fandom is no different. Man Ying-laam sees it as a 70/30 split between male and female in China vs. a more equitable 60/40 in the West. Dingz isn't as optimistic and estimates a 90/10 male-to-female divide due to furry's lingering reputation in many quarters as a kink scene. "The preconceived notion of what furries do scares people away," he commented to a reporter. "They overlook the fact that the furry lifestyle is multifaceted."[29]

LAND OF THE RISING FUR: JAPAN'S *KEMONO* CULTURE

If there's any place on the globe where "East meets West," it's Japan. With many anthropomorphic animals in the country's mythology (supernatural *kitsune* foxes, shape-shifting tanuki raccoon dogs, and the ancient "Animal Frolic" scrolls, medieval scrolls depicting animals such as rabbits and frogs behaving like humans, to name a few), it's not surprising Japan would develop its own indigenous anthro subculture: *kemono*. Nor is it surprising in this global age of instantaneous worldwide communication that American furry and Japanese kemono culture would mix, mingle, and cross-pollinate.

The organizers of the Japan Meeting of Furries (JMoF) were kind enough to fill me in on both their convention and local kemono culture:

> Even though Japan Meeting of Furries is currently the sole furry convention in Japan, they absolutely don't think of themselves as representing all of Japan's furries. The JMoF is just one aspect of Japanese furry fandom. Japanese furry culture is a blend of both Western and Eastern cultures. For instance, Pokémon's Charizard resembles a Western dragon, while Ninetales is reminiscent of the nine-tailed kitsune
>
> It's often said that cartoonist Osamu Tezuka influenced furry culture in Japan, while Disney shaped it in the US, but in reality it was their influence on each other that led to these works' creation.
>
> Both furry and kemono fandom are gatherings of people who like characters that combine animal and human qualities.

Kemono's original meaning is "an animal with hair all over its body that walks on all fours." It's often used as a term to represent all animals, including reptiles, birds, and others, even if they are imaginary.

Just as with furry fandom in the West, kemono's large growth was spurred by the spread of the internet, and helped develop both fan cultures. There are differences of course, kemono fandom built upon *doujinshi*[30] conventions like Comiket ["Comic Market"] and Kemoket ["Kemono Market"],[31] as well as companies' social media sites (Pixiv, Twitter, etc.), and personal websites. We think Western furry fandom originally developed through conventions, fanzines, and amateur press associations that helped form a network for fellow furries.[32] In Japan there were no conventions or venture companies by kemono fans. Instead, so-called otaku markets and personal-level networks created the original framework for the growing creation and distribution of kemono content, giving the impression that kemono is part of Japan's otaku culture.[33]

We think a lot of furries use their fursona to show their furry self. In kemono fandom, the predominant tendency is still to view kemono and the self as two separate entities. From our perspective, we think the concept of a fursona has yet to permeate the kemono fandom.

In Japan it's pretty much typical for everything to have its own mascot character. To a large part this was spread by department stores, amusement parks, and other entities that hold shows with people in costumes featuring anime or *tokusatsu*[34] characters (superheroes, *kaiju*,[35] *kaijin*,[36] and others) in an effort to draw in customers. From there and into the 2000s, local governments and organizations started creating their own mascot characters called *yuru-chara* as part of their promotional activities that gained popularity and are now widespread in Japan today. We think this mascot character culture has to a certain degree influenced Japanese furry culture.

Costumes for mascot characters and costumes (fursuits) for kemono characters look different, but in the 1990s and 2000s, fans of kemono costumes had meetups with mascot costume fans and many people were fans of both. Now there's ample opportunity to see mascot or superhero costume shows, so it's very possible they will have an influence on kemono culture.

In Japan, the impression is that people are more reluctant to talk while fursuited or take their [costume's] head off in front of people than they are in the West. Someone wearing a fursuit is seen as that fursuit character. This may be the influence of Japan's way of thinking about characters (they possess their own identity) versus cosplay culture (where one is portraying a character from a creative work).[37] We think the number of furries who wear their fursuit to "become" their fursona has increased.

Generally speaking, Japan's fursuits have the tendency to have big eyes and a small nose and mouth. Many characters evoke a *kawaii* appearance and will use a lot of stuffing to make their overall proportions look rounder.[38] Many think it's the influence of anime and manga culture.

People were very surprised at how quickly JMoF attendance increased, from one hundred in 2013 to 1,372 at the 2020 convention. The increased attendance may have been because of social media like Pixiv and Twitter, where the kemono community's visibility has increased; that had a large effect on making it easier to attract new people. Despite strict attendance conditions following the COVID-19 pandemic, there were still 556 attendees at the 2022 convention. They were exceedingly cooperative with the measures to prevent infection, like refraining from having parties with people moving between rooms, even though it was a convention.

One thing unlikely to be seen at an American furry convention: group calisthenics! "Morning Radio Exercises" was an event where people gathered in the hall lobby in the morning for calisthenics set to a piano accompaniment. Because the Japanese educational system has adopted this kind of event for its schools, many Japanese people know how to move their bodies to it. Among the participants in this event there were even some people who participated while wearing a fursuit.

Japan Meeting of Furries has been covered respectfully by local newspapers and TV shows. They [furries] still have their guard up after seeing how furries have been covered overseas. Their policy is to refuse admittance to any reporters who might have malicious motives in reporting on them.

When individual furries are shown on Japan's typical variety shows, they aren't unfairly attacked, but they're usually shown as "eccentric people." Most shows aren't respectful, however, [and] this isn't just limited to furries. The Japanese media has a tendency to not pay enough respect to any subject they report on, but it's their impression furries are treated more respectfully when they're covered as creators rather than fans.

"G'DAY, FURRY"

There's an old expression that a camel is a horse designed by a committee, with each member having added features until it became comically overladen. If there were ever an animal that might have been designed by a cartoon studio, it would have to be the kangaroo. Its upright, two-legged posture gives it an anthropomorphic semi-human appearance, for starters. And when kangaroos lie down leaning on an elbow or are relaxing while flat on their back, they look so human that their photos are easily edited to show them holding beer cans or smoking cigarettes. And those hops—did you ever see a more cartoony means of locomotion? All that's missing is a *"sproing!"* sound effect. And even though their pouch is where real-world female roos nurse their young, there's no reason a male cartoon kangaroo can't have one too. All of which leads to the question, why are there no Australian kangaroo fursuiters?

"Come to think of it, I can only think of one roo fursuit, although there might be others," Aussie furry Bernard Doove tells me over email. "It seems most local fursuiters want something a bit more exotic."[39]

A prolific furry author, Doove created the Chakat Universe centered on a race of feline centaurs he (as his fursona Chakat Goldfur) and guest authors have explored in numerous stories. Doove grew up in and still lives near Melbourne, Australia's second most populous city, located on its southern edge. Living not just "down under" the globe but down under most of Australia, he was far from the developing furry culture in the United States and elsewhere. He shares:

> I was just about as far away from the burgeoning [southern California] furry fandom as you could get. Seeing as this was the pre-internet era and personal computers were still a novelty, I had no idea that a fandom existed before around 1990. However, I could be regarded as always having been a furry because I assiduously collected any anthropomorphic material that I could get my hands on. I came across a small ad from Bear and Cat Comix, which was published by Scott Alston, who was famous for drawing extremely well-endowed furry ladies. I knew next to nothing about him, but I was curious enough to send off a money order for some of his material. This opened my eyes to what was available, and I sought out more.

At some point, I made a connection with some other Australian furry fans and got involved with Australia's first furry fanzine, *South Fur Lands*. The first issue was published in July 1995, and I contributed to every issue before becoming its publisher, and then until it ended its run in 2011. Basically, the internet killed it. Contributions of art and stories had become a trickle, and sales had plummeted—but thanks to it, I got to know other furry fans in both Australia and New Zealand.[40]

Like a moth to the furry flame, nothing could keep Doove away from the community he felt at home in. In 1994 he flew eight thousand miles across the Pacific to attend his first furry convention: ConFurence 5 in Irvine, California, forty miles south of Los Angeles. It would be his first furcon, but far from his last.

In 1994 the first Australian furry convention was still fourteen years in the future. In the meantime OzFurry, a mailing list of local furs, was established to help the growing community stay connected. In 1996 Doove and a group of fellow furs went to the Sydney OzCon5 pop culture convention where Doove met Craig "Jenner" Hilton, creator of the long-running *Doc Rat* web comic.[41] From there, just as in England (it must be a British Empire thing), various casual meetups evolved into a named event, and in 1999 Melbourne in December Furmeet (MiDFur) was born. According to Doove:

> It was just a meetup at a restaurant where nine or ten of us chatted about furry stuff, but it was fun and it was decided to do

it again the next year. And the next. And the next . . . . [As] MiDFur started growing in attendance . . . we had to move to a larger restaurant. By the ninth furmeet, the numbers had grown to something like fifty, and I was asked to help turn the furmeet into a full-blown convention. I agreed to be part of the staff and was put in charge of the dealers den and creating a "conbook" (the convention's souvenir magazine).

In December 2008, MiDFur 10 became Australia's first official furry convention. The event attracted 177 furs to a hotel ballroom and raised nearly $4,000 AUD for the Royal Society for the Prevention of Cruelty to Animals, an animal welfare organization. As with other furry conventions, MiDFur's attendance rate increased from year to year: 247 in 2009, 339 the following year, 399 the next, and maxed out in 2012 with 474 attendees. But with the growing popularity, it became impossible for the growing convention to find December convention space, making the "D" for December pointless when it took place in a different month. In 2014 MiDFur's name was changed to ConFurgence and this was used for its final five years, until the convention's organizers headed west to pursue career opportunities.

Meanwhile, what would prove to be Australia's largest ongoing furry convention was picking up steam. Furry Down Under (FurDU), first launched in 2010, is held on Australia's Gold Coast, a resort area on the country's eastern shore near Brisbane. With its profusion of theme parks—everything from the Dreamworld theme park to the Big Wedgie Inflatable Water Park— the Gold Coast is the Australian equivalent of Florida's Orlando. Starting with a mere ninety-two attendees in 2010, FurDU's attendance grew to eight hundred in 2019, and passed the one thousand mark in 2022, its first post-COVID year. Local gatherings in Perth, Melbourne, and Canberra round out the Aussie furry scene.

"Where I once was a significant part of the Aussie furry fandom," Doove reflects, "my role has become minor, and I'm relatively unknown among the younger fans. But it's the youth that grow the fandom, and I am happy to have done my small part in paving the way. Now I get to sit back and enjoy it."

2

MAINSTREAM ANTHROPOMORPHIC MOVIES AND TELEVISION

When did anthropomorphic animals escape kiddie cartoons and breakfast cereal boxes and start appearing in mainstream movies and TV series? Perhaps this dates back to the 2014 debut of *BoJack Horseman*, Netflix's show about a washed-up TV star who happens to be an anthropomorphic horse in a universe where humans and humanlike animals live side by side and is trying to get his life together and restart his career. Or was it the same year, when Marvel's *Guardians of the Galaxy* movie premiered, featuring a talking, bipedal raccoon with serious attitude issues as an equal member of a team of spacefaring outcasts?

Whatever the instigator, by 2019 things were really cooking when the American version of South Korea's *The Masked Singer* premiered. The show became an instant hit as celebrities in fanciful, identity-hiding costumes (mostly of the animal persuasion) tried to out-sing one another. *Singer*'s amazing popularity soon gave birth to a spinoff, *The Masked Dancer*, featuring similarly disguised celebrities showing off their fancy footwork.

Looking at the history of anthropomorphic animals entertaining folks shows that these animals have always found a home in the cartoon universe, dating back to at least 1914, when a tame brontosaurus named Gertie gave her creator, legendary cartoonist Winsor McCay, a ride atop her head in his vaudeville act. Since then, beasties of all varieties have been widespread. Some have been utterly forgotten (*Flip the Frog,* anyone?) while others are woven into the very fabric of world culture (there probably isn't a country on the planet where Mickey Mouse isn't instantly recognized). Cartoon animals are so ubiquitous, in fact, that there's no point in calling them furries. However, plenty of humans have been set on their personal furry path thanks to the subtle influence of cartoon animals.

The Merriam-Webster dictionary defines anthropomorphism as "an interpretation of what is not human or personal in terms of human or personal characteristics." Male cartoon critters meant to be attractive project a suave self-confidence but still resemble actual animals. When it comes to the ladies, however, those attributes are often more human in appearance: shapely legs, a noticeable bosom (often disguised as a ruffle of chest fur), and big eyes with long eyelashes are commonplace. For some, it's the best of both worlds: female, furry, and sexy. Miss Kitty Mouse, the shapely chanteuse from the Disney film *The Great Mouse Detective*, has a killer bod. Except for her mouse head and tail she'd be welcome in any human nightclub. But if you're of a certain mindset, even those attributes are pleasing to the eye. Her ears are quite shapely, and her tail has such a delightful curve to it.

DR. STUART SUMIDA

On the sliding scale of anthropomorphism,[42] Miss Kitty is much closer to the human end than the animal end, but if ever there was a go-to guy for animators wanting to depict animals with more realistic anatomy, it's Dr. Stuart Sumida. A paleontologist specializing in pre-dinosaur fossils (the forgotten reptiles that preceded the dinos), Dr. Sumida is based at the California State University, San Bernardino, where he teaches courses on animal and human anatomy. If you're one of those people who sits through the end credits of movies, you've seen his name roll by in *The Lion King, Brother Bear, Over the Hedge, Madagascar, Kung Fu Panda, Bolt, How to Train Your Dragon, Tangled*, plus a dozen or so more. He's also been a resource for many films that have not provided an onscreen credit, as well as the construction of the giant Yeti in the roller coaster ride at Disney's Animal Kingdom in Orlando.

When I say that Dr. Sumida helps those creating animal images to "get it right," I don't mean that he leads them to create a perfect replica of a real-world animal on paper or in pixels. I mean that he aids them in hitting that magical bullseye where the audience completely believes a four-legged critter can walk upright, speak, and display human emotions in body and face.[43] Go too far and you might as well be watching a human actor wearing an animal head; play it too safe and there's little for a viewer to empathize or identify with. In other words, anthropomorphizing an animal means giving it human qualities without causing it to lose its animal essence. It's a specialty that Dr. Sumida essentially lucked into, if you believe in the expression "luck is when preparation meets opportunity." He explains:

In many ways, it was serendipity. First and foremost, I owe a huge debt to my longtime friend Charles Solomon [chronicler of animation history and author of a number of *The Art of . . .* books, from *Toy Story* to the Disney Golden Book adaptations]. We met at graduate school at UCLA, and we've hung out together ever since. He was talking to animators at Disney back in the late 1980s, early nineties, when I was teaching at the University of Chicago's medical school. He noticed some of them were concerned about accurately depicting horses and wolves in an upcoming film and asked, "Why don't you talk to an animal anatomy specialist?" They asked if he knew one, to which the answer was, "Well, actually, yes." He convinced them to invite me to speak. The film turned out to be *Beauty and the Beast*. They asked me back for the all-animal *Lion King*, and the snowball started rolling from there.

Getting down to basics, I ask Dr. Sumida to describe the similarities and the differences between human and animal anatomy. He responds:

Ultimately, humans are very weird vertebrates, so they have much in common with other animals. That being said, our orthograde, which is a fancy word for upright, posture is so odd, it's very difficult to have a real animal stand up without making it look merely like a person in a suit. To sell an animated character, behavioral details can help, and lots of animation and VFX [visual effects] studios do try to do that. But one great strategy is to have the character spend at least some time in the animal's actual posture. This was done to great effect with the beast on all fours in *Beauty and the Beast* and with Remy through much of *Ratatouille*.

Even as a kid I noticed that not all cartoon characters were created (or at least drawn) equally. A rabbit might look as "realistic" as the ones in the *Watership Down* movie; semi-realistic like Beatrix Potter's real-looking but clothes-wearing Peter Rabbit; kind of cartoony but still resembling a real rabbit, like Thumper in *Bambi*; or even be a person-shaped rabbit like Bugs Bunny. Dr. Sumida gives me his own take on the subject, saying:

> There are four basic categories: one, looking real and acting real; two, looking real but acting like a person; three, cartoony-looking but acting like a real animal; and four, looking and acting cartoony. The first and last are easy, really. It's the middle two that are most difficult. Even if the character is stylized, giving it natural behavior helps a ton. Like the way a cat cleans itself is displacement behavior. But in the end, the story is key. If the story is brilliant, suspension of disbelief is easier. No matter how good something looks, a cruddy story can kill it.

With the significance he places on storyline, Dr. Sumida begins to sound more like a producer than a professor. This leads me to wonder aloud what it's like to work among and alongside animators and directors and what his best experience was; he replies thoughtfully, saying:

> Wow, it's difficult to pick just one. Of course *The Lion King* is an early favorite and [was a] lynchpin event in my consulting career. Tarzan was brilliant, it was beautiful, and we got to work on some heartfelt scenes in Paris with [award-winning animator] Glen Keane! *Ratatouille* and *How to Train Your Dragon* are at the top of the CG [computer graphics] projects I've been involved with. I've done photorealistic gigs too. I thought [the dragon-populated] *Reign of Fire* was a wildly underrated film—it was a great popcorn B-movie! *Life of Pi* was a brilliant accomplishment, and it was neat to be part of it, though I'm a bit ambivalent given how it signaled such poor treatment of CG artists worldwide. In the end, *How to Train Your Dragon* with DreamWorks may be at the top of the pile. It's my own boys' favorite, which is about as gratifying as it gets.

"What about the downside?" I ask. There's always a downside. Again he replies thoughtfully, saying:

> You can say all you want, but they don't have to listen. In my experience, the artists always want to get it as right as they can, given the constraints of time and budget. The directors often as

well, or at least usually. In my experience, the farther you get from the trenches, the less likely they'll listen to you.

I can tell you about the groups that really work their asses off to utilize what I have to offer. Top of the list are Rhythm & Hues,[44] Pixar, DreamWorks, and MPC [Moving Picture Company].[45] Depending on the constraints of the project, Disney and Sony try very hard. Walt Disney Imagineering is unique because its projects must function in the physics of our actual universe, so they're great too.

Given Dr. Sumida's experience in the trenches working alongside animators, directors, and producers, I ask if he's ever thought about joining in and pitching a project of his own to any of the studios he's worked with. He responds by sharing a different type of fascinating project he's working on, saying:

I've not pitched any Hollywood-style projects. I know people who do that for a living, and I could never endure what they go through. However, I'm currently doing computer modeling of some of our fossil animals' skeletons. This would never have been possible without my experience and access with folks at the studios. DreamWorks has been particularly helpful in this regard. What I'd really like to see is a library of high-definition slow-motion locomotion of animals. If anyone had the resources to do it, I'd be all over a project like that.

Our interview nearly over, I ask what he thinks of furries and furry fandom. "I've had very little experience with them to be honest," he responds. "However, I have a tiny bit of experience speaking with characters who've worked at the Disney theme parks—an incredibly hot, hard job."

Finally, I ask, if he were an animal, which one would he like to be, and if he's ever imagined himself as one—like the *Dimetrodon*, his favorite of those pre-dinosaur reptiles, for example? He responds that he's more or less all set in his current form, saying: "Well, as a biologist, my first response is, 'I am an animal; humans are just weird mammals.' Right now though, my primary animal role is as a dad and family man. So I think if I could choose another animal, it might be dad minus about twenty pounds and [getting] a lot more sleep."

FILM/TV ANTHROPOMORPHISM

There's a trailer for Wes Anderson's *Fantastic Mr. Fox* that promotes the film's stars. In it their names are onscreen in big bold letters: "George Clooney," then "Meryl Streep"—but the figures standing next to those names aren't people, they're foxes: clothes-wearing, upright-standing foxes. Is Clooney actually a fox? Is Streep really a vixen? Maybe they've been foxes all along and we never noticed, or maybe they're method actors who've gotten deeper into their roles than anyone could imagine.

Or maybe they've just lent their voices to Anderson's vulpine stars. The modern trend to feature well-known performers to voice-animated characters may have begun with Robin Williams's genie in Disney's *Aladdin*. Since then it's become common for animation studios to add a bit of adult sensibility to their films by hiring A-list actors to voice them, and promoting their contributions. This puts grown-up fannies into theater seats, and performers into virtual fursuits.

The question is, is the growing pop culture representation of anthropomorphic imagery furry-inspired (or a secret hat-tip to us) or simply responding to the same zeitgeist that gave rise to the furry community? Until I can cross-examine a *Simpsons* writer, I'll give the show the benefit of the doubt and assume the 2002 Halloween segment named "The Island of Dr. Hibbert," in which a town doctor turns Springfieldians into anthropomorphic versions of themselves (Walrus Homer: "This is the least I've weighed since high school!"), or the 2005 episode "Future-Drama," in which a plastic surgery center of the future offers "fluffy tails" (and leads to Marge's sister Patty sporting one) are happenstance. There's no question, however, about the panda-suited fellow "The furry, the ultimate expert on poorly-rendered CGI hair," in the 2021 episode, "Do Pizza Bots Dream of Electric Guitars." Once you've been spoofed on *The Simpsons*, you have arrived.[46]

Photorealistic animals created from computer-generated imagery (CGI) are a big step forward in movie and television anthropomorphic representations. Rocket, the raccoon with a bad attitude from *Guardians of the Galaxy*, helped make his movie one of 2014's top-grossing films. Bebop and Rocksteady, the Teenage Mutant Ninja Turtles's warthog and rhino adversaries, have been battling the four terrapins throughout multiple comic book and animated iterations. They made their CGI debut in the 2016 live action feature *Teenage Mutant Ninja Turtles: Out of the Shadows*, complete with an on-camera human-to-beast transformation. DC Comics, determined not to be left behind in the anthro-animal sweepstakes, CGI'd the character Cheetah from *Wonder Woman 1984*, as well as King Shark and Weasel from *The Suicide Squad* into their on-screen Extended Universe.

This brings us to 2019's live action *Cats* movie, a film that will forever be near the top of the "what the hell were they thinking?" list. To make it, less-than-awesome CGI effects semi-transformed actors into horrible mutant creatures, neither human nor feline, nor any attractive melding of the two. While some people may have assumed that the combination of human and animal features guaranteed that furries would love the film, we know what anthropomorphic cat people should look like and how they appeared in the film sure wasn't it. One fur commented, "I watched a couple scary movies this week, and the *Cats* trailer may have topped 'em all,"[47] while another called it "creepy,"[48] and a third said, "I would rather burn those fuckin' things."[49]

There are all sorts of ways of making actors look like animals, most of them a lot easier than applying a digital coat of fur. In the moviemaking world, prosthetics are often affixed to an actor's face to animalize them without resorting to costly CGI. The early *Planet of the Apes* movies might be the best-known films that have gone this route, but a far stranger one is 1989's *Marquis*, an all but unknown French oddity. The film is based on the writings of the Marquis de Sade, but performed by actors wearing amazingly sophisticated prosthetics designed by the film's scriptwriter Roland Topor (who also scripted the surreal animated feature *Fantastic Planet*). The film's eponymous Marquis de Sade is a spaniel imprisoned for his libertine literary efforts. In his orbit are a corrupt, camel-headed priest, a bisexual jailer rat, an arrogant, secretly masochistic rooster warden, an imprisoned pig-faced pork dealer, a boar tavern owner, a simian moneybags, and a shifty parrot. The two primary female characters are the innocent and perpetually victimized cow, Justine, and a noblewoman, Juliette, who is a free-spirited revolutionary equine handy with a whip and not afraid to use it. Episodes from the real-life de Sade's writings are clay-animated, deliberately separating those particularly nasty moments from the rest of the movie with an entirely different look and texture.

Of course, putting animal heads on human bodies is a time-honored theatrical tradition still with us. Amazon Prime Video's *Mad Dogs* featured a cat-headed assassin (the centerpiece of the show's ad campaign), and in the sci-fi and fantasy retelling of *Alice in Wonderland*, *Alice*, broadcast on SyFy and Canada's Showcase network, a porcelain-headed white rabbit is the head of an assassin's league.

Director David Lynch is no stranger to strangeness, so it's hard to see *Rabbits*, his "situation comedy" shorts as something out of his oeuvre, except for its cast of rabbit-headed performers. Actually, the only sitcom-y element of the miniseries (currently viewable on YouTube as a forty-three-minute movie) is an old-school laugh track, punctuating non sequitur, non-funny dialog. It all takes place in a nondescript living room, seen in a single wide shot as if Lynch was afraid to get close to the three rabbit-headed characters. A long-eared, suit-wearing bunny enters the room to the sound of eager audience applause and cheers. After several lines of meaningless dialog, a rabbit's "What time is it?" evokes the imaginary audience's laughter. One of the trio then leaves the room and the room turns a deep dark red as she returns holding two candles over her head and speaking in an *Exorcist*-style demon's voice.

What does it all mean? Media deconstruction? Creating a sense of unease? An exercise in alienation? Take your pick, or watch any of the several YouTube videos attempting to explain it.

Recent TV shows slapping animal heads on participants have definitely leaned on the furry button, but did they actually press it? Or just lightly touch it? Either way, they seem to have triggered a number of articles describing them as such. Take for example, Fox's *The Masked Singer*. Like its inspiration, the South Korean series *King of Masked Singer*, the American version features celebrities disguised by elaborate, fanciful costumes, most often of the animal variety. The costumed celebs—a leering wolf, a pink giraffe, a gas mask-wearing deer, a violet alligator, a junkyard rottweiler (backed up by dancers wearing fetish "pup" masks), and a panoply of horses, porcupines, peacocks, butterflies, and others—perform before a panel of strictly human celebrities sitting in judgment of their performance.

"Furries will love this" was the conclusion HuffPost leapt to with its article "*The Masked Singer* is Great Content for Furries, Hellish Nightmare for Everyone Else."[50] The article's author, Priscilla Frank (who confessed in it, "I might . . . identify as a furry"), referred to the show as a "dystopian circus" and speculated, "this show will probably be remembered as a massive step forward in the normalizing of furry fetishes."

The celebrity judges' fetishes, perhaps. According to the article, the panel oohed and aahed over the pretend beasts with comments along the lines of "There's something attractive about that hippo," and "Work them hips! Strut that thing!" which a judge said to a lion before going on to proclaim a unicorn to be "slim and pretty." Another judge reportedly described a lion's legs as "delicious . . . like Kelly Rowland."

New York magazine's Vulture section consulted Patch O'Furr, founder of Dogpatch Press, to get his thoughts on *The Masked Singer* as it relates to furries.[51] Patch's response, according to the magazine, acknowledged that the backstories the show created for its disguised singers were "pretty damn furry," and observed the producers are "very aware of stuff like Comic-Con and cosplay. And furry would be one part of that."

Another magazine that also weighed in, *MEL Magazine,* didn't mince words with a headline proclaiming, "No, Furries Don't Want to Fuck The Masked Singer (Any of Them)."[52] According to the article's writer, Joseph Longo, "A number of furries tell me that they don't want to fuck the buff rottweiler or any of the animals on *The Masked Singer* for that matter." Longo then quoted a furry weighing in on this who characterized the "buff rottweiler" by saying, "He looks a little like a mascot. He has a 'static' type of face and just looks a little goofy."

Importantly, Longo also took the space of the article to acknowledge an important part of furry fandom, noting: "furry fandoms are a rising safe space for queer youth. That is, teens are connecting online entirely through their 'fursonas,' sharing detailed fan art, short stories, and advice on coming out." He shared the words of Oliver, a trans teenager, who told him, "It seems like a silly hobby looking in, but portraying yourself in various pieces of art—and in all different forms—allows for a kind of introspection that I feel can't be found in any other place."

Then there's *Sexy Beasts*, Netflix's 2021 version of a 2014 British dating show wherein animal heads—most cute, some freaky—were put on contestants' heads to determine which was most important to them: looks or personality. The show was popular enough to earn a second season from the streaming service and now offers a dozen episodes, with capsule descriptions on its website along the lines of "He's sweet—and scaly for the moment. Can Nashville tour guide (and temporary dragon) Mick lead an armadillo, shark, or meerkat to love?"[53]

Even though Netflix never mentioned furries in its promotion of *Sexy Beasts*, articles and reviews were quick to describe the series as one that would appeal to furries. As one example, an article on the website The Face by Kemi Alemoru notes, "When the trailer dropped... one maligned and misunderstood group came to mind almost instantly: furries.... But comparisons between *Sexy Beasts* and the [furry] community happened mostly on social media, rather than it being an angle explored by Netflix explicitly."[54] This was predictable, as Netflix knew exactly what it was doing and exactly what it wanted. Even if no one from the network came out and used the "f" word, they were hoping that people, critics and viewers alike, would make that connection.

In response to *Sexy Beasts*, furs got their licks in as well. In a Slate article, Riley Black, a furry, described the show as a "Netflix-hosted mess... going for shock value with the costumes" and wrote that "early reactions to the show's trailer on social media were predictably sprinkled with 'haha, ew, furries' jabs." Black then stepped away from this dribble to make an important point on what is commonly accepted as "real' and authentic. He writes: "While animal headpieces are shown as 'costumes,' the polished, airbrushed, made-up contestants who 'reveal' themselves at the end of each episode are presented as real and authentic. But how is wearing clothing and eye shadow in order to fit a very specific and technically unnatural definition of *hot* inherently more real than going overboard with the spirit gum and body paint to look like a dolphin?"[55]

My favorite comment on *Sexy Beasts* is from Jason Tabrys, a writer for the website Uproxx, who suggested the series should push the boundaries even further, writing: "Personally, I think you gotta make it so everyone around the couples is also in full makeup and create a whole fairytale forest vibe with where they go on dates. Titillate my sense of fantasy, Netflix. . . . Also, let's up the stakes and keep the losing contestants in their costumes for six months and show them trying to navigate real life as a nymph-y beaver or an armadillo club kid."[56]

BOJACK HORSEMAN AND *TUCA & BERTIE*

Let's now step away from *Sexy Beasts* and over to *BoJack Horseman*, which we can consider one of the most successful and lauded TV series of the twenty-tens. An animated dramedy, *BoJack* was set in a world where human beings and anthropomorphic animals coexist as equals, and even marry each other. It received rave reviews with accolades naming it the "best show of the decade,"[57] the "best animated TV series of all time,"[58] "the best writing on TV,"[59] and "one of the greatest shows ever,"[60] and won or was nominated for numerous awards, including Emmys, Writers Guild of America Awards, Annie Awards, and French Annecy animation awards.[61] It also had a wealth of celebrity guest cameos, with the stars voicing cartoon versions of themselves, portraying other real-life celebrities, or voicing fictional characters. Among *BoJack*'s guest stars were Matthew Broderick, Hilary Swank, Lin-Manuel Miranda, RuPaul, Paul McCartney, and even "Weird Al" Yankovic,[62] and, in fact, the total count of its celebrity guest cameos way exceeds that of the 1960s *Batman* TV series. *BoJack's* anthropomorphic universe included products and businesses with animal pun names and sight gags of anthro animals acting like their real-world counterparts also abounded.[63]

With so much going for it, *BoJack* was a massive hit with critics and viewers alike, to say nothing of furs, always in the mood themselves for animated anthropomorphic characters. So why didn't I like it? I almost felt like a traitor to the furry community with my dislike, but it was simply too depressing for me. Still, I felt like I was being unfair, so I asked several friends for their opinions on why I found it challenging to appreciate a show so many people were raving about. All commented on the sadness element of the show being the reason. One friend opined, "The series is dark and depressing and painful to watch, so I understand people who don't want to, because it might be too triggering for them." Another weighed in, "I know the sad parts can be tough, but they're an integral part of why people enjoy the show, even if it is uncomfortable." A third said, "Many episodes have a nihilistic and depressing tone, and there are some major fuckups on BoJack's part that cause some very dark and depressing aftereffects."

While my friends were sympathetic, but still liked the show themselves, I'm far from alone in my inability to warm up to it. A *New York Times Magazine* writer described one episode in particular as "too harrowing" to watch a second time.[64]

But my *BoJack* problem shouldn't be yours, and given the show's popularity, you likely may already be as familiar with the characters as I am.

Either way, here's a cheat sheet on the characters: There's BoJack, the bitter, substance-abusing washed-up star of a generic 1990s sitcom, *Horsin' Around*, who is hoping for a comeback; Diane, the human ghostwriter of BoJack's autobiography, who is a principled, strong-willed but occasionally hypocritical feminist; Mr. Peanutbutter, BoJack's canine rival/friend with a very doglike, overeager personality; Princess Carolyn, a pink Persian cat and BoJack's tireless talent agent whose life is focused (often to her own detriment) on her career; and Todd, a young human who is a multitalented slacker and BoJack's houseguest.

The characters' foibles and shifting, often painful relationships drive the show, and very often reveal surprising sides to their personalities. BoJack, for example, is capable of showing concern for others when he's not narcissistically thinking only about himself. I was also surprised to see that my initial assumption that Mr. Peanutbutter would be the Road Runner to BoJack's Wile E. Coyote, the former always coming out ahead no matter how our star tries, was utterly wrong. Mr. Peanutbutter is as capable of screwing up as any of the show's other characters.

It's interesting to note that many of *BoJack*'s animal characters have the kind of names that humans give their companion animals, police officer Meow Meow Fuzzyface being a prime example. And *BoJack*'s animated, mixed-species world of humans and very human animals wasn't created just for beastly sight gags and puns, it gives the show's animal characters a universality where they're stand-ins for humans. In this way, we counterintuitively can see ourselves in them far more easily than if *BoJack* were a live-action show starring human characters. Series creator Raphael Bob-Waksberg explained this in an interview with NPR, stating:

People project themselves onto him [BoJack] more easily because he is not a person, he is a horse somehow. If you see Will Arnett in a show, you think, *Well, that's Will Arnett, that's not me.* But seeing a horse somehow feels more universal, or it feels more like, *That could be me.* . . .

One thing we've really found is that it is a very silly cartoon universe, but it can also, I think, maybe because of that, go to some very sincere, dark, melancholy, and even tragic places. Because it's animated and it's like a horse and it's bright and colorful, it just takes on a different feel. And you can kind of sneak attack into sadness in some fun, surprising ways.[65]

BoJack's "bright and colorful" palette is the work of Lisa Hanawalt, the show's production designer and producer and Bob-Waksberg's high school chum. Bob-Waksberg has described Hanawalt's art style and "whimsical flourishes" as keeping the show from feeling "completely insufferable."[66] In their Palo Alto school days, the pair was akin to a mutual admiration society and would meet after classes. Hanawalt would share her sketchbooks of anthropomorphic characters, and in a harbinger of their future collaboration, Bob-Waksberg would invent voices and imaginary conversations for the characters. After college, the friends went their separate ways: Bob-Waksberg heading south to Los Angeles, where he worked on TV pilots and experimental movies, and Hanawalt heading to hipster heaven Brooklyn, where she focused on her cartooning and created illustrations for various publications in a style reminiscent of Robert Crumb, Mark Alan Stamaty, or *The New Yorker*'s Roz Chast. Hanawalt's graphic novel *Coyote Doggirl* and her carefully rendered, detailed illustrations of animal-headed people, mini-comic stories, and assorted miscellanea were compiled into a series of books: *Hot Dog Taste Test, My Dirty Dumb Eyes*, and *I Want You*.

By the time Hanawalt first heard Bob-Waksberg pitch her on *BoJack*, they had previously collaborated on a web comic named *Tip Me Over, Pour Me Out*. Now he was calling to tell her about an animated show he was pitching, at that time titled *BoJack the Depressed Talking Horse*, and asked if she could send him art of the "horse-guy" she was fond of sketching to accompany his pitch. She did—and Bob-Waksberg's pitch and Hanawalt's art merged into the Netflix series *BoJack Horseman*. Hanawalt originally signed on to design the show's characters, but stayed on in a larger capacity.

Once acclimated to the rigors of producing an animated TV series, Hanawalt started thinking, at least according to Bob-Waksberg, "*Oh, I can make a TV show. Why am I making this guy's TV show?*"[67] This led to her working with two *BoJack* producers to create the show *Tuca & Bertie*, which she sold to Netflix. As Hanawalt is a known furry, the success marked her as the first furry to invent, create, and produce a television series.[68]

Hanawalt was born with the furry gene (according to the *New York Times*, "As a kid, Hanawalt was so obsessed with horses that she sometimes walked on all fours. Her classmates called her Horse Poop and Lady Horse"[69]), and she hasn't shied away from speaking on the furry community's reaction to her work. In a 2016 interview with *The Guardian*, she shared that "the lack of tails in *BoJack* has been controversial among furries." In the interview she also revealed her thoughts on identifying as a furry and what that means for her:

> I think I am technically a furry because I think about animals so much, and about what it would be like to be an animal, but it's not erotic for me[70].... You know when something's so cute that you feel internal pain? There should be a word to describe a certain kind of horniness that isn't sexual—I can't emphasize enough how nonsexual it is—but it's when something is so cute that you feel kind of aroused.[71]

The heart of Hanawalt's *Tuca & Bertie* series is the relationship between the eponymous characters: Tuca, a brassy, strong-willed toucan, and her bestie, Bertie, an insecure song thrush. Like *BoJack*, *Tuca & Bertie* examines serious emotional issues—such as self-confidence, codependency, toxic families, and men behaving badly—but the show doesn't suffer from *BoJack*'s downbeat vibe. Instead, the two titular avian characters (who first appeared in Hanawalt's online comics) care about and support each other emotionally. While far from perfect, they lack BoJack's self-destructive streak. If ever a show aced the Bechdel Test it would have to be *Tuca & Bertie*.[72]

Unlike *BoJack*, *Tuca & Bertie* is set in an entirely anthropomorphic universe and there is not a human to be found among its avian population, although the occasional anthro dog or reptile shows up, along with leafy-headed plant people. While *BoJack* maintained a consistent internal reality, anything goes in

Tuca & Bertie; buildings have breasts, trains are giant snakes, and the show's animation style can shift in any direction without warning to match a scene's emotional tenor. In the style of classic Fleischer animation,[73] everything in *Tuca & Bertie* is imbued with life, personality, and the ability to transform without warning. In this way, *Tuca & Bertie* takes full advantage of all the spontaneity and playfulness that being a cartoon allows. It's also laugh-out-loud funny and filled with warm-hearted characters. While I respect and admire *BoJack Horseman* for its brave storytelling and willingness to explore the darker aspects of a character's behavior (not to mention its very furry world of coexisting humans and anthropomorphic animals), *Tuca & Bertie*'s compassionate storytelling and playful animation are much more my style; I'd definitely enjoy hanging out with these birds.

"IF MONET HAD A FURRY PERIOD"

John Oliver may be the most fur-friendly—or at least the most fur-curious—person on television. In 2020, on his HBO series, *Last Week Tonight with John Oliver,* the host asked his viewers to help him locate an unusual painting, a fine example of a previously mostly unknown genre, which Oliver referred to as "rat erotica." (Within the furry community, artwork of that variety is more commonly known as "furry porn.") The painting Oliver was passionate to locate was *Stay Up Late*, an early 1990s painting by furry artist Brian Swords, a.k.a. Biohazard. It depicts two anthropomorphic white rats positioned on the edge of a bed and holding each other in a serious embrace. The closer figure sits on the edge of the bed with its back to viewers and its buttocks exposed, while its partner's genitalia is visibly but tastefully in view. A dripping jar of K-Y Jelly rests on the headboard behind them.

Oliver's team had somehow come across a 1992 VHS recording of a local PBS station's fundraising drive that featured the artwork. The station had regularly been putting Sword's romantic rat pictures in its late-night auctions for many years. The year of the auction, *Stay Up Late*'s winning bidder added eighty dollars to the station's coffers—and with Oliver's show, twenty-eight years later, he was offering the painting's owner one thousand dollars, plus a twenty thousand dollar donation to a food bank of their choice.

Why did Oliver deem it so important to acquire the painting and not one, say, of kittens on black velvet? In March 2020, the COVID-19 pandemic was just beginning to ravage the United States, and Oliver was venting his frustration at the Trump administration's inept handling of the crisis:

> "I want that piece of art hanging behind me on this wall next week," Oliver said, pointing to the white backdrop behind him . . . "and if I don't get it, I will keep looking for it, because this is America. Where, sure, you can't get a test for COVID-19, or Purell, or a ventilator, or a sense of empathy from the person in charge. But if you try hard enough . . . you can get a picture of two nude rats locked in a passionate post-fuck embrace hanging on your wall."[74]

Less than a month later, Oliver was the owner of the rat erotica he so dearly desired.

Locating *Stay Up Late* was not just a comedic victory, as Oliver pointed out, it was a diversion from the world events around us. Who knew early-nineties rat erotica could be so uplifting during a time of crisis? As Oliver said:

> What are the chances that in 1992, in south-central Pennsylvania, a man would've made an impulse purchase of high-quality rat erotica and then, instead of throwing it away at any point in the last twenty-eight years, kept it, cherished it, framed it—not knowing that one day far in the future it might cause HBO to donate twenty thousand dollars to Pennsylvania food banks in the middle of the pandemic?

Oliver ended the suspense and triumphantly displayed the painting to viewers, saying, "I believe I have something we've all been looking for—and it's called hope."[75]

Oliver's (or HBO's) generosity didn't end with *Last Week Tonight*'s acquisition of the painting. In 2021, he sent *Stay Up Late* (along with two non-anthro paintings) on a five-city museum tour titled *Last Week Tonight*'s Gallery for Cultural Enrichment. Each museum received a ten thousand dollar grant and its city received an equally generous food bank donation—even Grand Rapids, Minnesota, where the tour stopped at the Judy Garland Museum.

In a video introducing the tour, Oliver waxed rhapsodic over the painting's artistic merit: "Our pièce de résistance and of course where our collection began, *Stay Up Late*, a study of rat friendship, which really has to be seen in person to be fully appreciated. Just look at the brushstrokes there—it's as if Monet had a furry period."[76]

Rat erotica is far from Oliver's only interest in all things anthropomorphic. *Last Week Tonight* is notable for its full-throated embrace of suited mascot characters. At least twenty-four mascots created expressly for the show have appeared on it over its nine seasons to date.[77] Oliver's passion for mascot characters reportedly dates back to his childhood love of the Muppets, which he can now indulge in, thanks to HBO's deep pockets—just don't ask him how much of their money they cost. ("If HBO ever finds out how much we spent on this stuff, we're toast," he once told a reporter.[78]) The show may have to spend a few dollars on therapy, however, for the kids who visited Oliver's office and discovered the show's mascot suit stash. On an episode of *The Late Show with Stephen Colbert*, Oliver shared the story behind this, saying:

> We eventually moved them after, like, the third child who'd been brought to our office opened the door and screamed, because you know puppets and mascots, when they're animated, are the most magical thing on Earth. A decapitated mascot hanging from a hook like in a meat locker is something a child is not likely to forget.[79]

As a fur, I must take issue with Stephen Colbert's throwaway comment while interviewing his former *Daily Show* costar about his fondness for mascots, "I'll tell you who might get a little turned on by your show is anyone in the furry community." *Last Week Tonight*'s mascot mob might be cute or eye-catching, but I'm not sure I'd call any of them sexy.

The recent conservative hysteria over rumors of litter boxes in school restrooms for students who "identify as furries"[80] also has not escaped Oliver's notice. In a web-exclusive *Last Week Tonight* segment,[81] Oliver reported on a fringe-y, looney Georgia gubernatorial candidate whose "Jesus, guns, babies" campaign included a vow to stamp out furryism, litter boxes and all.[82] In his report on the matter, a frustrated Oliver exclaimed, "That is not what furries do. What furries do is use regular toilets, wear elaborate fursuits, and many offer art commissions where you can get yourself done up as a sexy river otter at very reasonable prices. They are harmless." At this point he presented his river otter likeness—presumably created by a staff artist who'd evidently been studying, *closely* studying, actual furry art—who was indeed quite sexy. The likeness, who furs quickly dubbed "John Ottiver," possessed a pair of impressive pecs, a solid six-pack of abs, and a snug pair of short-shorts that left little to the imagination. Later in the segment, Oliver displayed two furry responses to the candidate's delusions: one a joke about "supply-side economics fairy tales" and the other a butt shot of a cartoony, blue furred animal.

"If you absolutely had to reduce the furry presence online right down to its bones," Oliver summed up, "critiques of conservative economic theory and fuzzy butt shots really are the guiding principles of the whole movement."

You can always tell the difference between a cheap shot and poking a little friendly fun at something. Between his fascination with mascot suits, his enthusiasm for rat erotica, and his spirited defense of the furry community (although I would've preferred something a little stronger than "harmless"), Oliver is indeed the most furry-friendly guy on TV—if not also a fur himself.

3

MEETINGS WITH REMARKABLE FURS

SHARON ROBERTS, DOCTOR OF FUROLOGY, AND FURSCIENCE

Sharon Roberts has a lot of letters after her name (and a lot of degrees under her belt)—BA (Bachelor of Arts, Psychology), MA (Master of Arts, Sociology), PhD (Doctor of Philosophy, Sociology), and most recently, MSW (Master of Social Work)—and she's put that alphabet soup of credentials to work as one of the founders of the International Anthropomorphic Research Project—the IARP, or as it's known more colloquially, Furscience. The project has been studying the furry community since 2006 and is a fixture at the larger furry conventions where its members distribute surveys in which furs can provide information about themselves to help Furscience continue its study of the furry community. When I interviewed Dr. Roberts, I asked how she initially found out about furry fandom; she shared the following:

> Funnily enough, my first introduction to the furry fandom was the infamous CSI episode, "Fur and Loathing." I had no real

understanding of what I had watched, but I was interested to learn more. When I do personality tests, I consistently score very, very high on measures of "openness to experience." While I didn't question the fidelity of the show's representation of furries at the time, the furry fandom certainly stoked my curiosity. When YouTube was new, I scoured the platform for anything furry-related and came up empty-handed.

By about 2010, I had packed away the idea of studying furries because I could not see a way to access the community. However, my entire research career took a turn in April 2011. I was setting up the papers for a final exam and met my proctor, Courtney Plante, who at the time was a young master's student in psychology. I asked him what he studied, and when he told me—furries—I became so excited I could hardly contain myself.

My area of expertise is youth and the transition to adulthood, and my dissertation work included developing a measure of identity resolution, something the team was looking for as they prepared for data collection at Anthrocon 2011. Within the fifteen minutes it took to set out the exams, I had officially joined the team. That openness to experience trait has served me well.

Dr. Roberts and her team still use the IARP name to describe the research arm of what they do, but in 2016 they rebranded as a more public-friendly platform for research dissemination and began to use the name

Furscience. The Furscience team engages in both similar research projects and specialized activities related to the research. They conceive projects, collect data, and write up findings.

Dr. Stephen Reysen is the lead author on many of the Furscience team's publications, and Dr. Courtney Plante, Dr. Roberts's former proctor, is the lead quantitative analyst, preparing much of the data found on their website. Together Dr. Reysen and Dr. Plante interpret data collected at conventions, including differences between fandom groups (e.g. fans of *My Little Pony* and anime). Another team member, Dr. Kathy Gerbasi, who was a founding member of the IARP and is considered the heart and conscience of the team, mentors assisting graduate students and heads up data collection at the annual Anthrocon convention, which gathers around ten thousand furry fans in Pittsburgh every summer. Dr. Roberts is the "money person" on the team, securing funding through grants as well as overseeing the administration of the funds the team receives. To date, all this collaboration has allowed the team to publish more than fifty peer-reviewed articles, cementing Furscience's academic credentials and endowing furry culture with the anthropological legitimacy it had historically been denied.

In 2016–2017, Furscience produced a PSA-style campaign named "Just Like You★ (★But with Fur)," a tongue-in-cheek series of ads that educated the non-furry public about furries. When I asked Dr. Roberts about it, she shared the following:

> The goal was to get people to see that furries were just like everyone else—they just happen to have an interest in anthropo-

morphic characters. Specifically, we wanted to blow holes in the public's misperceptions that all furries have fursuits (only about 20 to 25 percent own them, as they are prohibitively expensive) and that they wear them all the time, which is categorically untrue. We conceived of the series by juxtaposing the public's misperceptions of furries and putting furries in everyday, mundane situations wearing fursuits. The final gag reveal was that *of course furries don't do these things in fursuits, but you can get the facts at furscience.com.*

The series consisted of five short videos: furries wine tasting, going on a date, doing yoga, parking a car, and going to the bathroom. The videos were largely well received, and furries and non-furries seemed to find them funny for different reasons. Furries were, of course, in on the joke. We conceived of these videos in consultation with members of the community, and all the furries in the videos are actually furries. The non-furry public found them funny because seeing a furry do anything in a fursuit is captivating and awesome.

Furscience loves to educate the public, but we also find it important to include furries in our activities and give a wink and nod to the fandom more broadly. The most surprising thing I've learned about furries in the course of Furscience's work is how invested the furry community is in the research, from conception to dissemination. I have been *floored* by the positive response from the furry community to our research. I've given a lot of academic conference presentations over the years and getting more than six academics to attend your panel feels like a win. In contrast, with the furry research, we have filled ballrooms at some furry conventions or had standing room only rooms filled with people who are completely engaged in a presentation on *data* on a Saturday night.

One of my colleagues attended his first furry convention with me a couple of years ago, and we gave a talk to a fully engaged, cheering crowd. It's hard to know what the future will be regarding the public's acceptance of furries. Nothing would make me happier than to have the public see this community for what it is: a fun environment for people with like-minded interests to connect with others, share their creativity, and contribute to a place of belonging.

In my opinion, the world could take some needed lessons from the furry fandom in how to be kinder and more supportive to others—especially toward those who face marginalization. However, I am hopeful that there will be an improvement in the way the world sees furries. A big part of that is because I see many creative, extraordinarily talented furries using platforms and tools of communication to showcase their talents and interests to the non-furry public. Part of that hope comes from a growing diligence of journalists, producers, and documentarians taking the time to understand the facts of the fandom.

LIASSUR: TURN AND FACE THE STRANGE CHANGES

There are many face changer apps available for your smartphone. They can be used to paint out zits, tweak your face shape, swap your face with a movie star's face, or even plaster funny stuff like animal noses and ears onto it. However, none I came across in the App Store can accomplish what the filters designed by the programmer who goes by Liassur are capable of: gradually transforming video of your face so that it appears to transform from human to animal while the new animal elements stay perfectly placed on your moving head. With the filters, faces stretch into muzzles, lengthy ears belonging to any number of beasts sprout, and your new animal mouth opens and closes as you speak. Liassur's effects are amazingly close to what high-end movie effects companies do—and not just at a fraction of the cost, but absolutely free of charge. It's a furry's dream to turn into an animal, and Liassur's filters make that dream come true.[83]

A twenty-three-year-old computer science student in Paris who plans to work in the cybersecurity field, Liassur first found the furry community on websites like DeviantArt, and later Fur Affinity, and became fascinated with the process of animal transformation. He shared his journey with me as follows:

> My first experience with computers outside of regular use was when I learned how to make a website in high school. Later on I became more interested in programming and applied mathematics, and started working toward a degree in computer science. I didn't know much about computer animation and 3D software before starting to make augmented reality effects, but

seeing the projects of other creators on Instagram and Snapchat, and discovering selfie-editing smartphone apps like MSQRD were also powerful motivators for learning.

Before starting, I didn't have much knowledge of the software used, or CGI in general. I learned how to create and modify 3D objects, how to texture them, and how to assemble an augmented reality effect using trial and error, and lots of YouTube tutorials.

Personally, my ideal TF [transformation] filter would be a full anthro lion filter, not only with the face changing, but also with a mane, a tail, paws . . . . In a way, it's already possible in virtual reality. To make it even more immersive in augmented reality [AR], you'd be using AR glasses instead of a smartphone, so you can directly see yourself and others with a virtual fursuit on, or being in the middle of a virtual shape-shift!

THE VIRTUES OF VIRTUAL REALITY

"It's a bit disorienting, as if you're visiting this strange, almost alien place. It's rather wonderful." So begins a 1993 episode of *Murder, She Wrote*, wherein mystery author Jessica Fletcher solves the mystery of a video game designer's murder using the virtual reality software he'd been working on.[84]

One could make a case that way before the first VR headset, Mattel's View-Master was one of the earliest virtual reality systems: just slide a disc in and enjoy stereoscopic views of nature and world landmarks. Or at least that was how many adults enjoyed it. For many kids, the View-Master's real delights were the miniature, painstakingly constructed dioramas recreating fairy tale and animated cartoon scenes that had been photographed by a stereoscopic camera. Looking at those scenes in a View-Master was like peeking into a miniaturized, frozen three-dimensional world.

The first head-worn VR viewer came to be in 1968. Invented by computer scientists Ivan Sutherland and Bob Sproull, the contraption could only display primitive wire-frame graphics and weighed so much more than a human pair of shoulders could support that it had to be suspended from the ceiling on cables. From there, VR evolved throughout the 1970s and 1980s, though it was primarily used in medical, military, and flight simulations, leaving the idea of personal VR headsets little more than a gleam in a futurist's eye. Finally, however, in the 1990s, VR began working its way further into the public consciousness, first through motion simulation rides in amusement arcades and theme parks, as well as early unsuccessful headsets, and later in a more expanded way.[85] In 2016 the Oculus Rift VR gaming headset was released to the consumer market. (In a *Wired* magazine article, its creator, Palmer Luckey, admitted the *Murder, She Wrote* episode with the video game designer's murder was part of his inspiration to create the Oculus.[86])

In Matt Baume's article "How Furries are Making Virtual Reality Actually Worth Visiting" for the website Input magazine, he writes:

> The revolutionary potential of VR was always just out of reach—until now. Over the last few weeks, I've spent countless hours exploring virtual worlds with a band of nerds who have figured out how to create the most satisfying, immersive social

experience I've ever found in VR. The subculture that made it happen? Furries.[87]

Baume credits furs with helping popularize MUDs (which you'll recall from earlier are Multi-User Dungeons, or Domains, depending on which history you read), which host text-based chat rooms or adventure games. MUDs were the predecessors of MMORPGs (Massively Multiplayer Online Role-Playing Games), in which thousands can play and interact in visually rich shared world games like *World of Warcraft* or *Final Fantasy*. (*Second Life*, in many ways a predecessor to VR, is likewise an MMORPG, and lets players construct their own realms where they can meet like-minded folks.)

When VR went mainstream, furs embraced it wholeheartedly; the reason for this is simple: there is a thrill that comes from putting on a headset and seeing ourselves *as* our fursonas, without wearing fursuits. All one needs for the change is an avatar—a representation of oneself in the VR-verse. Designers have generic ones available for a temporary visit, but furs who know coding often modify theirs to resemble their unique fursonas. The moment you don your headset, you're looking out of your avatar's eyes. If you look at your hands, you'll see a pair of paws instead of human digits, but back in the real world, your hands are holding pistol-like controllers festooned with buttons, switches, and trigger grips, enabling you to navigate and interact with an imaginary environment. When your real-world arms move, the controllers sense the motion and your virtual arms move in sync. Likewise with the headset when you move your head.

When you hang out with other furs in one of the many VR worlds online, others see you as your avatar, just as they appear as theirs to you. And although you're all in the same virtual location, interacting in real time with the fur next to you, your physical selves might be miles, time zones, and even continents apart.

Not long ago I became a cartoon rabbit at fellow furry Crispy Carrot's biweekly meetup, a popular place for virtual bunnies to gather. Eight or so other rabbits were on the scene too, many using customized variations of Crispy's generic bunny avatar, which is what I was using to be one of their number. But what good is being a bunny (or another critter) if you can't see *yourself* as one? Environment designers usually include a virtual mirror allowing you to do exactly that, and one was available at the meetup for this purpose. It was utterly amazing to stand at the mirror and see a rabbit staring back at me, his nose giving an occasional involuntary twitch. And what good is having a tail if you can't see it either? The thoughtful designers made it possible to step *into* the mirror to view yourself from the back as well.

Like any technology, VR is constantly evolving and constantly improving. Technical terms like "inverse kinematics" or "full body tracking" refer to techniques that make a VR character's movements seem smoother, more lifelike. If you watch those "making of" bonus features on effects-heavy movies, you'll often see performers dressed in tights festooned with dots for motion capture filming. As the actor moves, the person's motions are captured by those dots (highlighted points) and fed into a computer. The resulting data is used to give the CGI doppelganger—be it alien, monster, or something else—a sense of realistic motion.

Trackers are used the same way in VR, except they work in real time. The more trackers a person wears on their feet, knees, arms, and waist, the more closely their avatar will be able to mimic their every move, not just the moves of their head and hands. There's a huge amount of data crunching involved, which is why high-end video cards can get extremely pricey.

Haptics, which utilize the experience of touch, work in reverse. Built into a VR headset's handheld controllers or delivered via wearable gloves, belts, or other clothing, they provide the physical sensations of what's happening to your avatar to your real-world body, in the process magnifying the reality of the VR experience.

The COVID-19 pandemic gave VR a major boost in popularity. If people couldn't meet in real life, virtual reality was the next best thing. And for some people, VR was even better than reality. The previously mentioned Input article quotes a fur named Coopertom considering this by saying, "Some nights we'll go to somebody's world they made and hang out and chat about music, movies, conventions, traveling . . . . Other nights we'll be going out of our way to find the most crazy bizarre worlds to laugh our asses off at." Coopertom also says that he will sometimes "slip into VR after dinner, and realize when he emerges that it's 4 a.m."[88]

WARREN WOLFY

Furry fandom helped Warren Wolfy escape a heavily religious, guilt-ridden upbringing. In his teens he was, to use his words, "totally obsessed" with his faith, writing and performing sermons, leading services, and running a Christian outreach program. However, there was still something missing. As he told me:

I'd get home after finishing at the church for the week and crawl into bed and cry, because I must be broken. The reward for living a good life was supposed to be a nice home in the suburbs, a "Godly" wife, 2.5 kids, Bible studies on Thursday nights, etc., and I wanted none of that. When I was young, I related to animals a lot better than I did with people. Animals are pretty clear with expressing exactly how they feel and what their intentions are. That's basically me.

So I took refuge in anthropomorphics. Just like real animals, anthropomorphics in movies are typically portrayed as not very deceptive about their true feelings and intentions, so I could relate to them. [The movie] *Watership Down* especially affected me. Yes, they were rabbits, and yes the story was filled with horrors, but I could imagine being one of them. I could see myself fitting into their world.

Warren's "I'm not the only one" moment arrived when he was twenty-six and saw a report on TV about a furry convention. He had never seen people in fursuits wearing tails and hanging out together. It hadn't occurred to him that anybody else shared his secret animal obsession.

Warren eventually created a fursona: a brown-and-white rabbit (also named Warren, as it happens) with black arm and leg markings, and a fursuit to match. He wanted to take the rabbit into the virtual realm and tried *Second Life*, but found it left him wanting more:

[*Second Life*] just didn't feel like it delivered on the promise of letting you be your avatar. Instead it felt like it was filled with ghost towns of abandoned projects, and constant advertising for content locked behind paywalls.

I got the HTC Vive [virtual reality headset] about a month after it was released [in 2016]. I was one of the first to have a headset. It's a surreal experience when you start using it regularly for long periods. When you aren't wearing it, you sometimes find yourself unsure of how to do simple things like walk across the room or pick up objects. It's only a very fleeting feeling, probably because your brain is still learning to differentiate between which rules apply to which world.

I found that those momentary feelings went away completely after about six months, and after about a year I no longer get any kind of motion sickness from any VR games. It all just feels completely natural now.

Motion sickness is a definite drawback to the VR experience, and it is experienced by many users. It's the result of the brain's inability to reconcile two completely opposite sets of information being fed to it, moving and stationary, all at one time. Your eyes tell your brain you're in motion, but your stationary body is telling it otherwise, a conflict that can be nauseating. One can tough it out until acclimated, like Warren did, or consult the several online videos that offer advice, such as using ginger as anti-nausea medication, or simply eschewing motion-heavy games in favor of ones based in stationary or minimally moving environments. One popular suggestion geared toward visor makers is that they put a non-moving marker, known as a "reticle," in the center of the player's field of vision to give them a stationary point to look at.

My strangest moment inside Crispy Carrot's virtual bunny world was when I took a super bunny leap straight up, way off the ground. As I started to descend, my body instinctively braced itself against an impending landing impact that never came, as in the real world I'd never left the ground.

In spite of the challenges of acclimating oneself to the virtual realm, Warren is a zealous advocate of the VR lifestyle and shared with me that he's certain it's no passing fad:

> People who don't get it think VR is just a fad, but I see it as a glimpse into an inevitable future. At some point people are going to come home, throw on some VR glasses, and hang out with their friends' avatars. I look at the changes that VR will eventually have on society. I don't know what exactly the future will look like, but one thing I do find funny is that riding this oncoming crest of the future, in fact right at the very bleeding edge of it, are the furries.

ORGANIC, ELECTRONIC, . . . AND FURRY

Today, "fursuiting"—creating and wearing a full-body costume of your "fursona," (your imaginary animal alter ego) has become such an integral part of the furry community that many non-furs believe all furries suit up. Judging from the number of participants in convention fursuit parades vs. total convention attendance, it's more likely that 20 to 30 percent of furries wear fursuits.

Hybrid fursonas—fursonas that combine more than one species into, for example, a wolf-fox super-species— are very popular among furs and some furs take it a step further and invent not only entirely new species, but elaborate societies for them to occupy. Very often these original species become popular with other furs who want to get in on the action. But furs must be careful: some species are "open species," meaning anyone is free to create a new character for the species, but others are "closed," meaning they need the species creator's approval of proposed characters, and some are regulated, meaning furs can create new characters as long as they follow certain guidelines for their characters' attributes.

Out of at least two dozen invented species (I keep stumbling across ones I had no idea existed), Dutch Angel Dragons (DADs), a regulated species, is among the most popular, with well over two thousand art or fursuit variations of DADs on Fur Affinity, the premiere website for furs to post their creative efforts. Simply put, Dutch Angel Dragons are furry flying dragons. They have nothing to do with the Netherlands, but are named for their creator's beloved late horse, Dutch. DADs are literally guardian angels, invisible to human eyes but looking out for us nonetheless.

The most intriguing of these imaginary species is only partially furry. This species, "primagens," and its sibling, "protogens," are anthropomorphic cyborg alien species that arrived on the furry scene during the second decade of the new century. Like many imaginary species, they come with an amazingly detailed description, history, and mythology of their existence and abilities, the work of ancient creators to explore their alternate universe, which is also extensively detailed.

Here in the real world, furs with a knack for electronic design are creating working versions of primagen and protogen heads featuring streamlined molded plastic muzzles containing sophisticated multicolor electronic LED systems capable of displaying digitized facial expressions, mouth animation that syncs with the wearer's voice, and impressive animated graphics.

Coela Can't!, a protogen designer, is a systems administrator and engineer for a school makerspace with an undergraduate degree in software engineering and a master's degree in electrical engineering. As he tells me, "Making electronics with custom software fits quite well with my background, which is mostly what pushed me toward working on protogens. [In protogen mythology] they're created artificially and genetically modified to fit the goal of being a space-faring species exploring the universe."

While the primagens came along a couple of years earlier, protogens only entered the furry community around 2017 or 2018, and Coela caught onto them in 2019. He shared his story with me:

> While it certainly helps to have an engineering degree, it's not a necessity: the open-source community has been providing excellent resources for makers to use and design from. One that every protogen maker should know of is Adafruit.[89]
>
> The point of entry might be easier with a degree, but even with one you'd still be missing pieces. To conceive and create a protogen from scratch, you have to be able to mechani-

cally design the helmet with mounts for LED boards, vacuum form a visor ([by reshaping heavy plastic into] the shaded face cover on the front of the protogen), and create the electronics, which can vary in complexity from single color LED displays with an Arduino Uno [microcontroller board] to full flexible AMOLED displays with a full computer and GPU [graphics processing unit] in a backpack.[90] Then of course you have to be able to finish the design via painting, vinyl graphics, and making the fur ears and head. If you look at the full picture all at once it can seem quite complicated, but each task just needs to be broken down to its components and worked from there. If you're interested enough, there are plenty of online resources that will get you started.

While similar, the primagens and protogens differ in a number of serious ways:

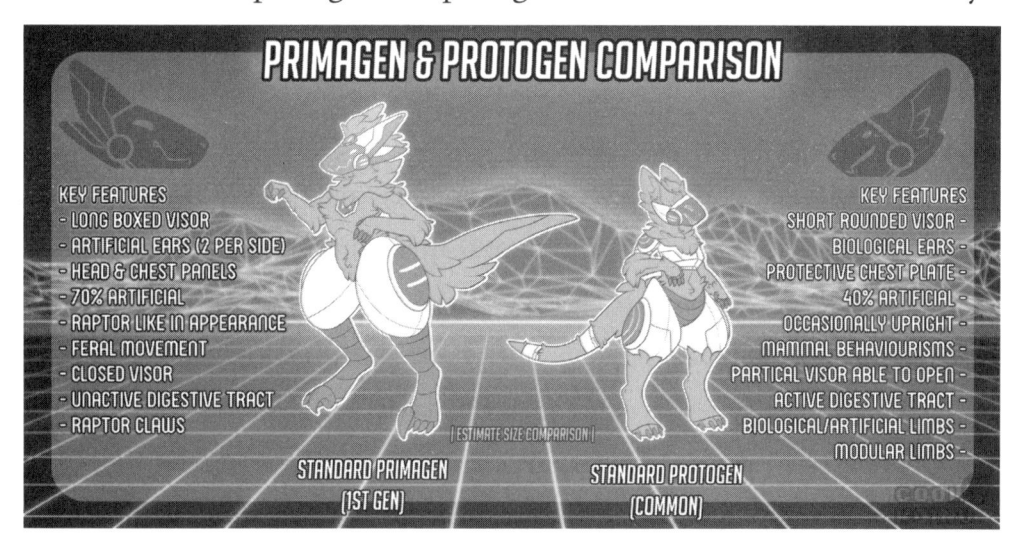

PRIMAGEN & PROTOGEN COMPARISON

KEY FEATURES
- LONG BOXED VISOR
- ARTIFICIAL EARS (2 PER SIDE)
- HEAD & CHEST PANELS
- 70% ARTIFICIAL
- RAPTOR LIKE IN APPEARANCE
- FERAL MOVEMENT
- CLOSED VISOR
- UNACTIVE DIGESTIVE TRACT
- RAPTOR CLAWS

KEY FEATURES
- SHORT ROUNDED VISOR
- BIOLOGICAL EARS
- PROTECTIVE CHEST PLATE
- 40% ARTIFICIAL
- OCCASIONALLY UPRIGHT
- MAMMAL BEHAVIOURISMS
- PARTICAL VISOR ABLE TO OPEN
- ACTIVE DIGESTIVE TRACT
- BIOLOGICAL/ARTIFICIAL LIMBS
- MODULAR LIMBS

| ESTIMATE SIZE COMPARISON |

STANDARD PRIMAGEN
(1ST GEN)

STANDARD PROTOGEN
(COMMON)

Why did Coela build a protogen and not a primagen? The primagens were a closed species carefully controlled by their creator, Malice-Risu. Until recently Malice-Risu would occasionally put a new design up for auction and it would fetch anywhere from a couple of hundred dollars to several thousand dollars. (Not the actual primagen head, simply its design; the auction winner was free to use the design to construct their personal primagen's helmet.)

By comparison, the protogens are an open species that anyone can create independently as long as they stick to the species' general guidelines. Speaking of which, Coela estimates that there are easily over a thousand furs with protogen fursonas, but only "around one hundred or so who have actually built protogen suits." You can see them on YouTube videos, but you may have to attend one of the larger furcons to catch sight of one in the electronic flesh.

PATCH O'FURR, FURRY'S DOGGED INVESTIGATIVE JOURNALIST

Patch O'Furr's Dogpatch Press website (which shares "Fluff Pieces Every Week") is unique among furry news sources for its deeply researched and detailed articles about serious (and occasionally not so serious) issues challenging the furry community.[91] On the scene since 2014, Patch and the site are regularly quoted and consulted by mainstream outlets covering furry news, including *Rolling Stone*, the *Los Angeles Times*, Vice, and *Newsweek*, and the site has won the Ursa Major Award, an annual award for excellence in anthropomorphic literature or arts, for Best Magazine.

While occasionally running guest pieces, the website's reportage is almost entirely written by Patch. Here is my interview with him:

Who are you?

I've been a furry fan since my teenage years in the early 1990s, and the main person behind Dogpatch Press. It covers news, reviews, interviews, and investigations about the furry fandom. When I'm not doing that, I'm a guy in the San Francisco Bay Area with a lot of hobbies that are sometimes jobs. I quit working for bosses years ago to write my own ticket. Working from home in a calm corner of the Bay is good for observing things during the pandemic, and I've luckily sailed through it with few effects besides putting social events on hold before getting vaccinated.

Professionally I've worked in media like animation, and made a lot of money with my own business. There's quite a story for starting it years ago: it involved losing residence, job offers, and friends in another country because I wasn't a citizen, landing on the wrong side of the border, spending my last five hundred dollars on a rusty old van, sleeping in it for a winter, and pulling my first computer from the trash while salvaging for income. I ate a lot of freegan meals then. [In time,] I raised the business to a comfortable level, but actually if I have extra means now, it goes toward making the world more interesting with events and culture. I can run a business well and don't have to separate "off" time from work, as career people do, so time I put into anything is very valuable in opportunity cost.

What was your first interest in anthropomorphic characters? Were you furry before you discovered the furry community?

In the early nineties, before knowing there was a community, I was drawing my own fan art of animal people from science fiction book covers, with an active imagination full of characters I would read and see in cartoons and a big collection of nerdy books. It led me to go to animation school. I lurked on the edge of 1990s furry, but only really made a fursona and got involved in [the subculture in] San Francisco around 2012-ish. It was like bringing an older person's appreciation to a new person's experience.

I didn't exactly follow the college animation program in Canada. The [assigned] final project was a one-minute all hand-drawn film, but mine was one of a handful of finished ones at several minutes long. I finished it in months, [working] after school [hours] while helping a friend make a TV show, staying in basements, and [sleeping on] a couch on a farm. It led to work on TV shows for Disney and MTV, storyboarding for music videos and commercials, and freelancing.

Why did you start Dogpatch Press?

I wanted to because I saw a strongly growing fandom with a big gap for all the untold stories, and nobody doing it the way I wanted to see it done. Since I mingle a lot of subcultures and experiences, and was already comfortable doing a personal blog that nobody saw, it felt great to start a DIY solution. As it went along, it was like overturning a rock. Tips would come in, and if you knew things from two overlapping areas, you could find stories in the overlap that weren't recognized and wouldn't get done by the mainstream. It wasn't meant to be for investigative stories, it's a hobby, but [it] became a crash course in journalism.

Other than occasional guest columns and reviews, is Dogpatch a one-fur show?
There are helpers who work behind the scenes to run the site, and private chat groups for it, and many sources and peers who make it possible by their incredible fandom support. But personally I don't fit in with corporate jobs who work by committee or avoid risk to keep the status quo. I put reporting first, and it isn't to grow readers, a brand, advertising, or income. That works most securely with the tightest trust among just a few people. It's not just a hobby, sometimes it means protecting sources and serving them to tell costly truths. However, anyone can submit a story, and guest pieces are some of the most important ones.

What story are you proudest of reporting?
Why pick one?

For insight: Hosting a guest history of the Cartoon/Fantasy Organization (1970s furry fandom roots) written by

Mark Merlino, founder of the first furry convention, and my stories on paleo furries (one-hundred-year-old theatrical animal costuming—like fursuiting a century ahead of time) and future fursuiting (high-tech innovations that inspired animatronics builders).

For effect: Publishing interviews and news about fandom in Sri Lanka, Iran, Latin America, Ukraine, and Kazakhstan that sometimes helped them connect and establish groups for the first time.

For how fun it was: On-the-scene stories about San Francisco's influential Frolic furry dance party, and furries in SF Pride, which I've organized since 2012 and helped put hundreds of furs on the street for millions of watchers.

For reach: Breaking national news about Nazis infiltrating furry cons, including leaders of violent terrorist groups, subsequently covered by *Newsweek, Rolling Stone,* Vice, and others.

For effort: Hundreds of hours of investigating a dark web and Telegram-based crime ring from insider leaks, including evidence of zoosadist and pedophile crimes tied to furry convention staff who try to cover up and retaliate. The story is ongoing.

For exposing secrets: Finding that an infamous furry troll was the main suspect in the 2014 Midwest Furfest chlorine attack, linking it to far-right hate. That was covered in the *Worst Year Ever* podcast "How the Furries Fought the Nazis and Won."

It sounds like you've crossed paths with some less than savory characters in the course of your reporting. Have you ever felt endangered by any of them?

Most of them had no real reach beyond social media harassment. However . . .

• A violent felon tried to find my home address. After I reported it to the FBI, he posted in a Nazi chat that police visited him and discouraged him from trying again.

• My reporting about furry Nazis led to the Furry Raiders hate group targeting me in a crime scheme. First, their founder was arrested for child sex offenses uncovered by a Dogpatch Press guest reporter (who kept it so secure I didn't even know until his arrest). Second, the founder's right-hand man targeted a witness in his case for intimidation. Third, someone tried to bait me to report false info against the witness to hurt both of us, which backfired when I reported the intimidation to police. This led to three arrests, many felony charges, and eight years in jail for furry Nazis who tried to retaliate at my reporting.

Are you worried that furry may get swept up in the rightwing attacks on gay and trans people, since they're a large and welcome presence in our community? The litter box rumor may have been a test run for such a campaign.

I think furry hate is old news and hoaxes, and haters look stupid doing it. Hoaxes work to an extent on stupid followers. Is their approval needed? If they have power, then we should keep debunking the same shit from the 1980s to today, and telling the story of the bad media period in the 2000s. I've said this time and again, and the media is helping with debunking too.

It's easy to ignore bullshit on social media after having real battles. It's better to introduce friends to what I like rather than put up with what much of the fandom may put up with to have as many events as it does now. And it's most healthy of all to get on my bike and ride in the sun, enjoying the beautiful world with friends off the net.

FURRY FOOD FOR THOUGHT: LAURENCE "GREENREAPER" PARRY'S THREEFER: FLAYRAH, WIKIFUR, AND INKBUNNY

The third millennium was still young in 2001 when the furry news site Flayrah was born. In the subsequent two decades, the site has posted over five thousand stories about and of interest to the furry community.

"Flayrah has always been something of a melting pot," explains Laurence "GreenReaper" Parry, its current head. "We've had over three hundred individual contributors in two decades. Twenty have posted fifty or more stories, and about sixty of them have posted ten or more."

Originally, a "story" on the site might have consisted of one or two sentences. Today, however, Flayrah focuses more on long-form work and less on press releases, newsletters, and one-liners. Parry explains:

I've just finished migrating it to a new server with significant upgrades to both hardware and web serving software. From a user and editor perspective, nothing has changed other than the site being faster and maybe more secure now.

YouTube has become a major means of furry news distribution, but I've always preferred text as a more content-dense means of communication, although I do listen to a few podcasts from time to time.

Parry took command of Flayrah in late 2009 after its original editor retired and no engaged successor emerged. *Watership Down* fans will remember "flayrah" as the Lapine word for what the book's rabbits considered unusually good food, or the "food of princes." The site's original editor, who was a fan of the book, imagined the word could also describe unusually good information.

Parry originally authored furry-themed articles for Wikipedia's Wikinews, then switched over to WikiFur's news page, where his stories would reach a more receptive audience. When it looked like Flayrah might vanish, he turned it into one of furry's main news sources. He explains: "I started writing news in 2007 because we had gone a long way toward recording the fandom's past at WikiFur and I felt there was a need to record the present as well, especially at such a dynamic time of growth in the fandom, with new conventions springing up all over."

Unlike most furs, Parry was born without the furry gene, but his first interest was as part of the *Creatures* Community, fans of the *Creatures* video game series where players create and raise aliens, some of whom resemble animals. When he started participating in the very popular role-play game *World Tree* (built around anthro animal characters), he took his next step into the furry community, and an interest in furry comics like *Kevin and Kell, Ozy and Millie, Freefall,* and *Dan and Mab's Furry Adventures* (*DMFA*) sealed the deal. Parry eventually became a regular at furmeets and furry conventions.

As contributors provide most of Flayrah's content, Parry, an experienced software developer and tester, is focused on maintaining the site's backend and can explain in great detail the role of servers, multi-file submissions, bulk uploads, resolution limits, and the like. Thanks to his IT interests, Parry also handles the technical aspects of both WikiFur and the furry art site Inkbunny, both of which his servers also host. He explains: "My background is primarily as a software developer—one shared by many in the fandom, but many tend to keep it to their work. For me it has been a key part of my contributions to the fandom, one which I saw would be far more valuable than any contribution I could make in terms of art or stories."

While Fur Affinity (FA) is the furry world's preeminent furry art repository, Inkbunny is one of several alternatives (along with sites like Weasyl, SoFurry, Furry Network, and until recently, Furiffic), and Parry speaks proudly about it, sharing:

> Inkbunny's a lot smaller than FA, at least five times smaller userwise. Even so, we've managed to stick around for well over a decade so far, with over two million submissions and thirty-one thousand daily users. We have better quality uploads with higher

file size, resolution limits, and better-resized copies. We don't necessarily want to be the first furry site you join when you're getting into the fandom, we want to be the one you join after that, but grow to prefer.

"DON'T ASK, DON'T TELL": TO BE GAY, FURRY, AND A SOLDIER

Kanic is a former member of the US Army. He joined right out of high school in 2006, when he was only seventeen. I originally met him at Anthrocon's traditional Milfurs [Military furs]/greymuzzles breakfast. I asked him what it's like to be gay, furry, and a soldier, and he shared the following:

> Patriotism and the thrill of adventure definitely played some part in my enlistment. The biggest motivator, though, was the lack of belief from classmates, and even a few family members, that I could "make it," so to speak. At that time I wasn't exactly a physically strong individual, nor was I into activities that many who join the military are into. I loved video games and gaming in general, computers, technology, and other things many would consider nerdy.
>
> It was quite satisfying to see how proud my family was of me after completing basic combat training. No one thought I could do it. The physical challenge in and of itself was immense, but the mental factors had their fair share. Joining the military as a gay man or an LGBTQ+ person at the time presented its

own set of unique challenges to overcome. The military is seen as generally masculine, traditional in its customs and culture. To say there isn't some homophobia or general disdain for such folks in the military would be a lie. The real kicker to the aforementioned unique challenges for LGBTQ+ folks in the military at the time? The policy known as Don't Ask, Don't Tell, or DADT as many boiled it down to.

To put it simply, it was a policy that was put in place in the nineties that allowed LGBTQ+ folks to join the military, with the caveat that no one could ask if you were gay (or lesbian, bi, trans, anything that wasn't strictly heterosexual), and you couldn't tell anyone you were either. To do so would get you a dishonorable discharge from the military (though many were given "other than honorable" discharges, which isn't exactly good either, but not as heavy as a dishonorable). To join the military at the height of the wars in Iraq and Afghanistan at the time was dangerous enough. Those dangers, along with the stressors of having to hide one's sexuality out of fear of discharge, was taxing at times. Why would a gay man want to join the military with such obstacles in front of him? Courage is the biggest one. To put aside fear of all of that and show that anyone is capable of doing this.

Furry and the fandom overall were a huge base of mental support and help, if you can believe it! When I got home from basic combat training in 2006, gained stable access to the internet, and began my journey into the fandom, I eventually bumped into other military furries, both online and in person, many of whom I'm still great friends with to this very day. Even nonmilitary furries were wishing me well, providing listening ears to vent to, and generally supportive. Furs I hadn't even met were sending me care packages even while I was overseas in Iraq! That made my combat tour in Iraq of 2009 much easier to get through.

I left the military in 2014 after eight years of service. While there was temptation to stay, I saw that another combat tour was on the horizon, and I felt I had done my part in service to my country and chose not to reenlist. I have no regrets though. I smile when I look back on my years of service. At the end of the day, joining the military and simultaneously being in furry gave me lasting connections and friendships that I may have never found had I not joined the Army—or furry, for that matter. For that, and all the lovely folks I met, I am truly grateful!

4

MAINSTREAM ANTHROPOMORPHIC LITERATURE

You may have loved *Peter Rabbit, Winnie the Pooh,* or *The Wind in the Willows* when you were a kid. Those animal stories meant something to you, but now you're an adult and it's time to put away childish things, or so they tell you. Well, to hell with them. Furry and non-furry adults alike still find comfort and wisdom in the storybook animals of their youth. Growing up doesn't have to mean giving up your childhood friends.

However, there are quite a few books about animals that behave, speak, or think very differently from the critters in your bookstore's kiddie corner. You can go as far back as that fourteenth-century staple of college English lit courses, Chaucer's *Canterbury Tales*, and its "Nun's Priest's Tale" of a vain rooster and a wily fox, or to China for Wu Cheng'en's sixteenth-century novel *Journey to the West*, based on twelfth-century legends of a troublemaking, godlike simian.

COMMUNIST PIGS AND PHILOSOPHICAL SEAGULLS

Here in modern times, books starring anthropomorphic animals have become bestsellers and literary classics. The best known has to be *Animal Farm*, George Orwell's 1945 allegory of Stalinist totalitarianism set on a farm where the animals have overthrown their human master. (Its original subtitle, *A Fairy Story*, is long gone from the covers of contemporary reprints.) In the immediate aftermath of World War II, when the Soviet Union was still respected as a valuable ally in defeating Hitler, *Animal Farm* was turned down by several publishers before finally finding a home.

Richard Bach's *Jonathan Livingston Seagull* has been derided as a banal self-help book in the guise of an animal fable, but this 1970 novel of a perfection-seeking waterfowl has sold millions of copies. It spent the better part of 1972 and 1973 atop the *New York Times* bestseller list[92] after being rejected by several publishers.[93]

QUESTING RABBITS, FUGITIVE DOGS

Richard Adams's *Watership Down* was likewise rejected by an assortment of publishers and literary agents before a small publishing house took a chance and watched an oddball work become a monstrous international bestseller.[94] (Are we beginning to see a pattern here?) It has since sold *fifty million* copies, become a movie, inspired a sequel, and had theatrical adaptations as well as an animated series.[95] Only twenty-five hundred copies of the novel were originally printed, and today used copies of the first edition go for as much as seventy-five hundred dollars.[96]

Adams's story of a band of rabbits traveling the British countryside in search of a new home is an imaginative blend of fact (courtesy of British naturalist Ronald Lockley's *The Private Life of the Rabbit*) and fantasy. Adams created a richly detailed secret world for his rabbits that includes their own language, assorted deities, and El-ahrairah, a trickster folk hero Bugs Bunny might envy, who appears in brief tales interspersed throughout the novel. As Adams explains in the novel's introduction, "I followed the idea of Rudyard Kipling, in his two *Jungle Book*s. That is to say, although my rabbits could think and talk, I never made them do anything physical that real rabbits could not do."[97]

Adams's later novel *The Plague Dogs* is nowhere near as ambitious a literary exercise—or as life-affirming as *Watership Down* (or commercially successful, for that matter). Its canine heroes, Rowf and Snitter, escape from the research laboratory that has subjected them to repeated, cruel experiments. Circumstance and a sensationalist reporter conspire to make the dogs appear as vicious killers and possible plague carriers, panicking the public and triggering a military hunt for the animals.

The film version of *The Plague Dogs* may have the distinction of sporting a tragic ending almost the exact opposite of its source material. The animated feature ends on an ambiguous note faithful to Adams's original conception, with the exhausted dogs swimming toward an island refuge off the Welsh coast that may not actually exist. In the book, however, Adams openly admits—in an imagined dialog with "the reader" (written in rhyming, thirteenth-century French ballade form, no less)—that he's given into their entreaties (actually, friends who had an advance look at his manuscript) to provide a deus ex machina happy ending to his doomed characters.

Make that a *deus ex Orielton*, the boat that Ronald Lockley—the same Lockley whose rabbit research helped Adams accurately describe his *Watership*

Down warren—is traveling on with a friend. Adams mocks himself in dialogue he's given Lockley ("Well-intentioned amateurs like that chap Richard Adams . . . know next to nothing about rabbits—hopelessly sentimental"), while his companion counters that "a certain amount of anthropomorphism's probably useful in helping them to arrive at feeling and sympathy for animals," just before the pair notices "something swimming over there" and rescues the near-drowned animals. In the end, Snitter is reunited with his heartbroken master, who adopts Rowf as well, while the scandal-seeking journalist turns good guy, merrily exposing the laboratory's cruel methods.[98]

Even the modern-day celebrity author David Sedaris took a plunge into anthropomorphism with his short story collection *Squirrel Seeks Chipmunk*. As he explained to Jon Stewart during a 2010 *Daily Show* appearance, he decided to write his own animal stories after being underwhelmed by an audiobook of South African animal folk tales ("They just weren't very good"), to which Stewart responded, "So you're driving along thinking, *I can do better than this South African oral tradition?*"[99] Stewart, however, went on to praise the book.

With *Squirrel Seeks Chipmunk* was Sedaris responding to a personal, atavistic, and anthropomorphic instinct using his literary chops? Not likely. Instead he described it as more akin to a case of descriptive shortcuts. When Stewart asked, "Is the idea through animals it packs more punch somehow?" Sedaris responded (in sentiments similar to Raphael Bob-Waksberg discussing his use of animal characters in *BoJack Horseman*), "If you were going to write a story, and you say, 'Phillip and Leslie had been dating for two weeks and they ran out of things to talk about,' as a reader I would need to know what Leslie's hair color was and what Philip was wearing and how old they were. But if you say, 'the squirrel and the chipmunk,' everybody knows what the squirrel and the chipmunk look like, so you can just start."

Though Sedaris's sardonic and somewhat condescending tales have found an audience, all but three feature unlikeable characters and downbeat end-of-story morals and they left this fur cold. While most are set in an all-animal universe, a handful take place in the human world with self-aware animals following Rudyard Kipling's *Jungle Book* rule of communicating only among themselves. In the title story, a chipmunk's family forces their daughter to break off her relationship with the squirrel she met through a personals ad. The decision leaves her filled with regret in her old age, thinking of the squirrel's love of jazz as "every beautiful thing she had ever failed to appreciate."[100]

In Sedaris's story "The Motherless Bear," the bear seeks endless sympathy for her loss, but alienates other animals when she is incapable of offering any sympathy in return. When she turns to an old, sick dancing bear for sympathy, she winds up taking the animal's place after it dies. In spite of being treated miserably by her owner and being in full view of an audience, she can only think of being motherless: "Every so often she'll spot someone weeping and swear they can understand her every word."

We have the Transportation Security Administration to thank for Sedaris's story "The Vigilant Rabbit," in which the power-mad guard of a forest community kills anyone who challenges his authority and lives (but not for very long) to regret robbing a unicorn of its horn. Promoting the book in 2010, Sedaris told Jon Stewart that an elderly TSA agent once aggressively insisted he remove his vest before letting him through security, leading the author to decide, "I'm going to make you into a rabbit."[101]

Squirrel Seeks Chipmunk also features a parade of smug New Age-y rats, narcissistic cows, judgmental chickens, conniving crows, and a mouse who, believing her pet snake is a loving companion, feeds it her neighbors' children until the snake consumes her as well.

Thankfully (and curiously) at the end of the book, Sedaris shares three stories that avoid a completely bleak view of existence. One is "The Parrot and the Potbellied Pig," wherein a feathered journalist at a party meets the insecure porker she once mocked in an article and apologizes for her cruelty. The two then begin a relationship she later calls "her days of swine and neuroses."

The somewhat redeeming story "Hello Kitty," is set in a prison's Alcoholics Anonymous meeting. There, an arrogant cat who never talks and thinks himself above it all is challenged by a rat who is in for serious crimes. The goaded cat finally angrily speaks up, and inadvertently admits to being an alcoholic. In appreciation he says, "That little SOB saved my life, can you beat that? Not a day goes by when I don't think about him."

The story "The Grieving Owl" is the strangest, longest, and final one in the book. In it, an owl offers to spare a mouse rather than have him for dinner if the rodent can tell him something he's never heard before. The mouse informs him that a species of leech lives inside a hippopotamus's anus. The pair then meet a zoo hippo who confirms the mouse's story and shares that she wants to rid herself of the colony inside her, whose singing annoys her to no end. Then a gerbil appears who offers to help, and great American humorist David Sedaris ends *Squirrel Seeks Chipmunk* with a gerbil up the anus joke.

WILLIAM KOTZWINKLE

William Kotzwinkle's first book was published in 1969, and since then he has written short stories, novels, screenplays, novels based on screenplays, and children's books, and has won scads of awards for his work. He's probably best known for his novelization of, and sequel novel to, Spielberg's *E.T.* He's also written several imaginative and provocative novels featuring anthropomorphic animals.

The cover of Kotzwinkle's *The Bear Went Over the Mountain,* illustrated by *New Yorker* cover artist extraordinaire Peter de Sève, depicts a confused bear in a rumpled suit holding a document under his arm while standing in the midst of traffic and a crowd of oblivious New Yorkers. It's a compelling cover image for a book with a surprising backstory, as *Bear* was conceived of as the result of a fire in a Maine farmhouse. Kotzwinkle and his wife, both writers, had left New York City in favor of a tranquil environment more conducive to their creativity—something that seemed like a splendid idea until the day they went into town and their farmhouse burned to the ground in their absence, incinerating the only copies of their unfinished novels.

Their farmhouse rebuilt, the Kotzwinkles decided to take no chances on their next trip into town and left their work in progress under a tree a safe distance from their new home. Another good idea, until a curious bear made off with the portfolio containing Kotzwinkle's wife's latest manuscript. Thankfully, the portfolio—while ravaged by ursine tooth and claw—was soon found, and its contents were intact.

"Years later, it occurred to me," Kotzwinkle reminisced on his website, "what if the bear had succeeded in opening the portfolio, begun to read it, and said to himself, 'This isn't bad,' and set off with it to New York City to find an agent and a publisher?"[102]

This is what happens in *The Bear Went Over the Mountain* when a bear, the self-named Hal Jam—who is by far smarter and more literary than the average bear—sees the potential in *Destiny and Desire*, a story into which Arthur Bramhall, a moody college professor, has poured his heart and soul. Dressed in a stolen suit, Hal heads for New York where, thanks to the purloined manuscript, he quickly acquires an agent, publisher, publicist, and glamorous Hollywood power player whom he'll eventually screw in the back seat of a taxicab. ("*If she had some fur on her face and the backs of her hands,*" Hal thinks, "*she might be good looking.*"[103]) Interestingly, despite his indulgences, throughout Hal's entire New York adventure—flopping on his back in a posh restaurant, diving into a Central Park lake in search of salmon, buying a supermarket's entire honey inventory—no one notices he's a bear, or at least no one chooses to notice, because as the book explains, "they were human beings."

Conversely, as Hal becomes enamored of civilization's niceties, back in the Maine woods, Bramhall is recovering from the loss of his life's work and finds himself growing attuned to the natural world Hal has left behind. This is evocatively described by Kotzwinkle:

> Then the beavers worked, and Bramhall, with a strange floating sensation, felt himself go to them, felt himself crouching beside them on the wooded hill above their pond. . . . Their eyes flashed at him, signaling a pact he could seal with them, if he desired. . . .

> Bramhall turned abruptly, sensing the direction of the invisible ripple. . . . Precisely where his gaze stopped, the weasel reappeared . . . . Bramhall could feel the little killer reassessing him . . . . [The porcupine's odor] was leaving a vivid picture of it in the night air. . . .
>
> [Bramhall was] suddenly aware that he was smelling a night rich with scents of every kind . . . . Bramhall felt the groundhog's uneasiness, even seemed to feel its thoughts—caution, suspicion—you never know who might shove a rat terrier down your hole.

In addition to connecting with the animals, Bramhall begins physically changing as well, turning burly, hairier, and semi-feral. In the midst of love-making with a nature-loving woman, he impulsively bites her shoulder "and felt an odd sensation at the tip of his coccyx, as if a tail were vigorously twitching there." He soon gives up human habitation in favor of sleeping in a cave where he dreams of bears: "their great dark forms rubbed against him, then led him down forest trails."[104]

What connects Bramhall to these images and sensations? It's an urge that runs through several of Kotzwinkle's works, and although it's not elucidated in *The Bear Went Over the Mountain,* Doctor Rat, the eponymous protagonist of another Kotzwinkle novel, is more than happy to enlighten us, saying: "I'm sure you are aware, we animals have wordless communication, based on sensory impulses more subtle than language."[105] Here Doctor Rat is describing the "intuitive network": the means by which the denizens of the animal world share their thoughts and feelings with one another in his novel. In *The Bear Went Over the Mountain*, this intuition enables the increasingly feral Bramhall to tune into his forest's beavers, bears, porcupines, and groundhogs.

The nonhuman animal world communicating through an imaginary worldwide telepathic network? An imaginative fantasy writer's invention, surely. Or is it? Kotzwinkle begs to differ:

> The intuitive wavelength is undeniable. It happens spontaneously under extraordinary circumstances. But it can also be developed if one has patience. And something else is required—sympathy.
>
> I can spend hours looking at insects for the very good reason that it breaks the boundaries of my ego. This is a startling surrender and during it insight occurs. You recognize that the insect and you are equal. The insect's concerns are absolute. It's involved at that very moment in an ultimate struggle exactly like your own. All of its senses, including some that we don't possess, are exquisitely active as it scans the world in order to survive. And the insect is there, it's really there in front of your eyes, with a claim to existence equal to your own. You are important to it only insomuch as you are a giant predatory shadow. You have no other claim in its kingdom. You're a stranger, a foreign element, a nothing that is something but nothing nonetheless.
>
> When you feel yourself to be momentarily *nothing* and the insect to be *something* then a huge shift occurs.[106]

The rodent mentioned is the title character and central narrator of *Doctor Rat,* one of Kotzwinkle's earliest works. (My yellowing forty-five-year-old copy is practically crumbling in my hands as I page through it.) The novel, poles apart from the whimsical *The Bear Went Over the Mountain*, is a pitch-black tragicomedy of the horrors not just of academic laboratory animal experimentation, but of completely *pointless* animal experimentation.

Having been castrated and "driven mad in the mazes," Doctor Rat cheers on and describes in gruesome detail the tortures inflicted on the dogs, rabbits, and his fellow rodents ("You'll be the tenth rat this week to have his brains sucked out by a pneumatic tube"[107]) in the name of science. Doctor Rat is a victim of the rodent equivalent of Stockholm syndrome, extolling the lab's meaningless "research" to its victims. When he hears their bewildered agony, he responds to their suffering with his cheerful motto, "Death is freedom!"[108]

And exactly what qualifies Doctor Rat to comfort his fellow rats? "It requires psychological understanding, of course. And having been driven insane, I hold the necessary degree in psychology," he shares[109]. For Kotzwinkle's part, he recalls his own similar experience:

> I saw behavioral science grad students thoughtlessly joking about a monkey they used in their experiments. They were completely unconscious of the monkey's nature. I watched them tap him on the head with a hammer and laugh about it. I had to leave, or I would've taken the hammer to them.
>
> All the other experiments came from laboratory literature. I've read of present-day scientific investigators who work

with birds. Birds sing through a unique organ called the syrinx. Among other things, it allows them to sing two notes simultaneously. These investigators remove the syrinx of birds, then inflate the syrinx artificially to find out exactly how birds sing. This is so monstrous and wrong-headed one can only feel sorry for the poor fools who are so dead inside that they can't recognize birdsong for what it is—the gift of the birds to the world. Some things shouldn't be taken apart.[110]

Counterpointing Doctor Rat's twisted soliloquies are chapters following an uprising of the animal kingdom, spread through the intuitive network, as members of every species migrate toward a great gathering. Kotzwinkle gives voice to many in the throng or trapped in cages, slaughterhouses, or factory farms and zoos—and all in poetic, often heartbreaking chapters. It's not as much a revolt against the human world as it is a protest, a yearning for unity of all animals, man included. In the hopeful words of a young chimpanzee, "Once we gather this way, man will come too. He will realize that we are all one creature, and he will stop killing us. His realization will be sudden and wonderful."[111] To spoil the ending, it doesn't end well. (Then again, once humankind is involved, what do you expect?)

The novel's one moment of hope comes from a visionary composer who has brought a sixty-piece orchestra to the middle of the Atlantic to communicate with a pod of whales, a species he considers the world's greatest musicians ("They're creative, wise, and they make no wars") via a symphony "constructed from the basic musical elements" of their songs.[112] The whales respond in kind, performing an even more magnificent version of his symphony, a success beyond his imagining, until whaling ships appear on the horizon to capture the animals.

In Doctor Rat's efforts to keep his fellow rodents from joining the animals' revolt, he discovers numerous rodent subcultures, all parodies of human behavior. A female rat attempts to seduce him, an event described by Doctor Rat in language no self-respecting fur would fail to appreciate: "She slinks slowly up to me, twirling her tail seductively . . . she wraps her tail around my neck and yanks me into the burrow." Visiting the other side of the street, as it were, Doctor Rat discovers a colony of pink-tagged gay rodents ("Male rats—dancing with each other, cheek to cheek, whisker to whisker!") and a rat army "marching all in file, all in perfect order, all armed with surgical picks, all wearing surgical-thimble helmets, which glisten ominously in the moonlight."[113]

With its gruesome, pointless lab experimentation on helpless animals, and the humans oblivious to the suffering they inflict upon the world, *Doctor Rat* would make an unbelievably powerful animated feature, but it wouldn't sell very many Happy Meals.[114]

Of all of Kotzwinkle's works, the strangest appearance of the extrasensory "wavelength" may be in his phantasmagoric *Herr Nightingale and the Satin Woman*, an illustrated fable that all but defies description. Set in a variety of exotic locales and taking place between the world wars, the book begins with a hard-luck Scotland Yard detective visiting a dressing gown-garbed mole (who is also a mole of the espionage variety) for information about his quarry, the elusive Herr Nightingale.

A human in spite of his name, Nightingale is a smuggler of machine guns, hashish, and a supernatural potion, the "attar of dreams" that affects almost everyone it comes into contact with. Nightingale's sometime companion is the glamorous Satin Woman, herself on the verge of a romance with a piano-playing cricket. The lovestruck animal tries to communicate with the woman through the intuitive network and as he does so, "a strange signal passes thru her nerves, and she draws back, shocked by the delicate sensation that only gradually subsides[115] . . . the voice of the cricket which she hears inside her forehead, faintly tingling, electric."[116]

Following their connection, the woman and cricket hope to consummate their love in a dream realm where she will take the form of a cricket herself, but both meet with frustration when she becomes a beautiful moth instead. She consoles herself by allowing the cricket to take up residence in her undergarments where "he roams freely . . . [and] at times she faints without reason, a sudden little gasp taking her mid-sentence, her eyes glassing over, then fluttering wildly."[117]

For Kotzwinkle, the border between the human world and the rest of the animal kingdom is permeable, if it exists at all. A bear and a man trade places, a rat adopts the worst values of humanity as his own, and an insect pines for a human woman who is smitten by his affection.

And what of the author himself? Where does he stand on that divide? If he could turn into a bear, or any animal for that matter, would he? Kotzwinkle answered this for me:

> [Yes,] on a nightly basis. I once had a most convincing dream
> that I was a fox. Moving beautifully through the moonlight, I
> rejoiced in my wildness.

We torture animals and we cherish them. There are more pets now than anyone could have imagined one hundred years ago. There are animal psychologists and psychics all over the place. Pets have become big business. Is it a sign of our warm hearts and spiritual progress? Or our loneliness?

As for the intelligence of the human race, one can be highly intelligent and still believe any sort of nonsense. But the intelligence of the human race remains what it has always been, an extraordinary example of what the cosmos can do when a planet is at the optimal distance from the sun.[118]

"WHISKED INTO A WORLD OF CASTLES AND TALKING ANIMALS": KIRSTEN BAKIS

Was 1997 to be the year of anthropomorphic fiction for mainstream readers? So wondered an article in the *New York Observer*.[119] The article referred to a handful of novels published around the same time—*Pig Tales*, *The Bear Comes Home*, and in particular, *Lives of the Monster Dogs*—and these musings surrounded an interview with *Monster Dogs*'s author, Kirsten Bakis, at that time a twenty-nine-year-old first-time novelist. The paper's headline writer must have had trouble taking seriously an author whose characters were anthropomorphic animals, as the writer referred to Bakis as a "dog-loving weirdo," but perhaps the name was partly Bakis's fault, as in the article she referred to her work as "a little weird" and then added, "I guess my take on the world is a little weird too."

The titular dogs in *Lives of the Monster Dogs* are a troupe of canines who have traveled from the far reaches of Canada, where they were surgically created by a certifiably mad German scientist, to arrive in New York in 2008. Dressed in elegant nineteenth-century finery, they speak using implanted voice boxes, sport mechanical hands, and walk on their hind legs with the aid of canes. Almost immediately, the dogs become New York society darlings, the object of breathless media attention. They treat the city to a fanciful Christmas parade ("artificial snow paved the way for gold and silver sleighs shaped like swans, dolphins, lions, and ships") and build themselves a Disney-style castle in lower Manhattan. There they throw an anarchic party and retell their violent origin for the public, some of whom are "wearing disturbingly realistic canine heads, with ears and mouths that moved awkwardly . . . operated by hidden strings and pulleys." (I believe I saw several at the last furcon I attended.) A young student to whom one of the dogs has taken an interest becomes their chronicler (and the book's narrator), the only human allowed into their inner circle.[120]

Monster Dogs earned rave reviews from newspapers across the country. Among them, a *New York Times* write-up most authors would kill for that described Bakis's novel as "a rich, resonant dream . . . a dazzling, unforgettable meditation on what it means to be human."[121] The *Observer* article revealed that Bakis's empathy for canines began during her time as a dog walker for New York's wealthy and deepened with the death of her dog Ox, who was struck by a careless driver not far from the fictional location of the Monster Dogs's castle. It also shares that Bakis spent years writing and rewriting *Monster Dogs* and her dogged determination to get the book right ultimately led to a thumbs-up from celebrated novelist Saul Bellow, and a fifty thousand dollar advance from a major publishing house.

When I interviewed Bakis, she admitted to thinking that Cleo, the book's narrator, was a stand-in for herself, and asked: "Doesn't everyone want to be picked up from the grimy streets by a limousine and whisked into a world where there are castles and talking animals?" Then she spoke of the overlap between human and animal worlds that the book touches on, saying: "There's something very moving to me about the way in which they're caught between the human and animal worlds. They want so much to be part of our society, to be in our company, but they're not like us."[122]

Personally, I think the same could be said of our feelings toward dogs—we want so much for them to be part of our society, to be in our company. We write books and make cartoons about talking and thinking dogs, buy them clothes and Halloween costumes, take them to pet therapists, call them our children, and, if you're a fur of a certain mind, don a multi-thousand-dollar fursuit and become one.

"I do think our culture is thinking more about the relationship between humans and other species," says Bakis. "Not that we have ever not thought about that, but clearly it's on the rise. We're reconsidering that relationship." She continues:

> For example, the idea of being vegan because of the suffering caused not just by the meat industry, but the egg and dairy industries, that was hardly around when I wrote the book. Now almost everyone at least knows what the word "vegan" means. Maybe my book is part of that trend. But also it's something I've always been interested in.

I don't like many books or stories about anthropomorphized animals. Too often they're just stand-ins for people, and I think the underlying assumption when you anthropomorphize is that only people can have feelings, can have stories about them that matter. For a story about an animal to matter, that animal has to be made human, or made into a symbol for something that humans care about.

We've done such unspeakable things to animals. I think sometimes we anthropomorphize and use them as symbols because we can't bear to look directly at them. When I wrote *Monster Dogs* I tried to avoid making the characters into symbols or stand-ins for people. I felt they were real in their own right. They seemed alive to me. Maybe they weren't exactly dogs—they were altered, they were different—but they were at least themselves.

The book was so widely influential that Bakis tells me about a swamp rock band from Atlanta whose members named their band after the novel. ("They're great," Bakis says.) And the novel was adapted, without Bakis's prior knowledge, into a stage play. ("A friend of mine got hold of the poster, but that's all I know about it. It's a nice poster," she says.) It also had its film rights optioned twice. The first attempt never got past the screenplay stage, but in 2010 *Monster Dogs* was optioned by Chris Wedge, former head of the now defunct Blue Sky Studios, the studio responsible for the *Ice Age* films, *Rio*, and *The Peanuts Movie*. According to IMDb, Wedge optioned the film rights to *Lives of the Monster Dogs* not for Blue Sky, but for his personal production company, WedgeWorks. A *Hollywood Reporter* description of the proposed film reads:

> A mad Prussian scientist engineers a group of soldier dogs in a Canadian village. The hyper-intelligent dogs, who walk erect and use voice boxes to communicate, revolt against their masters and, dressed in nineteenth century formal wear, show up in modern New York.[123]

The film rights have since reverted back to Bakis, and so Wedge's vision of the story will go unmade. Like Kotzwinkle's *The Bear Went Over the Mountain*, *Lives of the Monster Dogs* may be one of those projects destined to perpetually hover on the edge of "soon to be a major motion picture."

KRAZY KAT AND GOJIRO

Pop culture has always been fertile ground for mainstream authors who see in well-known, commercially successful characters metaphors for something larger than the characters' creators' original humble goal of providing folks with a bit of time-killing amusement. Two books in particular come to mind that employ appropriation, importing ideas and images from existing artistic works into new creations to better explore those concepts. These books, Jay Cantor's *Krazy Kat* and Mark Jacobson's *Gojiro*, have a lot in common. Both use pop culture characters to explore the anxieties of the atomic age created by the nuclear bomb, both feature the real-life nuclear scientist J. Robert Oppenheimer, one of the key architects of the bomb (as himself in *Krazy Kat* and as a fictionalized version in *Gojiro*), and in both books a Hollywood movie producer plays a key role.

In Cantor's book, which pulls its title character, Krazy, from George Herriman's early twentieth-century comic strip *Krazy Kat*, Krazy is a cat of indeterminate gender who interprets the bricks tossed at its noggin by the irritable Ignatz Mouse as expressions of love. Herriman's comic strip that inspired this was ripe with poetic dialog and surreal, ever-shifting backgrounds that made *Krazy Kat* irresistible to artists and intellectuals of his day, in the 1920s and thirties, including Charlie Chaplin and Pablo Picasso,[124] as well as contemporary cartoonists too numerous to mention who cite the strip as having influenced their own work.[125] Its biggest fan, however, may have been publishing magnate William Randolph Hearst, who ran the strip in all his newspapers and gave Herriman a lifetime contract and complete creative freedom.

In Cantor's novel, Krazy, now certifiably female, meets and develops a crush on J. Robert Oppenheimer and witnesses the atomic bomb's testing in a New Mexico desert that fills her with existential dread.

Cantor mimics Herriman's language (Oppenheimer and his scientists are "New Clear fizzyits"), but his efforts to depict the comic strip's surrealism in prose is often labored. ("The mountain you walked towards became a building as soon as you stepped on/in it.")[126]

Traumatized by the bomb, Krazy quits the comic strip, leaving Ignatz and the rest of its animal cast at loose ends. Ignatz tries a variety of methods to induce Krazy to return to the strip, including psychoanalysis and introducing Krazy to a Hollywood movie producer who promises to make her a star. Ignatz and Krazy eventually join the human world, first as psychiatrist (Dr. Ignatz) and patient, then as lovers, and eventually as accompanist and cabaret singer Kat—or are their human lives simply an agreed-upon and minutely detailed fantasy?

Krazy Kat: A Novel in Five Panels leaves its fan fiction premise behind to incorporate a heady brew of definitely non-comic strip subjects, including aging and death, sex and sexism, terrorism and class conflict. It's enough to make a comics fan nostalgic for a simpler time, when a cat and mouse's sado-masochistic relationship set against an ever-shifting, protean background was a new work of art every day.

Like Cantor, Mark Jacobson builds his novel around a "what if a pop culture legend actually existed in the real world?" premise. In *Gojiro,* his reimagining of Godzilla as an intelligent, philosophical, and suicidal five hundred-foot-tall, mutated monitor lizard named Gojiro, his prose is so dense as to be all but impenetrable and nearly impossible to follow ("But once the tabloid reflex locks and Luce's sluice flings loose, who needs proof?" runs a typical line.)[127]

Gojiro's plot defies easy summary, featuring "lizard philosophy," "psychic supplications," visions of the past and future, a "quadcameral brain" capable of physically absorbing the entire Earth, time travel . . . and a bomb capable of obliterating the universe.

In the novel, Gojiro, accompanied by Komodo (not an actual Komodo dragon, but a radiation-scarred Hiroshima survivor and scientific genius) live on Radioactive Island with equally radioactive, mutated children known as Atoms. Everything changes, however, when the giant 'zard (to use the novel's scaly slang) succumbs to a high-living Hollywood producer's offer to star in *Gojiro vs. Joseph Prometheus Brooks* (the fictionalized Oppenheimer) *in the Valley of Decision*. The film and its many sequels make Gojiro a movie star and the object of worship of children across the world who view him as their friend and protector. The success takes Gojiro to the decadent world of Hollywood power players and ultimately to the same place that changed Krazy Kat's life: the New Mexico site of the first atomic bomb test.

JONATHAN LETHEM

Not many authors combine high and low culture as easily as Jonathan Lethem. A highly respected novelist and short story writer, he's also written a graphic novel based on a Marvel Comics superhero,[128] interviewed Bob Dylan for *Rolling Stone*,[129] and authored short books about the Talking Heads[130] and the John Carpenter movie *They Live*.[131]

In the literary world Lethem is known as a genre bender, mixing superheroes, detective stories, and sci-fi concepts into his work.[132] His first novel, *Gun, with Occasional Music*, combines private eyes and talking animals to unique effect.[133] *Gun* takes place in an alternate reality where detectives are known as "inquisitors," the printed word is outlawed, people carry their "karmic level" on a credit card (if you let yours hit zero, you're in serious trouble), and "evolution therapy" has created intelligent, speaking animals. In classic first-person detective story lingo (with lines such as, "He couldn't have been more than twenty-five, but he'd obviously lived long enough to have things to regret"), private inquisitor and tough guy Conrad Metcalf narrates his attempts to solve his client's murder.[134] In the process, Metcalf runs up against an assortment of suspects and antagonists: an evolved kangaroo and thug in the employ of a major gangster, as well as dogs, kittens, sheep, and even rabbits dressed in tiny three-piece suits. Evolved animals do the menial jobs once performed by minorities, and "the rules barring the evolved animals [from human establishments] were slackening everywhere," Metcalf ruminates, "and bigots like me were just going to have to get used to it." In total, a fun, snappy read, *Gun* is also lush with oddball lines like "In Los Angeles it's illegal to know what you do for a living," reflecting its askew reality.[135]

Gun isn't the only time a talking animal appears in Lethem's work. In his short story "The Dystopianist, Thinking of His Rival, Is Interrupted by a Knock on the Door," published in Lethem's 2004 book *Men and Cartoons*, a writer (identified only as "the Dystopianist") who specializes in gloom-and-doom speculation is only mildly surprised to be visited by the character he is in the midst of creating: the suicidal Sylvia Plath Sheep. To his disappointment though, the sheep isn't particularly suicidal at the moment; instead he challenges his creator: "How many sheep have to die to assuage your childish resentments?"

The sheep leaves, to the Dystopianist's relief: "[he] was still proud of the Plath Sheep, and rather glad to have met it, even if the Plath Sheep wasn't proud of him."[136]

A COW, A TURKEY, AND A PIG WALK INTO A NOVEL...

"I WANT TO BELIEVE," reads the flying saucer poster on the wall of Fox Mulder's FBI basement office, the exiled home of the Bureau's resident oddball special agent, in the long-running sci-fi TV show *The X-Files*. But believe in barnyard animals who can talk and stand upright passing themselves off as human beings who steal planes and fly across the globe in search of refuge from the human world that considers them nothing more than food? If this is perceived to be happening, it would definitely be an *X-Files*-worthy case for Mulder. Resident skeptic Dana Scully might remind Mulder that these kinds of conjectures are strictly fictional—but *Holy Cow* author and *X-Files* star David Duchovny, who played Mulder, would likely disagree.

Or at least I'm led to believe so from Duchovny's *Holy Cow*, a 2015 novel that tells of bovine Elsie Bovary's attempt to elude the meaty fate destined for those of her species. Accompanied by converted-to-Judaism pig Shalom and willfully anorexic, Thanksgiving-dreading turkey Tom, Elsie escapes the farm and the trio travels to far-off lands where they believe safety awaits: India (where cows are sacred), Israel (where pork is definitely off the menu), and Turkey (what could be safer than a country that shares his name?).

The disparate species communicate through what Elsie, the chatty first-person narrator, calls "a kind of universal, beasty Esperanto" (not that far removed from Kotzwinkle's "intuitive wavelength"), a language in which all animals can converse with all other animals, regardless of the noises they make.[137]

Holy Cow can easily be described as a postmodern work: randomly, and for no obvious reason, Elsie shifts from first-person narration (directly addressing, even challenging the reader) to retelling her adventure and describing working with her editor, and between standard narrative-style fiction and screenplay-format dialog.[138] And Elsie (or more accurately, Duchovny) continually rubs our noses in the tale's impossibility, beginning on page one when Elsie admits her hooves are incapable of holding a pen or using a phone—despite the fact that the animals make extensive use of "hammerspace," that extra-dimensional cartoon realm producing maps, books, and yes, even a mobile phone seemingly out of nowhere.[139] Also pushing our imagination is how, like Hal Jam in Kotzwinkle's *The Bear Went Over the Mountain*, Elsie and Shalom walk upright to pass—surprisingly successfully—as human beings (Tom comes along as their "emotional support turkey"), and how Elsie continually interrupts her narrative to insert one literary or pop culture reference after another. As she does this, she references everything from *The Odyssey* and *The Iliad* to pop bands, *West Side Story*, *Star Wars*, vinyl records, and *Gilligan's Island*—all things a cow has no business knowing.

In a particularly meta moment, Elsie describes a conversation with her editor, who believes that adult humans wouldn't take a book about talking animals seriously before asserting that animated movies are often the most successful and often star animals. A skeptical Elsie comments, "We'll see if Hollywood calls."

Hollywood never called Elsie, but Duchovny called Hollywood. He originally pitched *Holy Cow* to Pixar and Disney as a kids' film, without success. On the book's acknowledgments page Duchovny thanks Disney and Pixar for "turning it down as an animated film and forcing me to write it out like a big boy."[140]

In the end, neither the cow nor the pig or turkey find their particular promised land. Like Dorothy, they realize that there's no place like home. But between all the postmodern magical realism and the fourth-wall shattering, Duchovny repeatedly returns to the idea that humans have isolated themselves from the rest of the animal kingdom, noting: "If they [humans] got it [the idea that we're all one] with their hearts and souls, they would change, they would change and rejoin the animal kingdom and once again be proud to be called animals."[141]

BRIDGING THE GAP

The gap between the human and animal worlds, and the aching desire for unity between them, is a chasm both Elsie and furry culture seek to bridge. And it's not just one book or one author attempting to do so: William Kotzwinkle in *Doctor Rat,* Richard Adams in *The Plague Dogs,* and many others, share similar sentiments. In *Doctor Rat,* it is a young chimp who believes that man would eventually realize that all creatures are related and would stop killing them. In Adams's book, one of the two supposed plague-carrying dogs, Snitter, has a near-death vision of the world as a "great flat wheel . . . forever turning and turning," with animals known and unknown to him at each spoke, and at its center a man who continuously whipped the creatures, not realizing that it was never necessary as the wheel would have kept turning even without his abuse.[142] Late in *Holy Cow*, however, Elsie sounds an optimistic note and cuts a little slack for us: "Humans can be decent and understanding at times. Which makes me think there's hope for them."[143]

5

SUITS ME JUST FINE

Most folks outside the furry community (and even some newbie furries) labor under the assumption that as a furry you're practically required to own and wear a fursuit. But even though a well-made suit is a wonderful way of bringing your fursona into the real world, of becoming your fursona, it's not a requirement. The only requirement for being furry is enjoying anthropomorphic animal characters.

The general consensus, judging from the ratio of participants in a convention's fursuit parade to the con's overall attendance, is that only about one in four furs fully suit up. For the rest, a much more budget-friendly furry T-shirt, belt-attached tail, or other accessory suffices.

Of course, human beings have been dressing up as animals for about as long as there have been human beings. This includes tribal rituals, cultural events, and just for fun, with a surprising number of non-furries dressing up as animals, from days past through modern times. Take for instance, the Romanian Bear Festival, a ritual dating back centuries. At year's end, dozens of people wearing bearskins over their heads (replacing actual bears who, decades earlier, were forced to "dance" on hot metal plates) congregate in the town square to chase away the departing year's evil spirits.

While we're on the subject of dressing up like a bear, fantasy authors C. S. Lewis and J. R. R. Tolkien once unexpectedly dropped in on a New Year's Eve party wearing homemade polar bear suits.[144] Their outfits might have been more appropriate for a costume party (or as they call them in England, a "fancy dress ball"), but perhaps the fact that both their works include talking animals predisposed them to become ones themselves.

And speaking of British dress-ups, Plymouth is fast becoming known as the United Kingdom's dinosaur central, as the inflatable dino suit has caught on in a big way in this small coastal city. According to HuffPost UK:

> On any given day in Plymouth, there may be a pterodactyl hovering at the bus stop, a couple of T-rexes in the tinned goods aisle or a stegosaurus at the school gates. In most places, this would be enough to warrant a fair few double takes—but in the port city, it's nothing out of the ordinary.
>
> Members of the Dinosaurs of Plymouth Facebook group, which has 5,600 fans, are locals—mainly parents—who bring joy to others by dressing up in inflatable dinosaur outfits. Many are women, and photos show them meeting up outside schools and nurseries, and pushing buggies, dressed in giant inflatable suits.[145]

The trend began with a local mother who originally bought one such suit to wear to her daughter's dinosaur-themed party and after decided to wear it as often as possible. Her Facebook page—Dinosaurs and Friends of Plymouth (UK) and Surrounding Areas—picked up a thousand followers in its first twenty-four hours and now numbers close to sixty-five hundred. And the craze is spreading to other British cities, with dino groups "evolving" in Ickenham[146] and Bolton.[147]

The mom who started it all, by the way, now owns three dino suits and wears them every chance she gets. As she told a HuffPost reporter, "It makes people smile and brightens up their day, which is all we want."[148]

The furry on a budget has a lot of alternatives to a full-fledged fursuit, including the inflatable dinosaur suits those Plymouth ladies are partial to. And then there's the *kigurumi*, colorful, open-faced onesies resembling fanciful animals. Originating in Japan, their name roughly translates to "wearing plush toy," and the Japanese use the term to refer to costumed performers. Except for the hood evoking an animal's face, these loose, comfortable, and baggy garments could pass for the outfits worn by the Lost Boys in Disney's *Peter Pan*. They're popular both in the furry community and out in the real world as well. Just ask Diana Ross, who dressed up her extended family—seventeen in all—in blue unicorn outfits for their Christmas photo.[149]

FURSUITING 101: BUILD OR BUY?

If you want the real deal, an actual full body fursuit, but don't have pockets deep enough to pay for it, your options are a bit more challenging:

1. Build your own suit. The most expensive cost of any fursuit is the labor necessary to construct it. Fursuits are generally built entirely from scratch, from the bottom up and the inside out, a process taking an incredible number of hours. If a suit's builder is particularly talented and popular, their work commands a premium price, and it may even be in such high demand that you have to wait a year or longer for the person to even begin work on your suit. By comparison, the cost of the raw materials to construct a suit is relatively small and the internet is chock full of tutorial videos that will guide you along. Some people take to the process so well that building suits for others becomes their full-time profession.

As one example, the Canadian suit builder known as Temperance graduated from creating simple cosplay outfits to full-fledged fursuits, which are much more challenging, beginning with Red XIII, a character from the *Final Fantasy* video games. As Temperance shared, "It led to my first commission with friends who had seen my work [and] wanted me to make suits of their own characters . . . . It became an actual career I could make a real living at." Temperance estimates she's made "a couple of hundred" since her first glimpse of Red XIII.[150]

2. Commission a "partial." More expensive than a do-it-yourself suit, but still way cheaper than commissioning a full suit, a partial typically consists of a fursuit head, paws, and tail, and often feet as well, and a commissioner typically has the goal of eventually ordering the other parts of the body to turn it into a full suit. A word to the wise: nothing makes a partial cooler than a wardrobe that fully brings your character to life. There's nothing lamer than a lion dressed in an ordinary pair of jeans and a T-shirt. Some amazing finds

can be discovered in thrift shops and secondhand clothing stores. (I picked up the tuxedo jacket that my Komodo dragon, Komos, wears for twenty dollars at one such establishment.) If your outfit really sings, you won't even need a furry body to complete your character.

3. Buy a secondhand or premade suit. This is where things get dicey. It's possible to find a good pre-owned full suit, partial, or other furry accouterments online, particularly through a site like The Dealers Den, but there are no guarantees, so tread lightly. If possible, make sure the seller will let you return the item if it doesn't live up to your expectations. If you're a first time shopper thinking, *Look what I found online: a really cool-looking full-body fursuit for only $360! How can I go wrong?* believe me, you can most definitely go wrong, tragically wrong. There are Chinese companies that specialize in producing unauthorized knockoffs of beautiful, custom-crafted suits and selling them online for a fraction of the original suit's cost. Very often the main photo in the listing is the original suit from the owner or builder's posting, but if you scroll through additional pictures (assuming the seller added their own version to the listing), you'll quickly discover an alpha-to-omega-sized quality gap between the original and the imitation.

Bogus suits abound on sites like Alibaba, AliExpress, and eBay. Apart from the too-good-to-be-true (because they never are) low price, another giveaway is the surfeit of descriptors in the listing's title ("Long Fur Furry Fox Wolf Husky Dog Fursuit Mascot Costume Adult Cartoon Character," etc., for example), which are included to reach a wide audience rather than highlighting the animal and qualities of the particular suit. Include any of these words in your search terms and a number of these suits are guaranteed to show up in your results.

Sadly, once a poor quality suit is purchased, there's not much the fursuit owner who's been ripped off can accomplish from the other side of the globe, at least not without a major law firm well-versed in international intellectual property laws backing them up. Still, Quartz Husky, a popular furry YouTuber whose adorable pink, white, and blue husky suit has been counterfeited numerous times, takes a surprisingly mellow view toward the entire affair and on Twitter noted, "I've seen some of the bootleg Quartz suits around on TikTok and social media. If you got scammed and now have the suit, it's cool. Continue to enjoy your suit! If you want more uniqueness, change a few features and make your own character! Either way, I'm not offended."[151]

A custom-made suit can cost as little as three thousand dollars, or as much as you're willing to spend for a more elaborate design featuring complex multicolored fur patterns, built-in electronics, cooling systems, and the like. If you have money to burn, there's always someone around to hand you a book of matches. That was probably the demographic fursuit builder AlbinoTopaz was going for when she launched her Zweitesich (a German word meaning "second self") brand of designer fursuits in 2019. The brand's slick website, dripping with snob appeal, launched with a six thousand dollar price tag on each of the three suits available at the time (Borzoi hound, lion, and lamb, all bearing a designer-y "ZW" logo on the suit head) and quickly rubbed furries' fur the wrong way. In point of fact, the "suits" weren't suits at all, merely partials: head, paws, "undervest," and "a three-view reference sheet of the completed suit vision" (emphasis on "vision"—in other words, a piece of paper in lieu of a full-body fursuit). Taken all together, the furry community, home to a do-it-yourself ethos and wary of commercial exploitation by profit-seeking entrepreneurs, was not amused. AlbinoTopaz went into full damage control mode at the uproar, admitting the marketing campaign was "poorly chosen." This was an understatement, considering the entire concept of a high-end, high-priced designer fursuit, complete with a Louis Vuitton-style logo of two overlapping letters. According to Zweitesich's website, the 2019 triad of Borzoi, lion, and ram heads have all been sold, but to date no additional suits or partials have joined the original three.

A sum of six thousand dollars may seem like a lot of money, but it's possible to spend far more than four figures on a fursuit. In 2020 furry YouTuber Odin Wolf posted a video[152] revealing the seventeen most expensive fursuits at the time.[153] The three most expensive suits went for $17,500, $18,250, and $23,500. And as it happens, all three are owned by the same person, someone who, according to Odin Wolf, owned twenty-five suits all together. But that was in 2020; today Spottacus Cheetah owns somewhere between thirty-five and forty suits, he's not quite sure, he told me, and that's not including the ones he doesn't wear anymore.[154]

SPOTTI

Inventor, entrepreneur, physician, and biophysicist Dr. David Benaron has a résumé that rivals those of Iron Man Tony Stark (genius, billionaire, playboy, philanthropist) and Buckaroo Banzai (physicist, neurosurgeon, test pilot, rock star). Dr. Benaron also happens to have the advantage of being a real person, not a fictional character, and the further advantage of becoming a cheetah named Spottacus—or any number of other fabulous beasts—when the mood strikes him.

PC Magazine describes the San Francisco-based Benaron as "a biochemist, inventor, and entrepreneur" and profiles him by noting, "He studied at Harvard and MIT, taught at Stanford, and has founded and served in the C-suites of multiple biotech companies. He developed the sensor that enables heart rate monitoring on wearables like smartwatches, and has made advances in the field of optical blood-oxygen monitoring as well."[155] If there's a greenlight heart rate sensor on your wrist, thank Spottacus, or Spotti for short. If anyone can afford thirty-five-plus suits, it's this guy. He prowls his office in a fursuit and wears one to venture capital meetings and business lunches in upscale restaurants.

Spotti, like myself and almost every other fur I've met, was born furry, crawling on all fours and meowing when he was still a toddler.[156] Here's the fascinating story he told me about identifying and cultivating his connection to the subculture:

> The things that I experienced on the anthropomorphic side are deep. I always crawled around the house, purring and meowing. I remember my parents and people commenting on this, not always favorably. I was always a cat, never a horse or a dog. I was a cat. It was just a natural thing, from as early as I can remember.
>
> The earliest memory I have that's sort of fuzzy or furry was a recurring dream about a giant insect. I had a friend called "B." I'd climb onto him and hold onto his warm, fuzzy, silken back, and he flew me places. I wasn't limited by speed or size, I

could go to enormous heights. It was never scary. It was always wonderful.

I wanted to read books in elementary school, and no one really wanted to read with me. I was bullied because I was small [and] I wasn't interested in boy things. I spent my recesses staring at the ground and dreaming about what could be. My dreams were where I had friends.

I always had this dysphoria in the sense that I never thought I was really cute, so I built fursuits. I was just more comfortable when I put on a costume, especially when my head and face were covered. My first suit was a wolf, then a cheetah. Don't ask for pictures, they weren't even "uncanny valley" scary, they were just scary—but they made me feel wonderful. I still remember how happy I felt at dances and concerts. I was suiting, but doing it entirely alone, never knowing anyone else felt this way.

I started putting on my suits and going to clubs, started looking online for mates. I stumbled across furries on LiveJournal. My new online friends encouraged me to go to [the convention] Further Confusion and I felt like I was finally home—I'd found my tribe.[157]

I'd risen to be a professor of medicine and physics at Stanford University. I felt that all the accolades that everyone was heaping on top of me had nothing to do with me.

Yes, I invented this. Yes, I discovered this. Yes, I pulled in this much funding. Yes, I solved a problem—but it wasn't me. I never felt my accomplishments were about me.

Of all the things I've done, I'm proudest of being a fur.

Sabertooth 2.0, from the renowned fursuit builders Clockwork Creature, is Spotti's favorite suit among the several dozen he owns. They take up space in his garage, in drawers, on shelves, and in a storage locker housing the eleven he no longer wears. His most sophisticated suit (one of the three most expensive ones cited by Odin Wolf) may be his namesake Spottacus Cheetah suit from the Primal Visions Design Studio, with each strand of fur *individually attached* to the thin-stretched fabric underneath. The fur alone accounted for $10,000 of the suit's $17,500 cost.

At $23,500, Rawr the Dragon, constructed by New Zealand costume artist Zarathus Dragon, is the most expensive suit on Odin Wolf's list. The deep blue and violet reptile suit is made of large, individually hand-painted and vented scales that, apart from the suit's beauty, help dissipate the sauna-level interior heat that can build up inside a normal fursuit.

And finally, Heuler Wolf, a scary, fur-covered lupine with glowing red LED eyes and claws sharp enough to climb trees, also from Clockwork Creature, set Spotti back $18,250.

So what is the payoff? What does it feel like to wear one of Spotti's suits? According to the cheetah himself, there's no feeling of wearing a costume once it's on. As Spotti said, "It's not, 'I'm wearing a fursuit.' It's, 'This is my fur. This is my skin with my fur on it.' It's not a distant relationship, it's a really intimate one. When I'm in that headspace, my words change, my emotional state changes; things are simpler. I don't worry about things when I'm in a suit."

6

MAINSTREAM ANTHROPOMORPHIC THEATER

IT'S ALL GREEK TO ME

Aristophanes, a renowned Greek playwright of the fifth century BCE, was known for his satirical comedies that often included attacks on powerful people of his time. This led his contemporaries to fear his powers of ridicule, and he was persecuted for his effrontery.

The Birds is probably the best-known of Aristophanes's surviving comedic plays. It tells the story of two Athenians who forsake the petty squabbles and disagreements of their fellow citizens. In the wild, they convince the birds to create a city in the sky between the human world and the gods of Olympus, proving the birds' superiority to both the gods and man. Birds from around the world, from the sparrow to the vulture—twenty-four species in all—gather to discuss the plan, and as they do, they are continually interrupted by comic interlopers, each with an agenda of their own. After much ado, the birds are victorious, and one of the humans (transformed into a bird earlier in the play) is selected by the gods to be the city's sovereign.

According to surviving accounts, *The Birds* was a spectacular production with a huge cast, special effects that must have been quite impressive back in the day, and dozens of performers feathered up for the occasion. (Perhaps Andrew Lloyd Webber, who produced the Broadway show *Cats*, will one day add songs to the show and turn it into a musical titled *Birds*.)

SOME SKIN IN THE GAME

Let us skip ahead a few centuries and continue on to the late nineteenth and early twentieth centuries, and the age of animal impersonators, known at the time as "skin players." Many considered the actor George Ali to have been the world's greatest animal impersonator.[158] Ali was best known for playing Nana, the dog nursemaid to the Darling children in the 1924 silent movie version of *Peter Pan*, but in the course of a decades-long career he also portrayed bears, lions, dogs, cats, wolves, horses, monkeys, jackasses, and *Peter Pan*'s crocodile.

Throughout Ali's career, his performances earned him accolades, often outshining his costars portraying human beings. Summing up his career, Mary Mallory of the LA Daily Mirror website wrote, "Ali's expressive, whimsical performances touched children and adults alike, giving dignity and humanlike qualities to pets or service animals."[159] Mallory's article also describes the Nana costume built to Ali's specifications: "From inside the costume, Ali operated the eyes, ears, tail, and mouth through a series of strings enabling him to cock an eye, wiggle his ears, wag his tail, and the like, enabling him to tug viewers' heartstrings as well."[160]

However, Ali had some serious competition for the number one slot: a contemporary observer crowned Canadian actor Fred Woodward "King of All the Animal Impersonators."[161] His menagerie included ostriches, jackasses, and, in particular, Hank the Mule in the play *The Tik-Tok Man of Oz*, which was based on a book and lyrics by L. Frank Baum.

While perhaps the best in their field, Ali and Woodward were far from its only practitioners. Among other top actors who took on "skin parts" was Charles Lauri Jr., who, according to an article on London's Victoria and Albert Museum's website, "was known as the 'Garrick of animal mimes" after David Garrick, a legendary eighteenth-century English actor.[162][163] Lauri was famous for his animal impersonations and regularly appeared in London theaters as one creature or another. Today Lauri might be considered a method actor, but in his day he simply viewed his connection to his characters as stemming from a personal fascination. He described this in an 1893 interview:

> Even as a child I was devoted to animals and always took particular note of their ways and doings; still a considerable time elapsed before I again thought of acting as an animal. All [of] London was running to see a performing monkey called Pongo. I said to myself I am sure that I could do as well as that monkey. Well I went to the zoo and spent hours in the Monkey House watching the creatures.[164]

In the interview Lauri also described the painstaking work that went into creating his monkey suit ("what is wanted when impersonating an animal is really a wig for the body"): the hairs that had to be attached separately, a leather mask with hidden threads to animate his eyebrows, and "more face makeup than any other beast character he had ever played."

History's numerous performers who have excelled in skin roles deserve a book of their own. Among them: Albert Felino, who particularly enjoyed playing Mother Goose's goose Priscilla (even though he claimed the constricting costume reduced his height by five inches);[165] brothers Fred and Arthur Conquest, who learned their craft from their father, George;[166] Arthur Hill, who among many roles portrayed the Cowardly Lion in a 1902 *Wizard of Oz* musical;[167] and a little person named Pat Walshe, who played the Wicked Witch's henchmonkey, Nikko, in the classic 1939 *Wizard of Oz* movie.[168] These performers were carrying on a British tradition of holiday pantomime shows, where performers wore simple masks and garments in place of elaborate costumes. (Even The Beatles took part in this kind of fun, turning into a hippo, bunny, chicken, and walrus on the *Magical Mystery Tour* album cover.) These shows birthed the beloved two-person pantomime horse, saluted in a classic *Monty Python* sketch[169] and now honored with an annual Pantomime Horse Race through London.[170] (God bless British silliness, long may it live!)

Modern times have seen stage adaptations of novels like *Fantastic Mr. Fox*, *The Wind in the Willows*, *Animal Farm*, and *Watership Down*. Unlike the skin players, these show's costumes make no attempt at realism, instead taking on a stylized approach to *suggest* the animal rather than recreate it. *Cats* (the stage musical and not the unpopular live-action movie) and *The Lion King* carry on this particular theatrical tradition.

EDWARD ALBEE

With works like *Who's Afraid of Virginia Woolf*, *Zoo Story*, and *The Goat, or Who Is Sylvia?*, the celebrated American playwright Edward Albee seemed to specialize in stories of alienation and hopelessness. One fascinating exception, however, might be his Pulitzer Prize–winning play *Seascape*, which premiered in 1975.

In *Seascape* an aging couple vacationing on a beach is reminiscing about their past and wondering about their future when they are joined by a reptile couple who have just emerged from the sea and are wondering if they should attempt to evolve upward and onto land. The four discuss their lives and try to understand each other's point of view. Several tense moments lead to near-violence, until the reptiles accept the humans' offer to teach them about surface life, and the play ends with the male reptile simply telling the humans to begin educating them about the human world. The play afforded costume designers on Broadway and in local productions the opportunity to create exquisite long-tailed reptile suits for the undersea couple, some with scaly textures, some smooth, some with crests running down their backs and onto their tails and dewlaps beneath their heads. Fursuit builders could have learned a few tricks from them—and perhaps shared some skills as well.

THE DOG DAYS OF HUME CRONYN

On October 12, 1969, the BBC broadcast the second episode of the sketch comedy series *Monty Python's Flying Circus*, "Sex and Violence." Its final segment was a no-holds-barred exposé of the Mouse Problem, a secret society of men who pretend to be mice.[171] The segment, a spoof of documentaries exploring the then largely hidden world of homosexuality, was written by the

Pythons's openly gay Graham Chapman, one of the show's creators and actors. It featured an interview with an abashed mouse-man (played by John Cleese) who confessed his secret rodential identity ("It's not a matter of wanting to be a mouse—it just sort of happens to you.") and a consulting psychiatrist and conjurer, Chapman as the Amazing Kargol, who sagely advises, "There's something of the mouse in all of us." The report ends with footage secretly shot at a weekend mouse party, as several Pythons cavort in somewhat ratty mouse suits, their fun interrupted by a mustached farmer's wife crashing the party, carving knife in hand. Such silliness and, entirely by accident, the very first look at furry, decades before its birth—or so I thought.

As it turns out, a Broadway play saw the fandom coming more than a decade before the Pythons. Return with me now to the 1950s, the age of the organization man in the gray flannel suit, lost in the lonely crowd after fleeing the big city with his family for the supposedly greener pastures of suburbia. When people weren't worrying about the commies dropping an A-bomb on us, they fretted about conformity: were we all becoming alike, sacrificing our individuality in order to fit in, look the same, and think the same as everyone else? Were you a conformist or a nonconformist? (In a few years, their kids would drop acid, go to Woodstock, and show their parents what nonconformism *really* looked like.)

The play was *The Man in the Dog Suit*, and I discovered it entirely by accident while skimming a 1958 reel of *New York Times* microfilm in search of long-ago Saturday morning TV cartoon listings. I stopped at a random page, hoping it was a Saturday, and that random page happened to contain the day's theater listings, where dead center was an ad for *Dog Suit*, which opened in October of that year.

The play's leads, Hume Cronyn and Jessica Tandy, were a celebrated theatrical couple whose film and stage career spanned an astonishing eight decades. In *The Man in the Dog Suit* they are Oliver and Martha Walling, a modest middle-class couple living in an anonymous suburb of look-alike houses. The mild-mannered Oliver is trapped in a life of dull conformity as a teller in the bank controlled by his wife's wealthy, domineering family. A costume shop mix-up prior to a masquerade party brings the canine attire into his life. Once ensconced within its furry confines, Oliver discovers his true self.[172] At the party, a liberated Oliver indulges in spontaneous self-expression, biting a gypsy and flirting with a rabbit.

The play opens as the Wallings return home from the party, eager to jump into the sack, with Oliver still suited up. If there were any doubts that it was a mutual pleasure spicing up a love life grown cold, Martha later admits she bought the suit as Oliver's birthday present "because he liked it . . . and I liked it."

Oliver's newfound furry freedom upsets Martha's staid family, who have his circumscribed career already in place, and the conflict strains Oliver and Martha's marriage. (In another prophetic moment, possibly the first reference to a man-cave on the American stage, the family matriarch remembers her late husband saying, "'Every man should have a den' . . . then he would go into his and lock the door.") During a heated conversation, Martha tells Oliver, "People don't go around as animals." To which he logically responds, "I'm an animal, same as a collie is."

Unable to resist its temptation, Oliver finds himself donning his dog suit more and more, transforming from Oliver to Oliver the Dog in the play's script. He even threatens to wear it to the bank ("Gets chilly sometimes—all that marble"), the country club ("Improve my game"), and indeed "all over town," and he eventually does wear it to all.

Oliver and Martha ultimately break free of Martha's family, thanks to the dog suit. As the curtain falls they leave for Oregon, where Oliver can pursue his long-postponed career in forest conservation and lead a natural life without the need of a dog suit. As they depart, a brother-in-law adopts the abandoned costume as his own, much to *his* wife's apparent delight.

Oliver's costume is a different animal from what one might expect, not so much a dog suit as a dog jacket. Apart from its oversized, tongue-lolling German shepherd head, shaggy fabric, and tail, the garment resembles an elegant, old-fashioned morning coat ending at the waist, with a pair of "tails" in the back that bracket the suit's canine tail. While Oliver is costumed, his well-pressed trousers and polished black shoes are deliberately visible, leaving no doubt whatsoever that there is a man inside the dog suit. (The published script informs future producers—or would-be Olivers—that the very suit worn onstage can be rented for the right price.)

The Man in the Dog Suit could only have been a labor of love for Cronyn. Its genesis was the novel *Three Ways to Mecca* and the novel's Oliver Walling is very different than the character in the play. Instead of a bank clerk stifled by suburban conformity, the novel's Oliver is a successful author who enjoys wearing a dog suit for reasons unknown.[173] Religion and psychiatry, in the form of a self-proclaimed bishop and a pompous psychoanalyst, offer to "cure" the perfectly happy Oliver at a neighbor's party; however, a friend who better understands explains that the dog suit allows Oliver to "astound and startle people" without revealing himself, the same balance of "boldness and shyness" that motivates many a fursuiter. Oliver's obvious happiness convinces their hostess, who gushes, "Why, the world would be a better place if we *all* wore dog suits! I've got a good idea to get one for myself."

At the novel's end, a visiting European film director finds himself intrigued by, and eventually donning, the dog suit. "Changes your whole point of view," Oliver tells him. "There's no experience like it. Try it once and you'll want one."

Cronyn commissioned a Hollywood producer and a screenwriter—neither possessing any stage experience—to turn the film script the pair had written (*very* loosely inspired by the novel) into a stage vehicle for himself and Tandy.[174] Cronyn and his writers worked and reworked their script for three years, presenting the show in endless out-of-town tryouts before its premiere in New York City on October 30, 1958—appropriately, the evening before Halloween. Reviews were, to put it politely, less than enthusiastic, the consensus being that the material was far beneath Cronyn and Tandy's talents. After thirty-one days and thirty-six performances, *The Man in the Dog Suit* was put to sleep and sent to live on a farm upstate where it could romp and play with other short-lived, labor-of-love stage plays.

It was a painful experience for Cronyn to see his puppy pass away—"a particularly bloody blow," according to his autobiography.[175] But why was it so devastating? Why did Oliver Walling's plight drive Cronyn to spend year after year bringing it to the stage? Was it because Cronyn viewed the play as a passionate commentary on the mediocrity that the conformism of the times called for? Was it that Cronyn identified with the put-upon Walling? Was it simply that it gave Cronyn an excuse to portray a man who finds himself at home in a dog suit? In spite of the time and passion Cronyn invested in the project, the only hint in his autobiography as to the source of his motivation is an enigmatic "what we undertook was not done frivolously"—a statement that only compounds the mystery.

7

AUTHOR! AUTHOR!

The world of furry creativity isn't limited to fursuits and illustrations. Dozens of furry novels and short story collections are written and published every year by publishing houses with names like FurPlanet and Sofawolf Press. Authors like Kyell Gold and Gre7g Luterman are as well-known to bookish furs as Danielle Steel, James Patterson, or John Grisham are to the average fiction reader.

Science fiction and fantasy, mystery, gay love stories, adventure tales . . . any genre one might think of (with the exception of books for elementary school-age kids, a demographic well-covered by mainstream publishers) can be found here, coated in fur, and are like catnip to book-loving furries. Many furs have created anthropomorphic fiction. A few of the best-known authors in the genre were gracious enough to sit down and talk to me about their work.

KYELL GOLD

Kyell Gold is one of the most popular and prolific authors of gay furry fiction. He has written several novels and dozens of short stories set in a wealth of distinct imaginary worlds populated by anthropomorphic animals. He's been feted as a guest of honor at furry conventions across the United States and in Europe, and he has won a dozen Ursa Major Awards for his writing. Gold's characters are gay anthros seeking love and affection, although occasionally, in works like Waterways *and* Out of Position, *the focus is on their struggle to accept their homosexuality.*

You have a very unique first name. Is there a story behind it?
There's not much of a story behind my name. It's a pseudonym I came up with when I started writing adult fiction. I liked the name Kyle, but I was deep in the furry fandom tradition of "spell a usual name in a different way," so I adjusted the spelling. Gold I got by flipping through a phone book, but I liked it.

Can you tell me a bit about your background?
I grew up in the northeastern United States. My parents separated early in my life and I did a lot of traveling with my dad—road trips across the United States, living in Europe for a few years, and so on. I went to college in Philly and then grad school in Minnesota before moving to California.

What turned you furry? What were your earliest anthropomorphic interests? I'm assuming that like most furs

you were into anthro stuff before discovering the furry community. If so, how did you come across it?
Disney's *Robin Hood* was the first furry thing I was into. I had the record of the story and listened to it obsessively. After that it was [the TV show] *Tiny Toon Adventures* that led me to a fan group, which then led me to the online game FurryMUCK and creating a character to role-play a fuzzy critter with a bunch of other people. That character creation, in 1991, is when I mark my entry into the furry fandom.

Despite the fact that my favorite *TTA* character is Furrball, I have never actually been a cat (except on a couple rare occasions when I played Furrball himself).[176] I thought I was a wolf for a little while until I read J. David Henry's book *Red Fox* and realized that I was a fox.

Similarly, when did you realize you were gay? Was it emotionally difficult to accept your orientation? As you explored your identity, was there any crossover between being gay and being a fur? Did either one influence the other? They definitely merged in your writing.
FurryMUCK was not my first exposure to gay people, but it was the first place where I was able to explore the possibility that I was also gay. The community there was so open and welcoming—in that aspect, at least—that it was a very easy exploration. So it's not a real surprise that it was

also in the early nineties that I started to explore that aspect of myself.

Being furry and being gay were definitely linked in my mind. The environment of FurryMUCK was not only accepting and open but forward, which helped a lot. I didn't have to make a first move, but I felt comfortable saying no to anything I didn't want to do. In furry, I could create an identity—my fursona—and I could say that my fursona was gay even if I wasn't sure about myself yet. There was very little risk in experimenting online.

How and why did you become a writer? Did you have any particular writing influences, either genre or mainstream authors?

My mother was probably the first and strongest influence. She was an English teacher and encouraged my pursuit of the written word, which was mostly in reading through my childhood. She got me my first favorite books, which started me on a path of loving stories. Anne McCaffrey's Harper Hall series was among the first that made me want to write stories like that—bold people with telepathic animal friends; what's not to like? I started making up my own stories and enjoyed doing it. In college I joined the SF [science fiction] club, which published a magazine, and I wrote a few stories for that.

Was it hard becoming a published/established furry author?

I helped found Sofawolf Press in 1999 with Jeff Eddy, who had appreciated some of the work I'd posted online and sent him directly. We wanted to create a semi-pro press for furry writing, and he was as interested in the business and technical aspects as the writing part. I liked the layout and design aspects of the press, so our shared enthusiasm served us well, and [we] brought our partners (now husbands) into it soon after. When I wrote my novel *Volle*, I brought it to him as though submitting it because I didn't want to just assume the press would publish anything I wrote. He made the decision to publish it, and it sold well enough that he took the next two books as well.

In the meantime I'd published a short story titled "Aquifers" to an online furry writing site, and it had taken off. I wrote a sequel novella called *Streams* and packaged the two of them with a concluding story in a book called *Waterways*. That was the first breakout book I published. The next year saw *Out of Position*, which featured artwork from Blotch, a popular furry artist, and won the Rainbow Award for Best Gay Novel.[177] Those things helped the book reach an even larger fanbase (outside of as well as within the furry fandom) and its popularity gave me the confidence to move to writing full time two years later.

In total, how many works (novels, short stories, etc.) have you written?
I currently have thirty-seven books out, including stand-alone novellas and story collections, with four more in various stages of "finished and coming out sometime." Short stories? I don't have a count. More than fifty for sure, maybe as many as a hundred if you count the free ones I posted to SoFurry or Fur Affinity. Listing them out would be a nice project to work on sometime.

What does writing about anthropomorphic characters add to your work? What would your stories lose if they featured humans in place of anthros?
The glib answer would be "tails!" But that's actually part of it. I'll go through a few of my favorite points about anthro writing:

- The fur and tails (or feathers and scales) are definitely part of it. That aesthetic has cultural resonance (foxes are sly, tigers are fierce) as well as personal resonance (foxes are cute, tigers are powerful) that can be leveraged into thematic resonances in the work.

- Creating furry characters allows me to bring in only those parts of our world that I want to use. If I made my characters human and tried to write a contemporary story, I'd have to figure out where they were from. I'd have to worry about accurately representing those cultures. I'd have to take into account a whole lot of things from the world that perhaps I don't want to. Furry characters, because they are fantasy, give me more freedom to create the world I want to portray in the story.

- Because furry encompasses a wide variety of species, there are a lot more ways to talk about prejudice and class topics. Disney's *Zootopia* did an excellent job of this, and in my stories I've used the predator/prey distinction, the native/exotic distinction, and general species discrimination. Prejudice boils down to preconceived notions about a person based on their group rather than the individual, and not only do furry groups offer more variety, they also offer a way to talk about prejudice in a more abstract way.

How would you describe your writing? What's your favorite work of your own?

I like to write character-based fiction, meaning that I'm most interested in how the characters move through the story and what they learn. Most of the time I start with a character journey and build the plot around it, and I let the characters drive the plot. It has happened that I had a plot element in mind and when the character arrived at that point, it didn't make sense to me that they would proceed the way I'd imagined, so I had to scrap a good chunk of what I thought the story would be.

My favorite work of my own is a hard one to pin down because usually it's "the thing I just finished writing," which in this case is *Camouflage*. It was written almost entirely in discovery mode: I didn't plan it out ahead of time, which is unusual these days. I like that one a lot. And I love all my books for different reasons. But there are a few in the catalog that I'm particularly proud of. If you asked me to talk about the thing I love about each of my books, I could probably do it, but I'll stop with that one because you did only ask about one.

MARY E. LOWD

Mary E. Lowd is one of the most successful and popular furry authors. She has written a dozen novels and more than two hundred short stories. Here she shares her journey in her own words.

I love science fiction and I was always looking for stories featuring uplifted animals or animal-like aliens. However, I didn't feel like I'd found a real home until I discovered the word for what I was missing, furry fiction.

I'd written my first novel, *Otters in Space*, and was trying to find an audience for it. I discovered an online forum called Furtopia where I heard about RainFurrest [a convention held in Seattle]. I went to the convention and was shocked to discover tables filled with furry books from furry publishers and writing panels filled with furry authors. I met FurPlanet's publishers there. The next year I asked if I could leave a few copies of my self-published book on their dealers den table. I ended up selling around twenty copies. They were impressed enough to offer me a book deal on the spot.

I've written about a dozen novels and more than two hundred short stories. The novels include three trilogies—*Otters in Space*, which is furry sci-fi; *The Entangled Universe*, which is space opera with a lot of furry characters; and *The Celestial Fragments*, which is furry fantasy. My novel *Nexus Nine* was inspired by *Star Trek: Deep Space Nine*, and is closest to my heart.

[At this point I asked Mary the same question I posed to Kyell:] What would your stories lose if they featured humans in place of anthros?
We get to know animals through stories and interactions when we're very young. So when you write about anthropomorphic characters, people already know what cats and dogs are like, how they're different, and how to picture them. Using animals gives you a head start, and sometimes you can tell a much harder-hitting story by using animal characters to give the reader a little emotional distance.[178]

I dedicate a lot of time to publicizing furry fiction. A lot of furries still don't know there's an active fiction scene in the fandom and a lot of mainstream writers and readers haven't heard about the genre.

THE SEVEN IS SILENT: GRE7G LUTERMAN

When furry author and illustrator Rick Griffin created his Hayven Celestia universe, he populated it with numerous unique species.[179] *Gre7g Luterman was fascinated by Griffin's creations. He began collaborating with Griffin and setting his own stories in Griffin's universe. Several of those stories have become quite popular with furry fiction fans. Here he shares his story.*

I started writing furry fiction in 1981, long before I knew furry existed. In the 1990s I discovered the furry community and I knew where I belonged.

I have aphantasia; I can't visualize [the situations I write about]. All my memories and thoughts are as words. I imagine dialog in words, things as descriptions. Writing comes naturally because I'm already thinking in that mode.

I met Rick Griffin around 2012 and read his short story, "Ten Thousand Miles Up." I loved it and got his permission to write stories set in his universe. It took a lot of poking to get him to read *Skeleton Crew* [and after he read it] I think he was genuinely surprised he liked what I had written.

I started promoting my writing at cons. I wrote *Small World* as a sequel to *Skeleton Crew,* and Thurston Howl Publications picked them up. They split *Small World* into two books, *Small World* and *Fair Trade.* The trilogy became their best-selling books. *Small World* won the Ursa Major, and *Fair*

Trade was the only book to ever win all three fandom writing awards.[180]

I write about personal triumphs and tragedies. I'm not going to tell the stories of wars and kingdoms. I'm going to tell about the guy who ran from battle and where his life led. I'm going to tell about the beggar in front of the castle. My characters fall in love, and though they'll change their fate, they won't change the world.

8

MAINSTREAM ANTHROPOMORPHIC SCULPTURE

Even though they're not furry themselves, numerous mainstream sculptors have chosen anthropomorphic characters as their subject matter.[181] I've selected three whose works share a common theme: rabbits.

SOPHIE RYDER'S BIG BUNNIES

What is it about rabbits that so fascinates sculptors? Take for example, British artist Sophie Ryder. As mentioned earlier, the English have always had a soft spot for bunnies, be they those of Beatrix Potter, Lewis Carroll, Richard Adams, or another creator, but Ryder's rabbits tower above those authors' two-dimensional fictional ones, and often by as much as thirty feet. In the course of her forty-five-plus-years career, Ryder has created enormous sculptures of an assortment of fantastical beings; among them, horses, boars, imaginary hybrid beasts—particularly minotaurs—and hares (dancing hares, standing hares, crouching hares, crawling hares). And more often than not, her fantastical beings have partly human bodies.

One long-eared hare that stands out from the rest of Ryder's rabbits is her Ladyhare. As Ryder explained to me: "I came up with the idea for the Ladyhare when trying to work on a half human, half animal to use with the minotaur. The hare seemed to work so well with a female human body. To me the long ears represent a mane of hair, and somehow the whole figure works and is so familiar to me. There is no legend behind the Ladyhare, of course, but plenty of myths about the hare itself."

Ryder's art has its occasional detractors. Her wire sculpture of two horses copulating was deemed "distasteful and offensive" by sensitive art fair attendees, and her minotaurs were banned from a Westminster Cathedral exhibition because, according to the cathedral, their generously-sized genitalia were a bit "too prominent." However, the sculptor is nonplussed by such criticism, telling me: "It's very odd to hide human anatomy from children or to say that it's offensive to different religions. We all have genitalia. I found that the animal masks allow me to show emotion without being sexually explicit. It's more acceptable if it's half animal. I don't make art to shock; I just make work that I feel driven to make."

MYSTERIOUS, ACROBATIC, AND UNPREDICTABLE MOVEMENTS: BARRY FLANAGAN'S LEAPING LAPINS

Barry Flanagan's slender hares are spindly to the point of emaciation. For connoisseurs of contemporary sculpture, they're reminiscent of Alberto Giacometti's equally withered statuary—only with rabbits instead of people. Flanagan's early, conceptual works featured piles of folded fabrics, sand-filled fabric "skins," or severed segments of heavy rope strewn across a gallery floor, but it was his hare sculptures, well over a hundred of them created over the last three decades of his life, that guaranteed his creative immortality before his passing in 2009.

Three factors set Flanagan on his personal bunny trail. One was George Ewart Evans's 1972 book, *The Leaping Hare*, about the animal in fact, fiction, and legend. A second was Evans's view of a hare dashing across the Sussex Downs, which left him mesmerized by the animal's acrobatic and unpredictable movements, as if dodging some invisible predator.[182] A third not quite as transcendental inspiration was when he began sculpturing hares in the late 1970s, and, according to *The New York Times*, was "working from a dead one bought from a butcher, partly because there wasn't much else to buy that day and partly because of a vivid memory he had of watching a hare leap across a field in Sussex."[183]

Whatever the motivation, Flanagan created his first Leaping Hare sculpture in 1979. Many, many more hares followed: dancing hares, drum-playing hares, hares in the style of Auguste Rodin's *The Thinker*, boxing hares, and acrobatic hares. Many of these hares are on permanent display around the world, and some are occasionally gathered for gallery and museum shows.

Apart from the near-mystical sight of a hare leaping through the rural British countryside, what else could account for the rich amount of imagery and humor that Flanagan was able to draw from the animal? An obituary of Flanagan in *Independent* quotes the artist describing the range of expressions he believed hares have, which is perhaps the source of Flanagan's inspiration. In describing this, he said:

[The hare] is rich and expressive, [carrying with it] the conventions of the cartoon and the investment of human attributes into the animal world . . . . If you consider what conveys situation and meaning and feeling in a human figure, the range of expression is, in fact, far more limited than the device of investing an animal—a hare especially—with the expressive attributes of a human being. The ears, for instance, are really able to convey far more than a squint in an eye of a figure or a grimace on the face of a model."[184]

Flanagan is not the only artist to describe this takeaway from animals. Many of the artists and writers I've spoken to have also expressed that an animal's universality—its generic appearance—makes it a better stand-in for humanity than any particular human's physical appearance.

Of course, not everyone appreciated Flanagan's sense of whimsy. In reviewing a 2020 retrospective of Flanagan's work Jonathan Jones of *The Guardian* described the artist's oeuvre as "a hare-brained scheme that wasted three decades," and Flanagan himself as retreating "into his forge to produce variations on the cold, even evil cartoon character he'd come up with."[185]

Spoken like a true Elmer Fudd.

A BRIDGE BETWEEN THE ANIMAL AND HUMAN WORLDS: MARGIT BRUNDIN'S RABBITS

Margit Brundin is a Swedish sculptor whose work, like that of Ryder and Flanagan, focuses on anthropomorphic hares and rabbits. However, instead of working on the gigantic scale of those artists, Brundin's rabbits are human-sized and thus much more accessible to the viewer. In our email conversation, as Brundin discussed her work, I was fascinated by how similar her thoughts were to what furry authors and mainstream entertainers have told me. Once again I felt I was speaking with someone who was born furry:

> I grew up in the countryside in a family with a mother, father, and two siblings, along with dogs, cats, rabbits, geese, etc. I loved spending my time with these animals. Another favorite thing was listening to children's stories and watching cartoons, whose characters were often animals with human emotions. I have always experienced a sense of communication with animals, an experience which I think led me to easily apply human personality traits onto them.

If anything, Brundin's anthropomorphic instinct and her identification with animals have grown stronger. Like William Kotzwinkle's Arthur Bramhall in *The Bear Went Over the Mountain*, she's able to mentally "become" a bear herself; like Barry Flanagan, she found inspiration in the sight of a hare racing across the landscape:

> I continue to use animals as my main theme, though they have gone from more animal-like to more human in their expression. Their anthropomorphic expressions have helped me express different personalities and thereby give the animals a stronger

narrative voice. I see my sculptures as a bridge between the world of the animals and the human world, that's for sure. My thoughts sometimes run wild when I think about an animal and its life. I may feel in my own body how a bear shuffles through the forest. I am inside the animal and the animal is almost always truly kind and innocent. If I'm not inside the animal, I often think of ways in which I can approach it and maybe stroke its fur and become its friend.

    The hare has been the only storyteller in my palette of animals. I remember seeing it run across the fields of my childhood home, and there are always rabbits on the lawn outside my workshop. My rabbits possess many human features; in their poses and how their eyes are centered, for example. Their ears convey their frame of mind. It is essential to me to apply a sense of dignity and sensitivity in the expression of this otherwise slightly naive or simple animal.

Like other creative people I've spoken with while writing this book, Brundin realizes anthropomorphic animals can represent humans more universally than an image of a specific, identifiable person ever could.

I also portray hares and rabbits rather than humans because an animal very clearly carries an element of familiarity that invites the viewer to recognize herself or himself and create a sense of belonging. It's much harder to achieve this sense of connection with a human portrait, which is typically experienced as a portrait of someone else, which can distance the viewer from the artwork. The sculpture's gaze is often rather focused, but with a tear in the corner of the eye. This invites the viewer to think about the personal history of the hare and perhaps try to look into its soul. Is it the case that we all carry a type of darkness inside us? Animals as well as humans? Or is it our own darkness or sorrow we see in the hare? To me, the sculptures express both strength and vulnerability at the same time.

I introduced Brundin to Barry Flanagan's and Sophie Ryder's thematically similar work and asked her opinion of them.

It was inspiring to acquaint myself with Sophie and Barry's work. There are, for sure, points of contact between our work. I would say mine can be placed somewhere between that of Sophie's and Barry's. Barry captures an enormous amount of movement in his work, and keeps a lot of the anatomy of the hare, even though they are clearly anthropomorphic. Sophie, on the other hand, captures still and calm moments in her sculptures. These sculptures are mostly human in their bodily expression. To me, Sophie's work also engages in portraying relations between anthropomorphic sculptures. I would say that this is a common thread in her art and my own. I believe we both work with self-portraits to some degree, that our sculptures portray emotional states that we have experienced. I also perceive that Barry's sculptures express a lot of joy and happiness, while Sophie's and mine carry sadness or melancholy. I really enjoy Sophie's large-scale sculptures, and find them incredibly striking.

9

I DIG A BRONY

"I feel sorry for any man who watches *My Little Pony*," says my former coworker. It's 2012 and we're chatting at a reunion party for Sunbow Productions, the TV production company we worked for in the 1980s. I've just finished telling her how much I enjoy a new series in the franchise, which is titled *My Little Pony: Friendship Is Magic* and has been airing for a while on The Hub, a cable channel of recent vintage. I've been enjoying the show so much, in fact, that I'm using a picture of the Mane Six, the show's starring ponies, as my smartphone's home screen, which I proceed to show her.

"This is Twilight Sparkle," I explain, pointing to the lavender unicorn with the magenta stripe running through her mane and tail. "She's the intellectual of the bunch." Then I move on to the others: "This one's Pinkie Pie. She's a party girl, a real space cadet, and she's got some sort of ESP. And those balloons on her side that look like a tattoo? That's her cutie mark. They all have one. It appears magically the moment they discover their role in life. And this blue one, with the wings and the rainbow mane and tail, she's Rainbow Dash, and she has a bit of an ego, but she's the fastest Pegasus pony in Ponyville...." I go on for another pony or two before I realize my former colleague is no longer standing there. That's what *My Little Pony: Friendship Is Magic* can do to a man.

The eighties and nineties were an era of "bartered" TV shows, first-run series that were produced as glorified toy advertisements and given free of charge to local TV stations. A few minutes of commercials were built into each episode, and the remaining ad time was sold by the station to advertisers. It was a win-win proposition for everyone, or so it seemed. For the ad agencies and TV studios that financed the shows, there was a healthy audience to view their commercials. For the stations who ran them, there was a brand-new show offered free of charge, guaranteed to grab more eyeballs than an old movie, and containing plenty of ad time to sell to advertisers.

For viewers, the appeal of these bartered TV shows depended on their interest in the show, but some series, like *Star Trek: The Next Generation* and *Xena: Warrior Princess,* have definitively become cultural touchstones. Others gave a generation of kids' toy-based cartoon series, like *Masters of the Universe, GI Joe, Transformers,* and *My Little Pony.* The latter three were based on Hasbro toys and Hasbro was the primary client of the ad agency that owned Sunbow, the company that produced the financed-by-Hasbro series and provided me with employment. Everyone high up on the Sunbow food chain insisted the shows weren't program-length commercials, but at the time of their airing, the GI Joe action figures, Transformer robots, and Pony dolls were selling quite nicely. The shows themselves were colorful, fast-paced, and appealing to their carefully targeted six-to-eleven-year-old audiences. To reach boys, action and explosions were used, and to reach girls, pretty pastel ponies took center stage.

I wasn't a fan of *GI Joe* or *Transformers*, but they didn't outright irritate me. On the other hand, I couldn't stomach *Pony*. It wasn't (just) the show's icky sweetness and abundance of butterflies and rainbows that unnerved me, it was the fact that the ponies were screamingly obvious knockoffs of the adolescent winged *pegasi* and unicorns populating the Pastorale sequence of my favorite movie, Disney's *Fantasia*.

LAUREN'S PONIES

Lauren Faust began her cartoon career as an animator on unjustly forgotten movies, like *Cats Don't Dance,* and justly forgotten ones, like *Quest for Camelot*. After directing a stack of *Powerpuff Girls* episodes for Cartoon Network, Faust hit her stride as head writer and supervising producer of *Foster's Home for Imaginary Friends*, but it was a project of Faust's own that led her to riding herd on Hasbro's pony-filled paddock. As she described it to me:

> It was actually pretty serendipitous. I met with a Hasbro Studios exec to pitch a series idea of my own. I told her about my background and showed her some art and an animatic I'd already produced. At the end of my pitch she pulled a *My Little Pony* DVD out of nowhere—*Princess Promenade*, one of the more recent *Pony* videos from 2006—and asked me if I liked *My Little Pony*. The ponies happened to be my absolutely favorite toy of my childhood. From what I understand it was completely on the fly; it had just occurred to her at that moment I might be a good fit for *My Little Pony*. She asked me to look at some DVDs

and see if I could come up with some ideas for where to take a new version of the franchise.

Faust already had some ideas of her own when it came to Hasbro's ponies.

My creative control for *Pony* was my inner eight-year-old. I still have my childhood pony figurines, I kid you not. I took out my six favorite ones, sat down, and remembered the personalities I gave them, the stories I made up when I was kid. My bedroom was their kingdom. I took that groundwork, fleshed it out, and made it more sophisticated.

The *Pony* product line had already gone through a few iterations since eight-year-old Lauren Faust played with hers, known today as the Generation One, or G1, ponies. Two more generations followed, each accompanied by its own cartoon series or animated specials, before Hasbro asked Faust to put a new spin on the franchise.

One observer of the animation scene was less than enthralled with the idea of someone with Faust's credentials coming up with a new cartoon spin on an old toy property. Amid Amidi, publisher of the Cartoon Brew website, was downright apoplectic, declaring the event: "the end of the creator-driven era in TV animation."[186]

According to Amidi, TV executives more concerned with money than magic were once again calling the shots, marking the end of a period spanning the early 1990s through the late 2000s. During this purported golden age, animation writers and directors had the freedom to come up with innovative shows like *The Ren & Stimpy Show*, *Dexter's Laboratory*, *Samurai Jack*, and *Rocko's Modern Life*. However, as the aughts drew to a close, studios were becoming more conservative, opting to back existing properties they felt were more likely to provide returns. In Amidi's opinion, "watching names like . . . Lauren Faust pop up in the credits of a toy-based animated series like *My Little Pony* is an admission of defeat for the entire movement, a white flag-waving moment for the TV animation industry."[187]

Was Amidi's judgment of Faust unnecessarily harsh? Amidi had no way of knowing, but Faust had a lot more in mind than helping Hasbro sell toys in exchange for a healthy paycheck, she wanted to create content that excited girls and pushed boundaries. According to Faust, "There's a perception out there, and I think you could argue rightfully so, that entertainment for little girls is a little eye-rolling. Usually it's not the highest quality, it's kind of babyish and overly safe."

If eight year-old Lauren's imagination kept inventing personalities and stories for her G1 ponies, it was probably because she instinctively realized that they had been given little characterization. "'One of them likes this, one of them likes that,' that was the extent of it," she told me. "My goal was to give them personalities. You need conflict and character flaws to distinguish them from each other."

Lauren spent six weeks putting together a forty-page show bible for Hasbro, one of the things she's most proud of in her twenty-year career. The effort led Faust's *My Little Pony: Friendship Is Magic* to become an amalgam of existing and new *Pony* characters that retained and updated elements of the previous series while adding some important new ones. The central character, Twilight Sparkle ("Twi"), is a socially inexperienced, intellectual unicorn sent by Princess Celestia, ruler of the realm of Equestria, to the small town of Ponyville in order to get her horn out of her books and make some friends. There Twi makes the acquaintance of a quintet of locals who become her pony posse: palomino farmgirl Applejack, high-octane Rainbow Dash, ditsy party girl Pinkie Pie, kind-to-animals Fluttershy, and fashion plate Rarity.

Guy ponies were few and far between in previous *Pony* programs, but while *FIM*'s focus is squarely on the Mane Six and other assorted fillies, this time around there's no shortage of male equines. Faust explains why:

> I didn't put boy ponies in there because I wanted boys to watch the show, I put them in there because when I was little I used to wonder why there weren't boy ponies. In fact, when I made up stories for my ponies, if I needed a boy I'd take one of my blue or green ponies and reassign its gender. [But] girls have brothers and dads, and even though most of their friends are girls, they have boy friends too. I didn't see any reason to exclude boys.

In addition to male characters, Faust gave *FIM* something else the franchise had never had before: an internal mythology detailed enough to serve as the springboard for numerous plotlines. Recurring villains like the shapeshifting Queen Chrysalis; mysterious Equestrian realms like the Everfree Forest (home to the deadly, and literally made out of wood Timberwolves); enigmatic characters like the reclusive zebra Zecora; and a variety of dragons who appear throughout the series all contributed to a richly populated world.

The heart of the show's mythology, however, may be the Elements of Harmony, six magical jewels that tap into the power of friendship to defeat evil. Twi and her friends each embody a different aspect of friendship: Applejack's honesty, Fluttershy's kindness, Pinkie Pie's easy laughter, Rarity's generosity, Rainbow Dash's loyalty, and Twilight's magic.

The Elements are put to use at the very beginning of the series, freeing Celestia's sister Luna, bitter from living in her sister's shadow, from her villainous alter ego Nightmare Moon. "I thought of the jealousy born of feeling ignored and left in someone's shadow," Faust shared in the *Pony* guidebook *The Elements of Harmony*.[188] "I thought that if we knew someone who was hurting that way, showing them friendship, showing them that they were loved and valued, would be the cure."

On October 10, 2010, *My Little Pony: Friendship Is Magic* premiered on the Hub. A lot of folks who might have ignored the invitation checked out the show thanks to Amidi, whose screed piqued their curiosity. They tuned in, turned on, and began generating thumbs-up, "you gotta check out this show" threads on message boards across the internet.[189] The most notable reaction may have been on 4chan's "/co/" board, dedicated to comics and cartoons, one of the dozens of special interest boards on the site. If there ever was an example of the internet's ability to send something viral, it was *My Little Pony: Friendship Is Magic*. Within weeks, hundreds, then thousands, of *Pony* threads appeared on the board and word quickly spread around the internet, leaping to other websites.

However, on 4chan's anything-goes "/b/" board, the reaction was quite the opposite. People who disliked the show tried to counter with a previously successful tactic: burying the threads under an avalanche of gruesome and/or grotesque images. However, they were no match for the show's fans (who now called themselves "bronies" as in "bro ponies") and used the motto, "We're gonna love and tolerate the shit out of you." The haters gave up and the victorious bronies were eventually rewarded with their own 4chan message board.

"I never thought a guy without younger siblings or children of his own would even give the show a chance," Faust reflects. "I'm just so thrilled they did and embraced it the way they did. Adult men who have a picture of Fluttershy on their message boards and stuff, not afraid to show it—it's more than I ever could've asked for."

Furs were of course among *MLP:FIM*'s first adult fans. For many, a cleverly written, attractively animated series featuring anthropomorphic animals was irresistible. But not all of the show's adult fans were furs. Many soon-to-be bronies had no inkling that furs existed when they discovered the show, and others wanted nothing to do with furs. For one thing, furry's kinky reputation was off-putting to no small number of people who didn't want to see their fandom tarred with the same dirty brush (and the appearance of pornographic *Pony* art confirmed their fears) or be considered a subset of furry—and many furs claimed the show, set in an all-animal, anthropomorphic universe was inherently furry.

By and large, adult male furs who enjoyed the show had no trouble considering themselves bronies. However, there were furs watching *Pony* who considered the show separate from their own fandom. They might watch it, but *no way* were they bronies! Furry would be kept "pure," they insisted, with no other fans, bronies or video gamers included, or given the right to call themselves furry, even if their anthropomorphic interests overlapped. There were also the furs who assumed *Friendship Is Magic* was simply a rehash of the juvenile 1980s series, and mocked anyone watching that "little girl's' show." Flame wars between the factions blazed and then thankfully died out. Except for the occasional trollish outburst, it became a matter of "We can agree to disagree, but we both love *Pony*."

So what was it about *Pony* that was turning all sorts of grown-up geeks, whatever they called themselves, into fans? In an email to me, Calpain, coeditor of Equestria Daily, the internet's top *Pony* fan site, offered a theory: "The world can be a cynical place, and with all the dark media out there it was refreshing to see something that bucked that trend. I think a lot of people were looking for a show with characters they can really relate to that was genuinely happy and promoted friendship."

Nobody expected *Pony* to be cleverly written, visually inventive, its characters funny and appealing—a show that embraced its non-targeted audience rather than chasing it away. Cartoon fans were drawn to the show's attractive character designs and inventive animation, furs tuned in to enjoy the anthropomorphic characters, and pretty much everyone was fascinated by the unpredictable storytelling. (Personally, my reason was "D, all of the above.")

On the show, Twi and her friends regularly shed their amiable personalities, turning eye-twitchingly neurotic, obsessive, or steam-coming-out-of-their-ears choleric at unexpected moments. And cartoon and pop culture references abound: anvils fall on heads, Pinkie Pie pursues a fleeing pony with Pepé Le

Pew-style hops, Twilight's magical abilities earn her a spot in Princess Celestia's School for Gifted Unicorns (an X-Men reference that a Marvel Comics fan can spot a dozen channels away), the *2001: A Space Odyssey* film's monolith makes a cameo appearance (complete with *Zarathustra* musical sting), a pack of canine villains are named after David Bowie's "Diamond Dogs," and an episode ends with a shot-by-shot recreation of *Star Wars: A New Hope*'s victory ceremony, complete with sudden iris into the closing credits. Together, this endless stream of winks and hints from the show's creators let fans know that they're just big geeks too.

The bronies returned the love, generating scads of fan art and thousands of fanfic stories, a lot of it taking the ponies to emotional heights (and sometimes naughty depths) the series dares not approach. Fan-created songs numbered in the thousands: the online Brony Music Archive contains some twenty-two thousand songs from two thousand different composers.[190] (An entire genre of fan songs consists of show dialog broken down into free-form poetry and set to original music tracks accompanying spliced montages of animation from the show.)

Videocentric bronies edited show footage to help ponies lip-synch pop songs and amateur animators created their own *Pony* cartoons, some indistinguishable from show animation, like "Ask the Crusaders" and *Picture Perfect Pony*,[191] others wildly original and insanely off-model, like hotdiggedydemon's outrageous "documentary" of Pinkie Pie as a dissolute celebrity.[192] They've collectively created and shared CGI models of the two-dimensional ponies that have appeared in numerous fan videos and ponyfied well-known visuals; one fan's version of *Casino Royale*'s opening credits is amazingly spot-on.[193]

Fan-created OCs—original characters—also abound, interacting with show ponies in fanfic and fan art, and occasionally becoming fandom stars in their own right, like Michael Chorney's mute ball of fur pony named Fluffle Puff.[194]

"The reaction to her was a really big surprise," Chorney admitted to me. "A lot of her is based off my own interests and personality. On the outside I find it really hard to express emotions—on the spectrum of autism is social anxiety. I like doing this, it pushes me to do more, it gives me an outlet for that so I can express what I actually feel."

DERPY AND DR. HOOVES

If you're a serious fan of a particular movie or TV show, you may have watched it numerous times. After a few viewings, you're familiar enough with the story and start noticing things like continuity errors (for example, a character was holding a book a second ago, but now he's not) and background details (such as, that kid has his hands to his ears like he already knows she's going to fire the gun).

Thus was born Derpy.

"Derpy was a character that kind of came from the fans," says Jayson Thiessen with a laugh during our interview. Thiessen was one of *FIM*'s original directors and later became its co-executive producer. He gives me the background on the character:

> She was a mistake. Someone along the way accidentally made one of the characters cross-eyed. She was way in the background

and nobody noticed her. It got through and onto the show. We were going on the fan websites to see what people were saying about the show. We saw fans had focused on background characters, so we started to personify them. Derpy was the most popular, and we liked her too. It was like, "Wow, we weren't even thinking about this."

Thanks to the bronies, the yellow-maned ditzy Derpy began showing up regularly, her absentmindedness usually leading to confusion.

Then there's another background pony, an anonymous equine, who, thanks to his hourglass cutie mark and a possible resemblance to onetime *Doctor Who* star David Tennant, was fan-dubbed Dr. Whooves. Hasbro, already hip to the brony crowd, trademarked the less-likely-to-upset-the-BBC variant Dr. Hooves and licensed it to companies happy to create plush and plastic doctor ponies for his fans.

Derpy and Dr. Hooves are far from the only ponies to have emerged from the herd to become show regulars. "To us they're just designs, Background Pony Number Two," story editor Mitch Larson confessed to the audience at a *Pony* convention. "You guys, *you* made them characters."

HEALING WITH A LITTLE HELP FROM PRINCESS LUNA

Cadejo Jones can't remember two and half years of his life. The young, round-faced brony with a bushy head of hair and a droopy moustache has been through hell. "The drinking was an on-and-off problem, but things went full-frickin'-bore the summer of 2014," he tells me. The drinking was a way for Jones to cope with a toxic relationship and other issues he'd rather not revisit. He does remember "the worst year of my life—basically the eleven-month hiatus between seasons four and five when I tried to kill myself. I'd been on board with the show since February of 2011, so yeah, I'm one of the original bronies."

Jones wasn't the only one going through a rough patch. In "Do Princesses Dream of Magic Sheep,"[195] Luna, younger sister to Equestria's ruling Princess Celestia, is tormented by guilt over her past as the villainous Nightmare Moon, guilt that takes the form of a powerful being that haunts her dreams called Tantabus.[196] At episode's end, with the Tantabus grown strong enough to become real and destroy Equestria, Luna confesses that it's her fault, as she created it to punish herself.

"But you're doing everything you can to stop it. Don't you see? That proves you're not the same pony you were then!" Twilight Sparkle tells her. The Tantabus, feeding on Luna's guilt, has grown into an enormous shadow version of herself and is moments away from escaping Luna's dream. This is a lightbulb moment for Luna. The Tantabus shrinks to her size and turns to face her. Luna does not destroy the Tantabus with a magical blast from her unicorn's horn or trample it under her hooves. Instead she smiles *and absorbs the Tantabus into herself.*

The 2015 episode was a lightbulb moment for Jones as well. "I was in dark place, and seeing Luna go through similar struggles to what I was going through was eye-opening. I was put heavy on the scent right at that moment. It was the big turning point. Soon after that I found a job and had the ground back underneath my feet."

"How can I forgive myself?" is a question Luna asks in the show. Jones, for his part, turned his experience into a presentation he's offered at several *Pony* conventions: "Living with a Tantabus: On *MLP* and Sobriety." The Tantabus is a metaphor for addiction and self-inflicted guilt, the episode an allegory of recovery. According to Jones, "What Luna goes through in the show is what a lot of addicts go through in real life."

One of the bullet points in Jones's PowerPoint presentation reads, "Learning not to let go, per se, but let be." As he explains, "It's the idea of not running from your past, but accepting that the past is the past. And learning from it instead of fleeing it is an important part of understanding one's self and healing."

Jones is far from alone. "At the end of my panel [as well as from] so many people I've talked to online, [people] have shared stories about how the show helped them. One brony who had only been sober one week told me my panel had been very helpful to him. Helping others is a terrific way to heal yourself."

PONY CONVENTIONS

When you have a fandom, you have conventions, and *Pony* is no exception. Over the course of *Friendship Is Magic*'s nine seasons and 222 episodes,[197] hundreds of *Pony* conventions were held across the United States and around the world, everywhere from Finland to Malaysia and points in between.[198]

BronyCon, the biggest of the *Pony* conventions, attracted ten thousand convention attendees to "Baltimare" in 2015. (Punny *Pony* city names are real groaners; until *Friendship Is Magic* premiered, I had no idea I lived in "Manehattan"). Before moving to Maryland, the first iteration of the convention, BroNYCon, was held in June 2011 in a mid-Manhattan rehearsal hall with one hundred people in attendance. The second was held in September 2011 and attracted three hundred fans to a Chinatown loft, and in January 2012, 850 fans gathered in a cramped midtown hotel ballroom. In June 2012, the convention took place in New Jersey over an extremely hot summer weekend with a sold-out first day attendance of four thousand guests eager to see Lauren Faust, several *Pony* voice talents, and each other. Some guests traveled hundreds of miles, drove across several states, or flew in from far-off countries.

I was at that June convention and can vividly remember people cosplaying as the show's ponies, many in exquisitely detailed costumes. There were numerous versions of the show's Mane Six, as well as secondary ponies, crowd scene ponies, and ponies that appeared in single episodes. There were also a handful of ponies in full-body mascot suits who were courageous enough to venture outside the exposition center into the ninety-degree heat despite the added warmth of their costumes.

The exposition center's convention hall was a vast, echoing space. A black floor-to-ceiling curtain physically separated the "Mane Stage" at the back of the hall from the rest of the building. The stage's anemic sound system was occasionally overwhelmed by competing audio from the nearby "Tail Stage." Before you could reach either stage you had to pass a gauntlet of dealers' booths. Most of them were occupied by vendors selling fan art, jewelry, posters, and the like, but the largest and most crowded one belonged to WeLoveFine, a prominent creator of *Pony* T-shirts, shoulder bags, and assorted merchandise. WeLoveFine produces dozens upon dozens of *Pony* tees, many designed by the fans and all approved by Hasbro. The tees highlight individual ponies, catch phrases from the cartoon, or replace pop culture icons with *Pony* characters (such as the winged Rainbow Dash in place of Led Zeppelin's Icarus logo or flying while generating *Dark Side of the Moon*'s rainbow in her wake).

A lanky fellow named Aaron was singlehandedly working the WeLoveFine counter and stuffing currency into an already overstuffed waist pouch bulging with cash. "We sent eight people to the anime con, and I'm here by myself," he told me while dancing between the emptying cartons behind him and the clamoring customers on the other side of the counter. Then, "I had five thousand shirts this morning. Right now, I'm down to my last hundred." At this point BronyCon 2012 was still in its opening hours.

Lauren Faust was the star of the show. When she stepped onstage, thousands of attendees gave her a cheering, standing ovation that brought her close to tears. As she brought her hands to her face, she was comforted by a hug from Twilight Sparkle's voice actress, Tara Strong. When Faust spoke she said, "I'm completely overwhelmed.... Thank you, thank you.... I love you guys so much."

A few hours later, Faust was a bit more composed and told the audience about the origins of *My Little Pony: Friendship Is Magic* and her desire to have an assortment of female characters with strong, distinctive personalities, sharing: "Most girls [in boy-oriented cartoon series] have the same character over and over again. I was looking for relatable characters. Usually the girl who wants to get good grades is the nerd, an unattractive stick-in-the-mud. My own mom was like Twilight Sparkle: she was too busy studying to make friends." The bottom line for Faust: "I wanted a respectable show for girls, not a girlie show."

The most imaginative *Pony* fans—the artists, writers, video makers, and musicians who use the show as raw material or inspiration for their own creations—have their own fans, as well as their own BronyCon sessions. (On the last day of the show, I met a fan who was ecstatic because the best-known fan composers had all signed his poster under their pony likeness.) This quality of brony fandom, that its top creator fans have their own fans, has always amazed me but raised the question of why *My Little Pony: Friendship Is Magic* has triggered a tsunami of fan creativity, from reverent homages to irreverent (but loving) send-ups, in both amount and quality beyond anything ever seen before. Perhaps there's some intrinsic, ineffable quality to the show and its characters, an openheartedness that speaks to every viewer personally and individually, and for many, inspires their own creativity.

The last day of the convention, John de Lancie, who voices the show's villain Discord, went onstage. With his neatly trimmed salt-and-pepper beard, de Lancie could pass for Dos Equis's Most Interesting Man in the World.

De Lancie has done a significant amount of voice work, and, in addition to *FIM,* his stentorian tones have been heard in the *Assassin's Creed* video games, the superhero TV series *Young Justice,* and the uber-weird sci-fi show *Invader Zim*. In response to my question of how he ended up doing voice work for *FIM,* he told me:

> One day I got a call from my agent to do a cartoon show. I looked at the script and thought, *Wow, this is pretty well written.* I went in and did the show. They said, "It's great to have you on the show, Mr. de Lancie, it's for . . . .'" [At this point de Lancie's voice trails off in a droning mumble. At the time he didn't give the role or even the show's name a second thought.] I did the show and completely forgot it. About three months later I turned on my

computer and there were four hundred emails. I begin reading one of them, and on top it says, *My Little Pony*. I asked my wife, "What is this?" She said, "It's a program for little girls."

That weekend I was in Vancouver at a *Star Trek* convention.[199] A bunch of people came up to me and said, "We're bronies." There must've been a hundred of them. I listened to their reasons why they liked the show, and they were really good reasons. I began to get a sense that this was the beginning of a new fan base. The next weekend I was in Calgary. The same thing happened, and I'm beginning to get a sense of who the community is.

But while de Lancie was increasingly excited about the show and how beloved it was, a snide, look-at-the-weirdos-style report on the January 2012 convention raised his ire. In response he told his cheering fans, "The world needs more of you. This group and more groups like you have got to be better than what we have now." For starters (and without endorsing anyone in particular), he urged the bronies to vote in that year's November election.

I was impressed by de Lancie's genuine passion. At that point, he had been dealing with fan boys and girls for years. There was absolutely no need for him to pander to this crowd, to pretend to share their love or recognize its importance to them. He was instead speaking from the heart.

FAUST DEPARTS

Faust left her creation after the show's first season, a result of the vague but all-encompassing stock reason: creative differences. Entertainment industry speculation attributed her reluctant departure to a lack of creative control over the property, and, in particular, displeasure with Hasbro's spin-off of *Pony*, *Equestria Girls*, which were direct-to-video movies featuring high school human analogs of the Mane Six.

The real reason for Faust's departure? She tells me she would rather not go into details, but I get the sense that she was denied creative control and that she seems to resent this.

"It's very complicated and I don't know if there's any way I can explain it quickly and simply enough to really answer anyone's questions," she tells me. "I can say it was my decision to leave, [but] I was very sad to leave. I didn't want to."

PONY REMEMBRANCES

It's early 2016 and I'm in Brooklyn attending another *Pony* convention. Earlier in the day Faust observed to a Q&A audience that the younger generation is much more comfortable crossing gender lines than their predecessors. I now come across a bearded young man in a skintight Rainbow Dash spandex outfit complete with a rainbow lightning bolt cutie mark on his hip. I ask him if he's cool portraying a female character. "I'm portraying the character as if she were male," he answers. "I'm male, so I look male. I'm not shaving my beard off."

A few minutes later I'm heading downstairs when a young dad and a son who looks to be seven or eight pass me on their way up. The kid is wearing Rainbow Dash's multicolored tail tucked into his belt. His dad has a set of pony ears atop his head and Fluttershy's pink tail emerging from the bottom of his denim jacket. This kid is growing up in a world where it's no big deal to walk around wearing a colorful tail on the back of your pants, just like dad. At this particular moment, I'm feeling pretty good about the future.

In August 2019 I'm in Baltimore for the very last BronyCon. The convention was originally going to run through 2025, but organizers decided to make 2019 the final one to allow everyone to remember the convention at its best, rather than let it fizzle out and leave memories of it being lackluster. Two months later, Discovery Family (successor to the now defunct Hub) is scheduled to air the final episode of *My Little Pony: Friendship Is Magic*, aptly named "The Last Problem." Nine seasons and 222 episodes are an impressive accomplishment for an animated series not named *The Simpsons* or *Arthur*.[200]

Once again, thousands of attendees have gathered for a brony convention, and this one marks a final weekend with series creator Lauren Faust and supervising director Jayson Thiessen, along with various episode writers, producers, and voice actors. Also present is Bonnie Zacherle, creator of the original generation of pony figurines in the 1980s. (Her expression turns sour when I mention I worked for Tom and Joe, the producers of the original series and owners of the agency that simultaneously created all *Pony* advertising, which I take to mean she had a less than harmonious working relationship with the pair.) Later, at a panel of the show's writers, I raise the subject of advertising when I suggest it's easy to tell the "using the products to tell a story" episodes from the "using the show to promote the products" episodes. One of the writers present, his days of scripting *Pony* episodes now over, pauses for a second, then advises, "Don't write for Hasbro."

In the lobby two young men are garbed in striped vests, bow ties, and straw boater hats. They're performing a pitch-perfect recreation of the similarly dressed Flim Flam Brothers characters from a season two episode. Nearby I meet someone costumed as the Smooze, a gelatinous green slime creature sporting a red bow tie and blue top hat from a season five episode. Soon it's time for my session, "Present at the Creation." One of my jobs at Tom and Joe's ad agency/production company was to produce promotional videos that would encourage companies to license Hasbro logos and characters for use on their own products, the idea being that the Hasbro brand would make otherwise bland products more appealing to customers.

Along with the GI Joe, Transformers, and *My Little Pony* licensing videos, I produced a short "behind the scenes" video featuring Tony Randall and Sandy Duncan promoting their voicework in the very first *My Little Pony* special, "Rescue at Midnight Castle," a one-shot half hour cartoon that introduced the characters while testing the waters for an ongoing daily TV series. As at other *Pony* conventions, I've brought along the *Pony* licensing and the behind-the-scenes videos to share with my fellow bronies.

A modest hundred people attend my session, a number I'm grateful for, especially because the group has chosen to forego the latest compilation of fan-made videos, always crowd pleasers, taking place at the same time. During the Q&A session following my videos, a woman starts weeping while describing her love for the series, then apologizes for crying. I offer what I hope is good advice, telling her: "Never apologize for your tears." It's not mere cartoon characters that bring someone to tears, but the thought of losing their companionship, their engaging personalities and surprising emotional depth, when the show ends its run. That's what *My Little Pony: Friendship Is Magic* can do to a person.

10

MAINSTREAM ANTHROPOMORPHIC ART

The visual arts, painting and photography in particular, are so loaded with anthropomorphic imagery as to rival the furry world. To even begin cataloging them could fill an entire book. In the meantime, here are a handful of examples:

Hieronymus Bosch's *Garden of Earthly Delights* triptych is chock-full of furry critters. People familiar with the painting may have already noticed the profusion of anthro beings in the hellish right-hand panel: clothes-wearing avian beings, a beaked creature consuming and excreting people, a hunter rabbit carrying its captured human prey, a pig-nun forcing herself on a distraught man—not very friendly furries. But in contrast, look closely at the pond in the Edenic scene on the left: among its inhabitants is some sort of aquatic being half out of the water. Its submerged half is a large fish while its half above the surface might be a duck or a platypus with dark fur, a prominent bill, and arms holding a book in its human hands. He appears to be the only anthropomorphic being in the entire panel but a well-educated one.

Furries may represent themselves as animals through their fursonas, but a heavyweight like Picasso repeatedly drew himself as a minotaur to represent his animalistic lusts.[201] Anthropomorphic goats are a recurring motif in Marc Chagall's work.[202] Even photography, a medium typically documenting reality, can be put to anthropomorphic use. William Wegman's whimsical Weimaraner portraits have been a pop culture icon for decades—but he's not the only artist putting animals in front of a camera.

LOOK INTO MY EYES: THE CREATURE PORTRAITS OF YAGO PARTAL

A website named Creature Portraits sounds as if it might contain classy animal photographs taken at various zoological gardens or wildlife preserves, pictures that might capture the essence of the animals' personalities.[203] Instead, it puts you face to face with row after row of extremely unusual images: dozens of head-and-shoulder shots of animals staring into the camera. Each one has a human name and is wearing human clothes that somehow seem like they would be appropriate to that particular beast were it human. Connor, a young domestic pig in a knit cap and thick, hand-knitted sweater, looks as if he were heading out to play in the snow. Àbakar, a sly-looking caracal in a striped T-shirt, has a sweater draped over his neck. Hubert, a dour Labrador, wears a green V-neck sweater over a white polo shirt.

Row after row after row, every one of them is staring straight ahead—cautiously, confidently, or defiantly. They could be posing for their driver's license photo or mug shot. Or perhaps they're looking into a mirror, dispassionately studying their reflection. Or is it *your* reflection? Perhaps you're the one looking into a mirror, seeing yourself.

The Creature Portraits are the work of Yago Partal, a Barcelona-based photographer, producer, and conceptual designer. I first came across them in a New York City card shop, but they're all over the world: on pillows and posters, calendars, clocks, clothing, mugs, magazine and book covers, mobile phone cases, and citywide ad campaigns.[204]

Taxing Google Translate to its limit, Partal and I enjoyed a haphazard online chat during which he shared his thoughts on how animals are usually anthropomorphized by caricaturing human beings into animals, or giving them human-like facial expressions, but Partal aimed to "depict animals in an entirely new way, different from anything that's been tried before." According to him:

> Many artists have humanized animals before me, but almost always via illustration. I tried to give each animal a human personality by creating a seemingly photographic, realistic portrait of it looking directly at the viewer—saying something with its eyes. Since many animals never make eye contact with a human, they're much more intriguing this way.

I marveled at Partal's ability to photograph or discover pictures of every animal looking directly into the camera. As it turns out, his technique was simpler yet more complicated. He explained: "The pictures are Photoshop montages. They're digitally assembled from any number of photographs, textures, drawings, and other reference materials." And each one's unique wardrobe? "It's a very fluid process that doesn't take very long. After I choose an animal and decide what its portrait should look like, I start researching costumes and fashion model photos until I decide what outfit would best suit it."

As one might imagine, some animals were easier to dress than others. According to Partal, "[An animal's] shape makes a lot of difference. It's difficult to adapt clothes to animals with very wide necks, for instance. Female animals are also a challenge; you can't use earrings, long hair, eyelashes, lipstick, or a neckline unless you want it to look like a cartoon character."

Partal traces his fascination with the nonhuman animal world to the multivolume animal encyclopedia he devoured as a child, a gift from parents who had no idea it would eventually inspire what was first named Zoo Portraits and today is Creature Portraits. He also credits the cartoons he watched back in the day and their anthropomorphic stars as another influence, "a reference point for many children"—as they are for many furs.

The portraits today have taken on a wider focus than they had when I first came across Partal's work in the mid-2010s. Partal is now the creative director of Creatures United, an international organization dedicated to preserving animal species and their habitats, and protecting the ecosystems that both human and non-human animals depend on for their survival.

Creatures United is using Partal's portraits to dramatize our interconnectedness with the animal world and the organization's website features an animated world map identifying regions where indigenous animal populations—as depicted by Partal—are at risk. (In the Arctic, walrus Joseph wears a red sports jacket and blue work shirt; in South America, tapir Gabriela sports a strawberry-colored scarf; in Australia, koala Cooper is dressed in a tropical-patterned shirt.)

Elsewhere on their website Creatures United makes an intriguing promise: "We, the Creatures, are going to tell a dramatic, compelling story: an army of animated, talking animals, voiced by some of the world's best-loved celebrities whose combined reach is in the billions . . . inspiring people to act." I for one can't wait to see Partal's Creature Portraits brough to CGI life—and there's already no shortage of A-list performers who don't mind lending their voices to animated animals.

I'm intrigued by Partal's dedication to the animal world, both emotionally and professionally, but I also have a biting curiosity to know what "anthropomorphism" means to him, so I pose the question directly. He responds thoughtfully, telling me:

> I think it's something that has always been present, whether in mythology, like the Egyptian gods, or cartoons in modern times. It goes way back. I think we have a basic need to become like the animals we love and experience abilities we lack, like flying. Moreover, there's something very magical about giving an animal a human personality and being able to communicate with him face to face.

Where does Partal's fascination with animals come from? Is it something triggered by the animal encyclopedia of his youth? He tells me, "It's a question I cannot answer. There is no why. It's just something that's lived in me since childhood, something that's always been there. I could spend my life observing animals. I'm fascinated by the blue whale, but my favorite animal is the moose."

Fascinated by the blue whale, fond of the moose; but if he could become an animal, or if he already is one, what animal is that?

"I'm a monkey," he tells me.

IN THE *NEW YORKER*, NO ONE KNOWS YOU'RE A FURRY

Since its birth in 1925, the prestigious *New Yorker* magazine has become world-renowned for choice literary fiction, in-depth journalism, coverage of the cultural scene, and its cartoons. Pick up any issue and you'll see a surprisingly large number of those cartoons are based on the antics of anthropomorphic animals. A rabbit wife opens the door to see her bunny hubby in an upturned top hat: "I got a job!" A human husband and wife look at their dog dressed in a tuxedo, cape, and top hat: "I think he wants to go out" A cat boss tells the dog standing in front of his desk, "Let's face it: you and this organization have never been a good fit." Outside his office we see all his employees are cats as well.

The magazine's covers are often equally furry, featuring animals in human settings: a kindly rabbit obstetrician administers an ultrasound test to a very pregnant rabbit wife, causing an easter egg to appear on the screen; a business-suited lion eating a salad in a vegetarian restaurant looks hungrily at the hoodie-wearing zebra walking by outside; the inside of a hollow Central Park tree is a veritable Whole Foods for the squirrels who are pushing shopping carts past bins of "gourmet nuts." But why does such a high-toned publication have a fondness for what could be argued are furry jokes? I was fortunate enough to talk with Robert Mankoff, who spent twenty years drawing cartoons for the magazine, and another twenty as its cartoon editor, choosing which ones to publish, to find out why.

Your magazine is known for its gag cartoons, many of which feature anthropomorphic animals, as do many of its covers. What's that all about?
Well, it's about being funny.

What makes talking animals funny?
It's a duality, that's what humor is all about. They're not animals, they're people, but they have animal bodies. It's easy to mash up the two ideas: it's a dog but it's not a dog, it's a person but it's not a person. That's the way humor works, it's an ideal way to mash them. It's why we like animals so much: because we act as though they're people.

Originally, the dogs didn't talk. In the 1920s and thirties the original dog cartoons were more about the people talking about their pets, *imagining* they were humans. It's not until about the 1930s and 1940s that the cartoons move on to talking dogs. By 1993 you have the great Peter Steiner cartoons with the two dogs in front of the computer saying, "On the internet, nobody knows you're a dog."

HOW LOWBROW CAN YOU GO? THE CARTOON CRITTERS OF ANTHONY AUSGANG

On an early evening in the year 2000, my family and I are at a New York City art gallery and performance space. We're there to catch a show by my then-twelve-year-old son's guitar teacher. Lining the wall to the left of our table are paintings by Anthony Ausgang, an artist who specializes in generic, yet often weird cartoon-style funny animal imagery. His recurring character is a cartoon cat vaguely resembling MGM's Tom of *Tom and Jerry* fame.

My eye wanders from the stage and catches sight of Ausgang's largest canvas. On it, in full glorious view of my twelve- and seven-year-old sons, is his cat depicted as enormously endowed and unmistakably at the climactic moment of a gargantuan act of self-abuse. (The spermatozoa-patterned wallpaper behind him was a nice touch.) My wife and our seven-year old didn't even notice the painting, but it fooled my older son: he thought it was a picture of an *elf* masturbating. Luckily, he was not sullied that evening by the pernicious influence of furry porn.

Anthony Ausgang was one of the first people I interviewed when I started writing about mainstream anthropomorphism. He's been called "one of the original godfathers of 'low brow art.'"[205] Ausgang was born to a Dutch mother and a Welsh father who emigrated from England to the Caribbean in the early 1950s in search of better economic opportunities. Here's Ausgang's story as he told it to me, followed by his responses to my interview questions:

> My family moved from Trinidad and Tobago to Houston in 1960. My father worked for Texaco on very early computer

science. He used to bring home hundreds of used punch cards, which I got to draw all over. They'd never owned a TV but once here they purchased a set so that my brother and I could watch a local kids' show called *Cadet Don*.

My dad discovered Saturday morning animated cartoons and soon we were watching them together, tripping out because neither of us had seen anything like it before. There were these weird shows like *The Banana Splits* that combined cartoon animals and live action. That particular show was psychedelic in the extreme, so watching it and *The Bugs Bunny Show* on the same Saturday morning made for a pretty mind-boggling start to the day—a stretch of morning TV time dedicated to weirdo juvenile programming that mostly excluded adults, making the whole experience a psychedelic clusterfuck of animated cartoon animals on one channel and live action actors running around in freaked out animal costumes on the other.

You were born in 1959, like myself, a part of the post-World War II baby boom generation. We were marinated in the classic animation (*Looney Tunes*, Fleischer, etc.) that filled kids' TV at the time. Some of it was quite surreal. Did any of it inspire you to use cartoon characters in your work?
I had no theory or manifesto. I just began painting cartoon-style animals, which seemed to fit somehow with the anti-humanist attitude of punk rock at the time. I'm sure my choice of imagery

was influenced by what I watched on TV as a kid, but I never sat down and decided to use cartoon-style characters. What I *did* decide to do was make my own characters and not use Bugs or Felix. I wasn't interested in being "ironic" and riffing on them like other Lowbrow artists.[206]

The first cartoon I remember was *Tom Terrific* on the *Captain Kangaroo* show. By today's standards it was utterly crude, but I still found it amazing. I was also impressed by *Clutch Cargo*, but a little freaked out by the human mouths superimposed over the cartoon characters' faces.

Back in the seventies, movie theaters would have outrageous midnight movie double features of rock concert films and offbeat features. One night I went to see Ralph Bakshi's animated feature *Fritz the Cat*, which was based on Robert Crumb's character. I had never seen an X-rated feature-length cartoon before, and I was struck by the fact that a cartoon could express such subversive and perverted sentiments.

In a magazine interview[207] you said, "In the early eighties I was one of the few artists that eschewed the human figure in favor of cartoon characters. I really felt I was doing something that would measurably improve the world if it were broadcast to a larger audience." It sounds like a tongue-in-cheek declaration, but...

No, I was serious when I said that. Most cartoon characters in the fine art world were familiar but used in some ironic way, like Mickey Mouse smoking a joint. I just decided to draw my own animals and use them to depict the human condition in nonhuman terms.

Did the rise of the Lowbrow Art movement help your art became acceptable to the mainstream art world? Do you feel you helped create Lowbrow?

Lowbrow Art began as a loose collection of disenfranchised artists who shared a visual vocabulary based on cartoon styles and tropes. The first wave of such artists included Robert Williams and Ed Roth, and it revolved around the connection between cartoons and hot rods. I was part of the second wave of Lowbrow artists who also used hot rods to build a narrative.

The first museum exhibition of Lowbrow Art was the Kustom Kulture show in Laguna Beach Art Museum in 1993, and as a result of being in that show my paintings became acceptable to the mainstream art world. Before this show I was selling my paintings to collectors, but none of them were connected to the mainstream art world. Not only were the artists obscure, but so were the collectors. It wasn't until rock stars began buying Lowbrow Art that "better" collectors began to take notice.

One art magazine journalist wrote, "His tripped-out, surrealistic narratives feature cartoon characters in exaggeratedly provocative situations."[208] **The 1990s were also the early days of furry fandom and a good deal of furry art features anthropomorphic characters in more than "provocative" situations (i.e., "furry porn"). Fursuiting is also popular in the fandom, and the characters in *Night of the Hunter* are humans in leopard suits. Did you know about the furry scene before I contacted you? If so, did it have any influence on your work?**

The Night of the Hunter [which features two people who have cornered a third in a leopard costume] is about "species bending" and the characters are obviously having a tough time dealing with the switch! I was aware of "furry porn" before I did this painting and decided to reference it in a painting of a nonsexual but potentially fatal situation.

How did you learn about or first come across furry porn?
Artists are cultural renegades, always looking for some subculture to pillage or mock. I first came across furry porn at an art show in the late eighties when a crew of kids dressed in animal costumes showed up and began pantomiming sex with each other. Right then and there I figured that they were doing it at home too.... I certainly would! In those days one had to go to the bookstore for offbeat (pardon the pun) porn, and once it was

on my radar I began seeing furry porn in magazines. But I still figured it was some "gay thing" and it wasn't until later that I understood it was a "nondenominational" fetish . . . .

What I like about furry porn is that it gives animal cartoon characters a definite sexuality. Most of them seem to exist with rudimentary (if any) genitalia in a weirdly sexless world.

Do you have any particular feelings or opinions about furry fandom or anthropomorphism in general, cartoony or otherwise?
I believe that many of society's ills are caused by sexual repression and I welcome any type of indulgence in that respect as long as it is consensual. If people were allowed to get off unimpeded by society's restrictions, there would be a lot less aggravation on the street. I'm also fascinated by furry porn because it's something I never would have thought of myself!

11
PRETTY AS A PICTURE (FURRY ART)

Anthropomorphism is inescapable. Every society, every culture throughout time at one point or another has created visual depictions of animals with human qualities and animals behaving like people. Artists in twelfth-century Japan (or perhaps we should call them cartoonists) created the "Animal Frolic" scrolls. (The English-translated version of their Japanese name is "animal-person caricatures.") In one scroll, frogs and rabbits stand upright, wrestle, and pursue a fleeing monkey, perhaps to reclaim the (stolen?) hat atop his head. The scrolls may have been the earliest ancestors of the Japanese comics known as manga.

Furry fandom began with cartoonists and amateur artists who created fan art of comic book and cartoon animal celebrities or art of their own characters. In spite of the fursuiters that represent furry to most people, the majority of furry creativity is still generated by those amateur artists on paper or computer screens.

A furry artist might draw anthro characters simply for fun—or, if they're good or popular enough, earn a living by taking on commissions from furs not quite as adept at putting pencil to paper. Simply describe the furry image in your mind and they'll do their best to bring it to life. If you're not sure what you want to see, artists have posted plenty of "Your Character Here (YCH)" rough sketches inviting your character to "fill in the blanks."

Although anime and manga have influenced a great deal of furry art, most artists' styles vary widely depending on their art school training or simply their intuitive talent. The best artists have cultivated a style so personal as to be uniquely their own. Subject matter may range from character studies to fun, "safe for work" scenes of anthro characters enjoying life, to most definitely *NOT* "safe for work" art of blushingly adult subject matter featuring anthro characters enjoying life in an entirely different way.

And just how anthropomorphic would you prefer your anthro characters to be—mostly animal or mostly human? "Mostly animal" might describe the beasts of Disney's *Lion King* family. While they have unique sapience, speech, and facial expressions, they're anatomically modeled on real-world animals. (So much so that the studio was able to swap them out for photorealistic CGI creations for movies like their pseudo "live action" *Lion King* remake.) Dial it back a bit and you might wind up (again to use Disney films as a reference) with the semi-realistic animals seen in *Robin Hood* or *Zootopia*: foxes, bears, rabbits, and the like that resemble their true-life cousins to one degree or another, but wear clothes and stand upright. Go further in that direction and your animals turn into the stylized, even semi-abstract cartoon characters currently dominating animated TV series. Depending on their setting, these particular critters might be semi-clothed or naked.

But to return to the realism, semi- or otherwise, that's popular today—animal heads on human bodies territory—clothed (of course!) characters are usually depicted living in a modern setting. *BoJack Horseman* is probably the best-known example of this style.

Finally we reach the least anthropomorphic "entirely human, except for" characters, such as the *nekomimi* catgirls of Japanese anime and manga. With only feline ears (*nekomimi* actually means "cat ears" in English) and a tail to put them in furry territory, they could just as easily be women cosplaying nekomimi as the real thing.

Why do furs find anthro animals appealing to the eye? Simply put, it's the careful mixture of human and animal forms, anything from applying a human facial expression or body language on a cartoon animal to giving a critter a shapely human form (a cartoon trope when an animal ogles a pinup of a female of his species). I think adding a shapely tail to that female form makes it all that more attractive to a fur. The tail enhances and adds to the curves the body already possesses. (This applies to the male form as well, but not to the same degree.) It's why skunk tails (much plusher in the cartoon universe than the real world) and husky curved tails (and the animals they're attached to) are popular in the furry community.

FINDING FURRY ART

Attend any furry convention and you'll find furry art abounding. In the dealers den, where vendors of all sorts rent tables to sell their wares, you'll see no small number of loose-leaf books containing art created by the person on the other side of the table. Many artists have both SFW (safe for work) and NSFW (not safe for work) books available for browsing.

Furry artists who can't afford a dealers den table (or didn't win the convention lottery to get one) make do with first-come, first-served free table space in the artists' alley. Many up-and-coming artists can be found here, the best of whom may develop a following that will someday help them afford that dealers den table.

Can't make it to the convention? Find great furry art on the internet. Numerous online image boards offer thousands of furry images, all free for the downloading. The boards usually feature a search function allowing you to zero in on exactly the species (or situation) you have in mind. If you're an aspiring artist you can open up a free account on any of these boards to share your art with the furry world.

To view furry art online, check out SoFurry (sofurry.com), Inkbunny (inkbunny.net), Weasyl (weasyl.com), Transfur (transfur.com), DeviantArt (deviantart.com),[209] and the like, or the best-known and by far the largest furry art site: Fur Affinity (furaffinity.net). Numerous pictures are posted to Fur Affinity *every second*, totaling well over *ten thousand* new pictures every day. And like the boards, Fur Affinity allows visitors to leave comments under the posted pictures.

12

FURRY AFTER DARK

Animals are metaphors for our human selves: our behavior ("He eats like a pig"), our self-image ("I'm a lone wolf"), how we see others ("What a jackass!"), and our physical selves, which includes our sexual selves. We refer to our genitals as beavers, pussies, lizards, and trouser snakes, and it's a lucky man who's hung like a horse. It shouldn't surprise anyone that in addition to more conventional forms of sexual self-expression, some people act out or access their sexuality through anthropomorphic animal imagery and roleplay.

    Other subcultures also have a sexual component. The term "slash fiction" depicting two same-sex characters as lovers originated in *Star Trek* fanfic of Kirk and Spock in a hot relationship, and there's plenty of anime and manga porn (*hentai*) overflowing with sex scenes. However, neither *Star Trek* nor anime fandom is regularly defined by its most extreme aspects. Furry is not as lucky. Even as our community becomes better known and media coverage grows less sensational, the word "fetish" is still very often attached to it. The assumption is that adults can't possibly be highly interested in imaginary animals simply because they're aesthetically pleasing or a creative form of self-identification, that it has to be a kink.

"Rule 34," a relatively recent cultural phenomenon of the internet age, states that if something exists, there's a porn version of it. "Rule 34f" is Rule 34 with "covered in fur" added on, and references the kinky or "naughty" side of furry that exists. If I had to estimate the percentage of overall furry creativity or products that might be considered kinky or naughty, I would say between 15 and 18 percent qualifies as not-safe-for-work, and that the vast majority of that can be found in furry art and storytelling. Many artists specialize in creating portfolios of their furry work that explore nether regions and publicly protruding areas, and very often where and how those two meet. And numerous furry authors are adept at spinning spicy stories of their characters enjoying each other physically.

There are, of course, non-furry kinks that overlap Venn-diagram-style to whatever degree with furry, but are still their own unique thing, like pup play or pony play. But other than the fact that they both involve pretending to be animals, they're actually quite different. Pup and pony play involve a person behaving like and "becoming" an animal (zoomorphic) by wearing leather or rubber hoods and masks (and not much else). In the furry world, putting on a fursuit "raises" the animal the wearer is pretending to be from four legs to two, from animal to near-human, turning it anthropomorphic. When there are BDSM or sexual elements involved, they generally (but not entirely) fall more in the pup/pony portion of the diagram than the furry one.

Now it's off to the sex shop, where all sorts of sex toys or marital aids—depending on your parlance of choice—can be purchased for your private playtime. Bad Dragon, the best-known vendor of such items, was created by three furries.[210] The company offers a huge assortment of vividly colored animal-themed dildos and related paraphernalia. A photograph on their website of their items that are trophy winners in their industry shows a dildo that resembles an octopus tentacle, a few sedate looking ones, and a dangerous-looking transparent one with sharp edges. (Oh wait, that's not a dildo, it's the trophy they won.) A look at their website can be a daunting experience for someone easily grossed out (like me), but for those into this stuff it's a visit to technicolor heaven, with its assortment of vividly colored, elaborately shaped, textured, and creatively detailed merchandise.

I'm not here to kink-shame anyone. For me, kinks are an expression of someone's personality and their secret desires, and a highly creative form of self-expression. They're also deeply personal, which is why most people keep them secret, unless they're among like-minded people who understand and possibly have identical or similar kinks, and who, thanks to the internet, are a lot easier to find than ever before. I invited several kinksters to tell their stories of what turns them on—and why.

VIRGOSE

Virgose is a furry in his forties living in the upper Midwest.

My furry kink? That is both a tough and easy question. Fur allows me to explore sexual interests that wouldn't appeal to me any other way. In real life I am very much a straight male. But fur gives me an outlet to enjoy bisexual fantasies, as well as play around with my gender.

My furry start was with the *ThunderCats* [sci-fi cartoon show] in the 1980s. I was seven and didn't even know what "furry" was. I just saw these nude cat people in the show's first episode, and they looked amazing. There was no sexuality to it, but my love of how they looked gave me the ability as I grew to see beauty and sexual desire in artistic expression.

As I grew, the internet happened. I started seeing furry porn in my late teens. The wild cartoon nature of the images and the daring color combinations were amazing. It wasn't that a generic image of a random tiger buried groin to groin with a rabbit specifically turned me on, it was that two extremely unique ideas were enjoying sexual pleasure together. Pure creativity having sexual encounters with pure creativity, [something I found my way to] thanks to a childhood love of a 1980s cartoon show.

I [also] enjoyed seeing the cartoons of my childhood sexualized. We all do this to some extent. We get pleasure from what we enjoy, and that pleasure often merges with our developing sexuality. What started as a childhood fascination with anthropomorphic feline characters grew to define how I see myself. I am not a dom or a daddy, or any of those terms, I am a furry. So even outside of *ThunderCats*, my desire to see myself in a sexual light grew to encompass how others saw my identity in a sexual light as well. [And] their creativity in how they expressed themselves aroused me. If I saw art I found attractive, I tried to contact the artist. Knowing the source of the creativity made the pleasure I got from their art more intense.

TF FREAK

TF Freak is a greymuzzle living in the Northeast.

My kink is animal transformation [TF]. Ever since I was a little kid, transformations excited me. Every time I saw a TF, whether it was on TV, in comic books, or movies, I felt weird in a way I knew I couldn't tell anyone, because it felt embarrassing to talk about it. Even though I had no idea why, I just knew I had to keep it secret.

The first TF thing I remember was an old, cheap cartoon from the 1940s called *Johnny Learns His Manners*. I was really young, maybe six or seven. In it, a spoiled kid turned into a pig a little bit at a time, without realizing it, whenever he did something rude or greedy. As an adult I wondered if I'd ever see it again or if I had just dreamed it, until it turned up on YouTube. I'm sure this cartoon triggered my TF thing. Every time I watched it I wondered what Johnny felt like when he was turning into a pig, what it would feel like if it was happening to me. The idea of happily wallowing in mud seemed appealing too, but that's a whole other kink. I think cartoons trigger kinks because weird stuff happens in them all the time, and little kids see them at an age when they're really impressionable.

My third grade classroom bookshelf had a book about Greek mythology and in it was a picture of a witch named Circe turning Odysseus's soldier into a pig. He was half-transformed and already had hooves instead of hands, which made the picture more exciting. I wanted to meet her and let her turn me into a pig too! And as before, I knew I had to keep it secret.

A grade or two later I had to write a book report about *Voyage of the Dawn Treader* by C. S. Lewis, who wrote all the Narnia books. I made sure *not* to talk about Eustace's dragon transformation in my book report. Him slowly realizing he was now a dragon was so exciting, I remember holding my breath the entire time reading it. I was probably blushing too.

I started thinking up my own ideas for transformations, not just by Circe and not just into a pig, but all sorts of animals and the different things that might cause it, what TF fans call a "trigger." What would it feel like eating a magic peanut butter sandwich and bursting out of my clothes (that's called "rippage") as I turned into an elephant, or vanishing under them after eating enchanted cheese and turning into a mouse, as in *The Witches*?

I never felt self-confident around women and had trouble dating, but I never thought of myself as gay until a furry told me in an email he enjoyed transformation drawings I'd posted the same way I did. This is when I suddenly realized I was in a way having sex with another man through my drawings! This opened a lot of doors for me. I met him for real a couple of years later at Midwest FurFest, along with some other furries who also liked my TF pictures. Outside of conventions, we still chat and role-play online, where we text each other how one of us is transforming the other, or how we're both transforming at the same time.

I always wonder why I like TFs so much when most furries don't care about them, or why some furries enjoy kinks that don't do anything for me. But I like to say that you don't choose your kinks, they choose you.

JACK

Jack is a fur in his thirties who lives in the Midwest.

How old were you when you first saw *The Jungle Book*?
Probably eight or nine. I would reenact the movie with myself as Baloo pretending Shere Khan bit my bare butt. I did this either in my bedroom or the bathroom with a *Harry Potter* toy basilisk that has a retractable mouth.

Did you begin reenacting the scene right away, or did that take a while?

It was almost immediate. Of course, I did the entire movie.

Was the bite the only thing that resonated for you? Did you feel any connection with Baloo because of your weight [of three hundred pounds] and his physical bulk?
Yes, definitely. I have to figure out how to put it into words . . . it's almost a spiritual connection. Anytime I put a little spring in my step, I feel him. Anytime I cook, I feel him. Being naked, I feel him. I occasionally let out a little "doobie-dee-doo," even do a little dance as I walk along. But sexually, yes, it was the bite.

Did it register as a sexual thrill at the time—or did that come later?
It didn't immediately, but it made me blush.

Did you feel guilty about it happening? Did you think, *I shouldn't be doing this*?
Maybe once or twice about the [scene]. Ultimately, no one knew what I was doing, so I felt fine. It honestly felt right, like I should have been doing it sooner, so it was easy to continue.

Were you already heavy at that point? I'm wondering if there was some body guilt involved.
People tried to make me feel guilty, but I was always content with who I was physically.

Do you remember exactly what it was about the moment [when Shere Khan bites Baloo] that made it so special for you? Was it the suspense of knowing it was going to happen to him?

It was the suspense and the moment itself. It seemed like it was fated to happen considering how much he threw his butt around throughout the movie. I just wish it happened more as some kind of punishment, like Bagheera could have spanked him for being an oaf. I think I phrase it like that because that's what that bite was treated as. Baloo defied Shere Khan by not letting him kill Mowgli, so he was punished by getting attacked in the spot he showed off the entire film.

Have you ever found anyone with the same or a similar kink?

I have! I found art of a woman in Baloo's position in 2015. It led to me talking to people and ultimately joining a Discord server.[211]

Or folks with a similar (or the same) kink but related to a different movie, book, or TV scene?

All of the above.

That must've felt wonderful.

Absolutely! I converse with people about it and even send shots off the TV screen to show I'm watching it while we chat.

JACK NEWHORSE

Jack Newhorse is a fifty-four-year old furry living in the Netherlands.

Believe the furry PR. For the majority of us, furry is an arts and social community, not a sex or kink thing . . . but as with any arts and social community there's a sex/kink side. Online it comes out on art sites like Fur Affinity, furry Twitter, and the many NSFW furry chat groups. Larger conventions have adult sections of the art show and dealers den. The convention might also have late evening, adult-themed sessions where entry is over-eighteen only, with a mandatory ID check at the door.

I am fully and unapologetically a "yiffy" fur (one into the sexual side of the culture). I'm in a bunch of NSFW chats, I check out adult events at cons, I go to furry plays—and I believe the yiffy side of furdom should be carefully kept separate from the rest of the convention so it's not in the faces of the majority who find it a turnoff.

Ongoing conflicts between the SFW and adult sides are long, legendary, and ongoing, but in short, the sexy side of furry is alive and well. But thanks to the media, it's what non-furries usually hear about, just as fursuits are in every photograph and news report about furry events. Only about one in five furries has a fursuit, but they're interesting and photogenic. Most furries aren't in it for the porn either, but for many, that's what's interesting and eye-catching.

Sexy/kinky furry really thrives at room parties during cons. I've been to furry parties featuring rubber, bondage, puppies, fat fetishists, ass stuff, drugs, cuddling, and just plain old fucking. And, yes, I've fooled around with fursuiters.

Furdom lives mostly online. When someone says they're a deer, they are a deer—or at least the archetype of one. We see their deerness more than their real-world incarnation. When we meet offline—at parties, BBQs, gaming nights, conventions—their deerness remains. To some extent we remain ethereal beings, free from "the heartache and the thousand natural shocks that flesh is heir to," to quote *Hamlet*. We meet, instead, as us.

Last night I went to a naked furry party in a trailer park in New Jersey with a crowd I met through the Mid-Atlantic Furry Hookups Telegram group. I was in an intimate moment with a fellow furry while surrounded by twenty-plus others playing video games and yelling jokes at each other in between weed breaks.

There are about twenty-five hundred furry Telegram groups, about half of them labeled NSFW where you'll find just about every fetish. The top ten groups are all art reposting channels, led by Yiff Factory, Gay Yiff Pictures, and Lady Furs (eighteen+). Then there are discussion groups. Some kinky ones I'm in are about size difference, weed, and transmasculine furs.

So yeah, furry kink is a thing—but what makes it different from other kinks? For me, it goes back to the way furries approach incarnation. We meet on the internet, our avatars representing us. And that's who we become friends with and get close to. Of course, furries have physical preferences: big, small, AMAB [Assigned Male At Birth], AFAB [Assigned Female At Birth], whatever. But I find furries to be more flexible about their preferences—I know I am! I'm a lot more likely to make out with someone who doesn't fit my usual preference if they're a furry. Because we meet in a world where our bodies are as we say they are.

13

MAINSTREAM ANTHROPOMORPHIC PERFORMANCE ART

Performance art is a notoriously difficult medium to define, given its wide-ranging practices and outcomes. A performance piece might include the artist sitting at a table in a museum for days on end, inviting people to sit in the opposite chair,[212] splattering paint on an art gallery wall,[213] sitting in a plexiglass booth while reading a novel as fan-blown money and baseball cards swirl around the artist,[214] adopting an animal fursona, or another creative activity. Performance art might take place in a gallery, museum, or other public space where the artist engages in unique, unusual, or even quite ordinary activities, but ultimately the keys to performance art are the artist's body, which becomes the medium, and the presence of onlookers, which gives the medium value.

ALEX KOVAS: PUTTING THE HUMAN IN "HUMANIMAL"

Alex Kovas has been widely seen as a Dalmatian: not sporting a Dalmatian suit, but with his lithe, toned, and apparently naked 6´2´´ body covered in white body paint and black spots and wearing a set of floppy ears and a prosthetic dog muzzle. This is how Kovas appeared on a 2009 episode of the NBC show *Community*, when he was viewed on a computer screen by college dean Craig Pelton who wistfully remarked, "This better not awaken anything in me," portending a series-long obsession with Dalmatians.

Off television, Kovas is the lead performer in the British performance group Humanimal, whose members, thanks to a team of makeup artists and prosthetics designers, appear as a variety of canines, felines, equines, and horned or antlered creatures.

"This undeniably unique act is guaranteed to turn heads, no matter what the occasion," claims the Humanimals website, "so use Humanimals to show the wild side of your event, conference, opening, or launch."[215] It's good to know that they're available for a variety of occasions.

JASON MARTIN AND THE POWER OF THE POWER ANIMAL SYSTEM

It's November 11, 2011, a dusky late Greenwich Village afternoon. I'm on my way out of Washington Square Park when the window display in the New York University art gallery across the street catches my eye. On view are a variety of furry half-masks, dog and fox muzzles, top-of-the-head animal ears, and, behind them, several large blown-up photographs of canine-faced models. One model sporting a Rod Stewart haircut gestures mysteriously, arms extended, as if casting a spell; a second model, in a tight-fitting woman's spandex exercise suit and a red swim cap, stares defiantly ahead, arms akimbo, as if daring anyone on the other side of the glass to judge. It's the kind of costuming that might be more at home at a furry convention, but I'm not at a furry con, I'm in

New York City, gazing at a public display of anthropomorphic art in a major university's storefront art gallery.

There's a title printed on the gallery's window, "The Power Animal System," and below it is the name Jason Martin. But what is the Power Animal System? And who is Jason Martin?

On Martin's website, he describes himself as "artist, musician, wolf-person, consultant"[216] and Power Animal System has its own Facebook page where it defines itself as a "species and gender queer trans-missional-dimensional experiential service."[217]

Jason Martin is a self-confessed "wolfperson," but, I ask him in an email, is he a furry?

"That is a great question. I'm surprised no one has asked [before]," begins his response. Then he elaborates:

> The answer is complicated. I don't identify as one, but I share many of the traits. It's one of the reasons why I use the word[s] "species queer." It speaks to a wider segment of the culture, and places it in the continuum of queer culture and its broadening definitions and meanings, beyond sexual preference, gender, and other traditional lines that have come into question. Furs easily fit into that larger continuum.
>
> "Queer culture" includes works of art, literature, and nonfiction created by members of the LGBTQ+ community, exploring and representing our lives and lifestyles. As gays become increasingly accepted into the mainstream, our experiences,

history, and identity have become legitimate subject matter for historical research as well as self-expression.

I want to engage people and press whenever I can, inside and outside the art world. This work has sparked some amazing conversations, collaborations, and the like. As I found out early on, if I start using the word "furry" in my dialogues, that's it, case closed, it's going to be the term that wholly defines the work, coming with a set of presumptions I'm not interested in debating or trying to parse out. And while the fur-centric stuff is very important, it is not the heart of the work.

When he was young, Martin had an awakening beyond what most furs experience when they connect with their furriness. In a 2016 interview with *New Noise* magazine, he described the "erotic animal entities from other dimensions" that were part of his awakening and inspired his anthropomorphic performance art:

Sometime in my youth, I realized I was pretending to be animals and that it was more than a game. There was a focus on wolves and dogs, but not predominantly so. They started to have attributes that seemed separate from me even though they were me.

My first tangible contact with these entities occurred at [an outdoor] evening festival, while I was staring at a toy that held up little cars and spun them in a circle. I couldn't have been more than six years old. I looked down at the toy, then up at a giant treble clef composed of lit-up office tower windows. Past the tower, stars were coming out. I looked up, down, up again, thinking I knew something about the wolf people and I was one of them. Or I was a helper.

These are the words I use now. Back then, no words. It was a visual message in bolts, wheels, light grid, treble clef, stars. I make drawings of them. They were ambassadors from another dimension. As I matured, erotic gateways opened though which we communicated.[218]

Martin gave more context in his email to me, sharing:

I was an active, producing musician and artist for over a decade who kept this material secret, a secret body of work within a body of work. I worked on drawings and thoughts connected to it regularly, secretly, and felt a contact with an otherworldly presence coming through all this. It was a place to experiment with things I wasn't seeing in the world. Its power scared and embarrassed me, I thought it was quite abnormal. Life changed when I came out with it.

A Power Animal System performance can best be described as enigmatic. In one that I attended, Martin is dressed as his lupine self, with a furred cowl descending to his shoulders, topped with a pair of pointed wolf ears, and a combined muzzle/mask covering his face. He's wearing a silver-painted leotard over a gray body stocking, with gauntlets covering his wrists and lower arms. Judging from its shape, the outfit seems to suggest the wearer is female. He's joined by two identically dressed performers and the three strike various poses, with a shared yards-long orange rope taking on different shapes with each pose. Later, each holds a rectangular mirror overhead, angled so audiences can see their faces from above. A viewer unfamiliar with performance art might find the piece inexplicable or even preposterous, but tonight's Power Animal System show earns an appreciative round of applause from the audience.[219]

Even though so many of Martin's experiences and emotions were similar to ones many furs have dealt with, he finds the trappings of the subculture—the fursuits, the conventions—unrelatable. And not furry's essence. As he told me, "These are gross generalizations, some of which could be incorrect, but for the sake of not writing a many-page essay let me just say: I wholeheartedly support it all, finding many intersections with my life and work, and see it all as incredibly fascinating, still-developing social norms and trends."

NAYLAND BLAKE AND THE 147-POUND BUNNY SUIT

Nayland Blake is a nonbinary multimedia artist whose creations and performances have been presented in museums and art galleries across the United States.[220] Blake has worked in drawing, sculpture, assemblages, and costumed performance art. The artist has a fursona,[221] and a serious thing for rabbits.[222] They've taken rabbit plushes and turned them into bondage bunnies, leather daddy bunnies, and satanic sacrifice bunnies.[223] (In one piece, *Birthday Present*, a big Bugs Bunny buggers a smaller Bugs Bunny; they both look extremely happy.[224]) They've also created a kaiju (monster)-sized sleeping bag in the shape of a bunny rabbit,[225] dressed in a 147-pound bunny suit (their lover's exact weight), and tap-danced until they collapsed onstage.[226]

The bunnies are Blake's way of addressing their uninhibited pansexuality and mixed-race heritage.[227] A late 2019 Los Angeles retrospective of their work was titled "No Wrong Holes,"[228] and masochism plays no small part in their art, as seen by the aforementioned weighted tap dance and videos of them being force-fed for an hour nonstop[229] or being randomly, repeatedly slapped across their face.[230] A *New York Times* art critic described the videos as "visceral, durational performances that draw upon the visual language of kink, which Blake uses as a tool to meditate on the complex nature of queer and racial identities."[231]

Earlier in the book I introduced several furs who describe their personal kinks as highly creative, but also deeply personal and sometimes secret. Blake suffers from no such inhibitions. Instead, they've turned their kinks into public performance art.

Blake has yet to be invited to a furry convention as its guest of honor, but just about every write-up of "No Wrong Holes" mentioned the furry community, and as part of their repertoire, Blake created Gnomen, a gender-transcendent bear-bison fursona. It seems likely that Blake researched furry fandom before creating Gnomen. Apart from referring to it as their fursona, hybrid animals are very common among furries, but rarely appear elsewhere.

In an appearance at New York City's New Museum, Gnomen stepped out of the building's elevator and into its lobby. The bear-bison held a tray of ribbons that people were invited to pin onto Gnomen's furry body and the animal also invited viewers to pose for selfies with them. The action reminded me of people posing with, or bringing their kids to pose with, fursuiters at furcons.

If you're interested, you can be the proud owner of one of Blake's bunny suits (not the 147-pound one, but a lightweight nylon bunny suit of gold and blue nylon) and it will only set you back thirty-five thousand dollars.[232]

MARCUS COATES: TESTING THE LIMITS

"I've always been interested in where the limits between human and nonhuman are," shares Marcus Coates in an interview. Coates is a forty-four-year-old British ornithologist, naturalist, and multidisciplinary artist whose career-long mission has been to explore that mysterious realm between man and beast, trying to put the human in the mental space of the animal. He's participated in or organized programs with the names *Dawn Chorus*,[233] *Conference for the Birds*,[234] *The Human Zoo*,[235] and *The Animal Gaze*.[236]

One of Coates's more ambitious projects was 2007's multi-channel video installation *Dawn Chorus*,[237] which began with a multitrack field recording of nineteen different species of birds' morning cries. Their audio was slowed down and given to people to mimic while being videotaped in their homes or other locations. Back in Coates's hands, their video was sped up to match the original speed and pitch of the bird recordings, matching their calls to an astonishing degree. Each person's accelerated performance was played back on individual monitors, the increased speed turning their casual movements into sudden, start-and-stop moments mimicking avian body language. In effect, Coates turned them into birds.

Shamans were tribal mystics who among other abilities mediated between the human and nonhuman animal worlds. In 2004, with a weekend course in shamanism under his belt, Coates featured a handful of elderly tenants concerned about the uncertain fate of their apartment building in his video installation piece *Journey to the Lower World*.[238] Gathered in a cramped living room, the tenants listen to the sound of recorded drumming and wait uncertainly for whatever is about to happen. Smiling, a gentleman mimics playing a drum, then a laugh is heard in the background.[239]

When Coates enters the room, he's wearing a deer head atop his own. The animal's hide is draped over his shoulders like a cape, and its legs are attached to his wrists and ankles. He sits in a chair in front of the group, silently meditating and seemingly falling into a trance. After a minute or so, he slowly rises and takes small, sluggish steps in a circle. He has entered the lower world, a spiritual realm where the boundary between human and animal is permeable. Crouched over and swaying, he begins giving out a series of yips and barks, pounding his chest as he does. Several people are quietly laughing, but a woman in the back has her hand over her mouth and an expression of disbelief on her face. Does his display frighten or confuse her? Or has she seen something the others haven't noticed?

Coates readily accepts the silliness of the situation, performing a ritual meant for a community thousands of miles away and likely centuries in the past. One might forgive his audience if they thought they were watching a Monty Pythonesque loony.

A trio of short films demonstrate Coates's desire (or ability?) to become a real-life shape-shifter. In *Stoat,* he imitates the mustelid's twisty, bouncy leaps as best a human can.[240] In *Goshawk*, he is hoisted to the topmost branches of a tall tree to experience the sharp-beaked raptor's aerial perspective.[241] And in

Finfolk, Coates returns to solid ground after a swim in England's chilly North Sea where he speaks the language of seals (a tricky language to pick up) as if he were a selkie.[242][243]

In *Conference for the Birds* (a title reminiscent of Aristophanes's *The Birds*), Coates gathers seven naturalists and bird enthusiasts for a roleplay session.[244] In a scene worthy of Aristophanes's comedy, the seven, surrounded by large recreations of different avian species, take on the identities of those birds and enjoy a spirited discussion of their life in feathers, from long-distance migration to avoiding hungry predators

In a series of events under the collective title *Ask the Wild,* Coates takes his "talk to the animals"-themed art public. In one, he encourages the mayor of a seaside Canadian city to apologize on behalf of the human race to the long gone great auk penguin for causing its extinction. In another, possibly inspired by Ylvis's *The Fox (What Does the Fox Say?)* music video, Coates gathers an impromptu chorus at a Netherlands train station to imitate the cries of foxes in the wild. (He also organizes a countrywide media campaign welcoming migrating birds home.)

Coates also took part in *A Duck for Mr. Darwin*, a collaborative video project set on the Galápagos Islands, where Charles Darwin formulated his theory of evolution based on the local wildlife.[245] Wearing a haphazard blue-footed booby bird costume constructed out of cardboard, he rides standing up in the back of a pickup truck as if he were a parade float or a returning war hero, then later asks schoolchildren if they were animals who had come to the island, what would their opinion of human beings be? The general consensus among the kids' conclusions was that humans are all just parasites and would die off soon.

Hopefully, their prediction will prove wrong in the long run. Elsewhere in the video, Coates muses about humans' relationship with our nonhuman brothers and sisters, and the limited ability of science to bridge that gap:

> Scientific studies prove we're related to these animals in a much greater way than we thought, but that still is very objective, very separating. It doesn't really talk about that subjective experience you have as an animal.
>
> You say you share 80 percent of your genes with your pet dog, but your relationship is so much more than that, it's on an emotional basis. You'd think science would open up this whole area to relate to animals in a different way, that the subjective experience of animals has created a very close relationship. I think we've always been aware of that, and I think scientists are starting to prove that it's in there and why it's in there.
>
> I think we should've trusted ourselves in the beginning.[246]

The creative urge, the philosophical underpinnings of Coates's work, using our human imagination to see the world through an animal's eyes—in a sense, to *become* the animal—is to try to rediscover, as an observer of Coates's work wrote, "something wild and ancient, buried deep within ourselves."[247]

ROB ROTH AND CRAIG

It's a Saturday night in April 2014 and I'm in a rehearsal space in a midtown Manhattan loft building on an all but deserted side street. Once upon a time, when a good chunk of America's wardrobe was manufactured in New York, the neighborhood I'm in became known as the Garment District. The "rag trade" has long since forsaken New York City in favor of cheap overseas labor, leaving plenty of room for venues like this.

A few rows of folding chairs have been set up for the small crowd waiting for an evening of performance art to begin. I'm there to catch another Power Animal System piece. When the show begins, a young woman dances in lingerie, a young man nervously, haltingly reads a poem from the screen of his smartphone, and Jason and his canine collaborators do their rope and mirrors thing. Then a violinist takes a seat in the corner of the dimly lit stage (in reality an empty space in front of the chairs) and begins playing a mournful, dirge-like melody. A few moments later a derelict enters from the opposite corner. He's dressed in dirty, ragged clothing, carries a crumpled plastic bag, and clutches a mostly empty bottle of booze. His face is covered in black, matted fur save for a shiny black nose. His hands are likewise furred and his fingertips end in long claws. Even his eyes, which appear overwhelmed with sadness, seem, at least to me, more animal than human.

After entering, this wretched being begins singing (between occasional swigs from his bottle) in an aching, heartbreaking falsetto. I can't make out the words, but it's obvious that he's singing about the loneliness and meaninglessness of his existence. Falling to his knees, he reaches into his bag and pulls out a glamorous silver high-heeled woman's shoe. The incongruous footwear triggers a few surprised snickers from the audience. Then the semi-human derelict raises the shoe over his head and tilts it, releasing a cascade of glitter that lands sparkling in his fur and on his ragged garments. He rises to a half-crouch, clumsily puts on the shoe, and then repeats the process with the shoe's mate and concludes his song.

I've just witnessed *Craig's Dream*, a performance piece by Rob Roth starring his "shadow self," a damaged wolf creature whose mournful dirge was in fact the Go-Go's "Our Lips Are Sealed."[248]

A few weeks later, Rob and I are sitting across from each other at a table in a Whole Foods on the Lower East Side, drinking orange juice and diet soda to justify our use of the space. I'm still trying to process the fact that *two* artists, Jason Martin and Rob Roth, offered anthropomorphic performance pieces on the same bill that night. I'm also trying to process the fact that when he isn't Craig, Rob creates music videos for Debbie Harry and Blondie, created a sophisticated video installation based on David Bowie's *Life on Mars* music video, and transformed Lady Gaga into Petga, a virtual recreation of the singer for her worldwide fan website.

The continually evolving *Craig's Dream* is Rob's most personal work. He's performed it solo, appeared as Craig in others' performance pieces, and posed for a dreamlike photo spread in the avant-garde magazine *Out There* that included Debbie Harry as the High Priestess.

So who are they, Rob Roth and Craig? I interviewed the artist to find out.

When did you start performing as Craig?

A very early form of him was . . . God, when that was? I'm

gonna say . . . [circa 2010] in an old dive bar in the East Village that had been there forever. I did one tiny thing, I sang "House of the Rising Sun" with a cellist for accompaniment.

Who is Craig? A homeless alcoholic?
Yeah. In my mind he's a representation of me [in 2010], living outside of me. He hasn't been taken care of. He's like a bum, hobo, whatever you want to call him.

What sent Craig into the gutter?
I think it was . . . he was probably discarded, tossed away, neglected, brokenhearted. All of these things.

It's open to interpretation. To me he seemed to be singing about his lost love—the shoes, the glitter—trying to recapture the love himself.
Yeah, totally. The drag stuff is fun, the glitter shoe is amusing. He's also come out in this big gown and becomes calmer. The idea is his feminine side vs. the beast. He's longing for beauty, and whether he gets it or not, it's just about—whatever the interpretation might be—kindness. It's a search for that. It's always about the search for magic—where are you going to find the glitter?

And his singing?
All those songs are from my teen years. Some people ask, "Why

don't you sing something from today?" It doesn't work for Craig. It always has to be that time because it's so personal for me. The music has to be very personal—that genre, New Wave from the eighties. When I was sixteen, that was the music I was listening to.

I was up for the lead in high school musicals. I had the lead, then I quit. I knew I'd be harassed terribly at that time in my life, so I just cut it off. I stopped immediately. I just couldn't put myself out there then. It would have been sort of . . . difficult.

You had a rough time in high school because you were gay?
A very, very, *very* bad time.

And openly gay?
Well, it wasn't my choice. [Rob laughs.] I was sort of forced out, it was sort of a witch hunt. [He pauses for a moment.] At that point you don't know what the fuck to do. I had some crutch people who helped, these amazing wild rock chicks I met. They would do crazy things like move all the furniture out of one of their parents' living rooms and onto the front lawn exactly like it was arranged inside. They protected me and introduced me to all this music. It just saved my life—[I thought,] *OK, this is cool, I'll stick around*,—but I was really on my own. It was rough, very rough. That's why I stopped singing.

I think Craig's a representation of that part of me. That's why he's so geeky and meek. He can't speak, he can only communicate in song. He's sort of a beaten, sad creature, a representation of that part of me at that time, coming out now. That kind of thing is really how I felt then, not understanding and really hating yourself. I think Craig has a lot of self-loathing within him, but when he sings—that's the thing I really like—something that's either comical or sad, dirge-y, something really riveting, and then I just sing with minimal accompaniment, like a violin. I like the purity of doing that, trying to sing the history of that, and not making it a joke.

Craig is a very elaborate tactic for me to think. It allowed me to feel more confident about myself on stage. I couldn't go up there by myself then. I think Craig really helped me do that.

It's a safe place to be.
I've had friends not even know it's me. That's when I know it's totally working.

Early on you were visualizing a wolf or cat for Craig, but why an animal?
I always liked little creatures. When I was young I had a very wild imagination. I still do, and I imagined creatures living in trees, in mines. I just sort of kept visualizing these things. There wasn't

anything like, "Oh yeah, I know why he's an animal." I think it has more to do with Frankenstein, the misunderstood monster.

This creature, or character, started developing. I kept seeing an animal, a cat or a wolf. Signs started happening that seemed to say, "Oh, this is the right thing."

What kind of signs?
Weird little things. One night I was walking in Chinatown, trying to explain the character to a friend, when I saw a discarded figurine of a cat person standing on a dumpster. I said, "It's like that!" and pointed to it. Those weird kind of things are always happening.

When Craig sings, you can feel his heartache. You can't help but pity this guy and the tragedy of his life. But when the high heels and glitter come out, it triggers some laughter in the audience. Were you expecting that, or does it throw you off?

I never mind the laughter because I think it's funny: this guy with hair, putting on high heels and pouring glitter over his face. You can find it amusing, or some people find it beautiful, but it depends on your perspective, your story. Everyone else's story is in how they interpret it. Like a painting, some people see one thing and other people see something else.

So it doesn't bother me when people laugh, but there are some I could tell were laughing in a condescending way. It's usually younger kids who don't know what to do. It's very confusing to them. They're like the kids in high school who want to make fun of you. It's happened maybe two or three times. What I do with it is really funny. I'll go up to them and just stare them down, give them a what-are-you-laughing-at look, not threatening, but in a really wounded way. It weirds them out, and I'll do it until they stop. It's funny, really. It cracks me up, makes me laugh inside. It's sort of like revenge.

You talk about Craig being amusing, but even with the shoes and the glitter, my heart goes out to him. I really feel his pain.
I make people cry, which I don't know I'm doing until somebody tells me later. I think that's so grand, to make somebody start to tear up.

The term "multidisciplinary artist" could have been created to describe Rob Roth. His website lists impressive credentials: director, creative director, art director, animator, artist, and he's an awesome singer as well.

Rob was active in New York City's alternative nightlife scene beginning in the 1990s, when he became involved with the once-a-week Jackie 60 nightclub and helped create its heady mix of costuming, music, and immersive environmental installations. In 1996 Rob and his collaborators created Click +

Drag, an ongoing themed event that from 1996 to 2000 explored the "interface between nightclubs, future-fetish lifestyles, and computers."[249] According to his website, "With each installment Roth created photography, video projections, installations, decor, and performance, making Click + Drag a completely unique New York club experience and contributing to its place in nightlife history."[250]

Screen Test, a feature-length film that combined video installation and rock concert, merged 1950s Hollywood glamour and post-9/11 paranoia to investigate the confusion and longing that drive one to transformation. In a video previously on his website, Rob elaborates: "To survive, you have to have a certain amount of fantasy that you create, that I think is real because you created it. . . . It's a survival mechanism, which I don't think is necessarily bad. If the world is shit, pretend it isn't and make your world." Transformation and fantasy, creating a world of your own, are elements far from unknown in the furry world.

Rob's impressive alternative and mainstream work made him a regular freelancer at The Mill, a world-famous London-based digital post-production facility and effects house. When Lady Gaga's director turned to The Mill for the project, The Mill turned to Rob, who became creative director for Lady Gaga's ARTPOP app. His work would give the app its ethereal look, and he also designed Petga, the app's ghostly virtual host. (The app would access album art, music, interactive chats, and a variety of additional content, including "Gaga-inspired games.")

Even though Rob had never met Gaga, there was only one degree of separation between them. Lady Starlight, the makeup artist from Rob's *Screen Test* days, would go on to design Gaga's attention-getting fashions early in the superstar's career.

A lot of people would kill to make something for Lady Gaga, and it just happened for you?

The thing about me is I'm very, very blue collar, so I had to survive. I went into art school as a painter and started doing video, film, and installations. I came out knowing computer graphics and video, all that stuff. I had to make a living.

I'm not privileged, I don't have a trust fund, it was do or die. I didn't want to be a waiter, but I had a talent and I knew I could use it. So I've been working for a long time in that area, building my way up. I was designing, then creative directing, then art directing, and now I'm directing. That's why I'm doing more high-profile stuff now.

You know how all the weird channels of worlds suddenly collide, like this one over here with that one. Years ago Starlight said, "You should work with Gaga." [I thought,] *If it happens, it happens* . . . and it did, and eventually the commercial world mixed a bit with some of my outside stuff.

I've always believed in living poetically in whatever you do and however you present it. A lot of performance art today, which I love, is really about shock value, or it's aggressive, with a lot of fake blood and screaming. I like a lot of it, but what's always lacking is something that's a lot harder to do, I think, something that's sincere and raw, and quiet. You're telling the audience they have to feel something, and that's way too depressing. They don't like feeling that way, they think it's too sentimental for the downtown performance art world. That's when you have the ones who laugh, who look uncomfortable. They're waiting for a pop song to play, which is great, and there's a lot of that, but I'm purposely trying to do something rather different.

The nomenclature in the gay world, "otter," "bear," that kind of thing, is so funny to me. I think a lot of that is about the tactile too. I think people don't know it yet, but there's a definite struggle between this new world of digital technology and the tactility of fur. I can't put my finger on it, but I always thought there was going to be . . . not a backlash, but a need for something. It's like a shtick now—Lady Starlight uses vinyl records in her performances. There's something about a physical thing, and it might be in there with that. . . . [There also] are transitions, a lot of transitions, obviously transsexuality and all, but there's also . . . I think people want to be other creatures because of their dissatisfaction with the human condition, the modern world.

People talk about transsexual, transgender, and gender reassignment surgery. I sometimes joke about people who'd like "species reassignment surgery."
Oh, totally. I've known people who've wanted that. [Singer-songwriter] Genesis P-Orridge talked about the future of it all, like getting gills. There's no end to it, really. It's all binary.

Has anyone ever been sexually turned on by or attracted to Craig?

I've had several people tell me, "Oh my *God,* I'd really like to have sex with the wolf," and I'm like, "Well, that would be horrible for me," because it's so uncomfortable in that suit.

It must be hot in there.

It's terrible, it's like being suffocated by a rug—but it helps with Craig's emotions!

The summer of the following year, in the back room of a Chelsea bar, a performance space somewhat fancifully named Sid Gold's Request Room, Rob—as Craig—is onstage. Mid-song he begins peeling off one paw-glove, and then the other. Finally, he removes Craig's face to reveal his own. An assortment of romantic ballads, sung in Rob's beautiful, natural tenor follows. For this night at least, Rob sheds his elaborate mask.

MARK WALLINGER AND THE NIGHTMARE BEAR OF EAST GERMANY

In the late fall of 1964 the BBC broadcast an East German children's movie, *The Singing, Ringing Tree*. It scarred a generation of British kids for life.

In this dramatization of an obscure Grimm's fairy tale, an actor portrays a prince transformed into a bear, and not just any bear, but an exceptionally creepy-looking one covered in matted brown fur that resembles old, chopped-up carpeting, except around his morosely staring eyes. There is also an unnerving, giant, bug-eyed goldfish and a scary dwarf that burned their way into kids' cortexes. One critic called the movie "one of the most frightening things ever shown on children's television,"[252] and a second accused the show of "giving us all the screaming habdads for years."[253]

The artist Mark Wallinger was one of those kids. "I discovered that *The Singing, Ringing Tree*, a children's program that fascinated and traumatized my generation, was something known to people brought up in the former East Berlin, but the West Germans had no knowledge of it."[254]

Wallinger spent 2001 and 2002 in Berlin for an artist residency and developed a strong affection for the city that prompted him to return to live there from 2003 to 2004. "I had this kind of primal psychic link with people beyond the wall [between East and West Berlin] for all those years. I found that kind of strange and moving in a way," he tells me.

The memory of that East German film tied into Wallinger's other thoughts about Berlin, and bears. "The bear is sort of an inescapable symbol of Berlin. The city's name even derives from that."

For nine nights in October 2004, Wallinger, wearing a baggy rental shop bear costume, wandered, prowled, crawled, and paced the glass box ground floor of Berlin's Neue Nationalgalerie. Passersby occasionally stopped to observe the "animal" as if it were in a zoo enclosure. "Some nights I'd rush at the window and people would run off," he tells me. "I actually managed to elicit a couple of screams. But on other nights people would just go, 'Yeah, so?'"

Even though he didn't do much snoozing during his ursine evenings, Wallinger named the piece *Sleeper*, a reference to undercover spies living seemingly normal lives in other countries until they're "awakened" for their mission. The word held resonance in a city that was once a hotbed of Cold War intrigue.

The experience and the concept of sleepers gave Wallinger a few vibes familiar to fursuiters. He told me, "It's weird. In a way I was the artwork, but I was sort of hiding as well, so that was very strange. In a sense, it's how far we can get within the consciousness of someone or something other, that was intrinsically of another culture." About the bear suit he shared, "At the beginning I couldn't wear it for more than a quarter of an hour without freaking out. Sometimes I was that hot, and feeling kind of faint. I didn't know whether I was overheating or coming down with something serious. But in the end I just sort of relished doing it every night."

A three-camera crew filmed Wallinger for several nights and assembled the footage into a 154-minute movie that was screened at the Venice Biennale art exhibition in 2005. In 2007 Wallinger submitted *Sleeper* to Britain's Turner Prize for consideration.[255] However, the Turner judges had ideas of their own and shortlisted a more recent Wallinger project, *State Britain,* a meticulous reconstruction of a famed antiwar protest site outside Parliament, which went on to win the competition.

As with any creative work, opinions on Wallinger's victory were mixed, and often flat-out contradictory. A London *Times* critic called *State Britain* "boring and unworthy,"[256] while *The Guardian* exulted, "I can't think of a better winner, nor of works more deserving of a wide audience."[257]

Even though *State Britain* took home the Turner, coverage of Wallinger's victory was told through a furry filter, focusing more on the artist than the art with headlines like "Bear faced cheek wins the Turner"[258] and "Bear man walks away with Turner."[259] My favorite headline ran in the British tabloid *The Sun*: "Bungle wins the Turner," referring to a bear in a kids' TV show portrayed by an actor in a much more charming suit than Wallinger's—or the one in *The Singing, Ringing Tree*.[260]

14

IS EVERYBODY HAPPY? (WELL, NOT QUITE)

When one feels at home in a community that shares their beliefs and values, the natural tendency is to assume everyone in that community is equally comfortable with those beliefs and values. Unfortunately, that's not the case in any community large enough to contain all sorts of people with differing opinions, and the larger the community, the wider variety of opinions and people can be found in it. The furry community is no exception. At one point, furry was largely the province of people who not only loved anthropomorphic animals, but felt like outsiders of mainstream fan communities and perhaps of society in general. Many of us were bullied as school kids because we behaved differently from "normal" kids.[261] Perhaps this helped us develop our creativity and our appreciation of furry characters and furry universes, as opposed to the one we were trapped in. But as furry grew and became more popular, different ideas of what furry is or should be became more apparent.

THE BALLAD OF THE BURNED FURS

In 1998 a small but passionate group of furs fumed that "lifestyler" furries were giving the furry community a bad name. These angry furs who would become known as Burned Furs consisted of some of the earliest furs who were cartoonists and fans of comics and animation. They believed lifestylers—furs with a more personal connection to anthropomorphism than merely being fans or creators of anthro art—were attending furry conventions to, among other misdeeds, flaunt their sexuality in search of quickie hookups. I regularly attended the early furry conventions of the 1990s and perhaps I'm naive or willfully blind, but I never noticed any flagrant public displays of sexuality. Evidently, however, numerous people saw behavior that upset them enough to come together and push back.

In the words of one of its founders, Burned Furs was composed of "furs who have spoken up against fandom perversion and been burned at the stake for it." A second founder, a close friend of mine who turned their back on furry years ago, went into more detail in a conversation with me:

> Burned Furs was basically a reaction by artists, writers, and some of the very first furs against the dominance of fandom by people who were there for sexual reasons and not creative reasons. We resented seeing a fandom that we had built as creators being appropriated by people who saw it as sexual, or a way to hook up or whatever. At a certain convention we realized all of a sudden, "Hey, there are a few people selling art—and more people walking around in tight pants and weird fetish wear."

We were wondering, who are these people? Because they aren't buying art, they aren't contributing toward what we had built. We believed we built this fandom through our creative efforts, our collective creative efforts.

One of the Burned Furs posted "A Sordid Little Business," a.k.a. the Burned Furs Manifesto, online, which was even more impassioned, taking exception to the perceived over-sexualization, spiritualization, and "lifestylism" of the furry fandom. In it, the writer proclaimed, "'Live and Let Live' is an excellent, tree-hugging philosophy, but it doesn't do much when the ones you refuse to kill are dragging you down with them. If you like animal-based stories, cartoons, or art, you're a furry. And like it or not, 'furry' means 'pervert.'"

The Burned Furs wanted lifestylers to leave the Usenet message board alt.fan.furry—in its day a hotbed of furry messaging and endless thread conversations—in favor of alt.lifestyle.furry. Unsurprisingly, there was no mass exodus of "lifestylers" heading to their designated board. Instead the Burned Furs found themselves on the defensive, with some furs calling it a hate group, as well as accusing some of its members of being anti-gay and prone to violent rhetoric.

Burned Furs's short but passionate life came to an end in 2001. Fifteen years later, with the benefit of hindsight, I asked my friend to share their thoughts on what might have gone wrong. According to my friend:

Maybe if we had focused more on community building rather than condemning, we would've had more success. In a way we were looking to perhaps create our own community once again, like it once was. Maybe we were the stodgy old people saying, "Why couldn't it be like it once was?"

Before we ended our conversation, I had to ask one last question: "Did you really think you could chase those people away?"

My friend replied, "I thought we could appeal to the angels of their better nature, while me and [another Burned Fur] had fun insulting everybody."

Like water, furry finds its own level. Because it's a self-created community, there are no gatekeepers. If you call yourself a furry, you're a furry. People bring their own level of furriness, along with their own quirks, kinks, and interests, when they join the scene. By and large, furry has made peace with its NC-17 side: adult convention events are held late at night, with IDs carefully checked, and lewd behavior is kept safely behind locked hotel room doors. (I guess it's an improvement that we're now often called "fetishists" rather than "perverts.") It's how and why furry has grown tremendously beyond that late eighties/early nineties kernel of "artists, writers, and fans of comics and animation."

MILO YIANNOPOULOS'S FURRY (NON)ADVENTURE

So much for internecine furry drama. Let's move on to a few problems furry has with the rest of the world (or vice versa).

Milo Yiannopoulos may be the most vocal right-wing agitator there is. The England-born provocateur leaves a trail of outrage and insult whenever and wherever he directs his efforts, and feminism, Islam, and general all-round political correctness are among his favorite piñatas. After resigning from the hard-right news site Breitbart after pedophilic comments from his past resurfaced, he lost a book deal and was banned from Twitter,[262] Facebook,[263] and all of Australia.[264]

In search of another minority to antagonize, Yiannopoulos declared himself a furry. This didn't go well either.[265] In 2019 Yiannopoulos registered for Midwest FurFest (at the higher-priced Shiny Sponsor level) and offered to do a panel on "The Politics of Fur." Everyone already had a good idea of what Yiannopoulos's politics were like, and the outcry was immediate. Numerous furs contacted the convention, protesting him based on his background. Shortly thereafter, FurFest refunded Yiannopoulos's Shiny Sponsor contribution and let him know he was *fursona non grata*. According to the organizers, "The board of Midwest Furry Fandom, consistent with our posted code of conduct, has rescinded Mr. Yiannopoulos's registration. He is not welcome to attend this or any future Midwest FurFest event."[266] In response, Yiannopoulos was taken in by a group simpatico with his beliefs: the far-right and controversial Furry Raiders.

SIEG HEIL, FURRIES!

Per the Furry Raiders's Twitter: "The Furry Fandom will always be a [sic] open and free place to express yourself. We're happy to welcome Milo Yiannopoulos to the Furry Fandom and the Furry Raiders. #theycantbanusall" Below the text of the tweet was an illustration of a sunglass-wearing, sneering snow leopard with hair similar to that of Yiannopoulos.[267] With this tweet, Yiannopoulos suddenly had a fursona courtesy of the Raiders (whom some suspect of putting Milo up to the FurFest stunt).

Truth be told, the Raiders's reputation among furs in general wasn't much better than Milo's reputation, in no small part due to the Nazi-inspired trappings they surround themselves with, including a red armband with a white circle containing a black paw print in place of a swastika.[268] In a 2017 interview, Foxler Nightfire, the Raiders's leader, claimed their symbol had absolutely nothing to do with Nazis, and that people were foolish to think otherwise. He described himself as "uneducated in history and politics,"[269] evidently suffering from a bout of amnesia and forgetting his 2014 YouTube paean to Adolph Hitler adjoining a film clip from one of the dictator's speeches:

> Time heals the pain, Hitler pushed for what he believed in, if more people did that we could solve the problems of this world. I stand by Hitler and the German people for showing the world there [sic] something to fight for. Doesn't matter what the rest of the world thinks, the will of a burning fire is what drives the human soul.[270]

The Furry Raiders's mission statement is pretty scary too, light years from the claim that their main goal is to embrace furry culture.

> Our Mission statement is clear: We are committed to upholding the values of free expression within the furry community by

providing an open and welcoming organization free of exclusion and prejudice based on race, sex, creed, gender, identity, sexual orientation or political affiliation. Our aim is to further establish our presence across multiple venues and platforms in order [to] achieve this goal.[271]

And the section on their history includes this gem:

With our signature icon on our sleeves, we made our presence known in events for furries, for special interest communities and those of our own design. Where to from here? Only time will tell. The Furry Raiders will carve out the next pages of our history.[272]

Things took a turn for the worse in 2016 when the Furry Raiders allegedly stole a huge chunk of the hotel room block set aside for the 2017 Rocky Mountain Fur Con when no one was looking. In a January 2017 Twitter thread discussing the dispute and the Raiders's ties to the far right, a fur named Deo joked that she was looking forward to punching Nazis, and in response someone wrote that they would enjoy seeing Deo get shot at the convention. Word of the threat got back to the hotel, which asked Fur Con to spend some twenty thousand dollars on a security force.

Deo received a letter from a member of the Fur Con board essentially blaming her for the affair, but some suspected ties between the board member and Foxler himself. A little digging revealed the convention was hiding the fact that it had lost its tax-exempt status, and that the board member who had sent the letter was a registered sex offender. The charges and counter-charges escalated until the Rocky Mountain Fur Con shut itself down in 2017.[273][274]

Fortunately, the furry community at large is keeping a sharper eye on the furry fascist crowd, who are still around but keeping a lower profile these days. Deo has become a prime player, quietly keeping an eye open at conventions for possible troublemakers or Nazi recruiters. She has also been active in helping younger furs break free of fascist groups that have preyed on their insecurities and given them a sense of belonging beyond simply being part of the furry community. "When your life is this thing, this hate group," she told an interviewer, "that's all you have."[275]

FREE FUR (ALMOST) ALL

In 2019 Tulsa, Oklahoma, had one furry convention known as Tails and Tornadoes. In 2022 it had two. The story of how the city acquired a second furcon begins with a convention head who wasn't sufficiently "woke" and was therefore bounced out by the con's "politically correct" board. At least that's one story that was told. Another story ties the rise of a second convention to the organizer of the first convention's deliberate blindness to the city's historic treatment of people of color, as well as making light of one fur's sexual assault.

That organizer left the original convention and launched Free Fur All, a new local convention, as well as an organization to run it, AWOO, the Anthro West(ern) Open Organization.

On the Free Fur All website, the organizers describe the convention as "America's Anthro Convention," which must have come as a surprise to organizers and attendees of long-running furry conventions in cities like Chicago, Pittsburgh, San Jose, Denver, Memphis, Reno, Seattle, Dallas, and Orlando, to name a few.[276] The name jibes with Free Fur All's America-themed identifiers, which are hard to miss and include a gray-and-black version of the US flag built into its promotional materials and the convention's lion mascot, who wears a kerchief featuring white stars on a blue background, and wolf pal, who sports a red-and-white striped kerchief, as if they've disassembled a US flag to make a fashion statement.

Perhaps because of the America themes, rumors began to spread that the convention was tied into the alt-furry/Furry Raiders nexus. The rumors were lent credence by the convention's first guest of honor, 2, The Ranting Gryphon, a furry stand-up comedian who had not been welcome at other cons due to his history of racist and sexist outbursts, not to mention callous statements mocking suicide victims and a generally contemptuous view of anyone who disagrees with him.[277]

Outside of AWOO, the consensus has been that 2, The Ranting Gryphon is free to express himself any way he pleases as long as it doesn't bring harm to anyone—but that no one is under any obligation to listen to him or give him a platform to speak from.

AWOO, the convention's parent organization, offers an invitation to become an AWOO "associate." However, the web page warns that such an opportunity is not for the faint of heart:

> In an age when the popular thing to do is to bully and "cancel" others, this sometimes makes us unpopular. Please consider

that being a part of this organization may bring some social stigma. All associates will be expected to show each other respect and kindness to each other and to the Association, regardless of any social pressures to do otherwise. If this pressure to do the popular thing is too much, the AWOO Association may not be for you.[278]

After considering the extensive association rules and nondisclosure agreement documents, one is left to wonder if whatever perks and pleasures come with being an AWOO associate are worth the risk; after all, as also noted on the application web page, AWOO believes "the furry fandom is supposed to be one of the most loving and accepting communities in the world, and we plan to lead by example."[279] Apparently by NDA as well.[280]

THE GREAT LITTER BOX PANIC OF 2022

It's July 2012 and I'm in Pittsburgh. Anthrocon is over and I'm about to get on the Megabus back to New York City, but I'm taking a few minutes to chat with my nephew David, a local ambulance dispatcher. I start describing how much fun the convention was when David interrupts me, saying: "I heard they found a litter box in one of the hotel rooms."

It's the first time I've heard this claim, but sadly it won't be the last. In 2021 this rumor, which I touched on earlier, began to spread from America's right-wing echo chamber. It quickly metastasized into the mainstream media, with hundreds of news reports across the United States describing the supposed bizarre behavior of furries who "identify" as animals and the schools putting "protocols" in place for them, including litter boxes in gender-free bathrooms ("gender-free" is a clue to what these demagogues' real issue is), and cafeteria tables lowered so furry students could eat without holding utensils.

The rumor made its way to Australia, where a reporter for Sky News claimed it was taking place at a local Brisbane school.[281] Hundreds of comments appeared beneath the report, almost unanimously from people who accepted the rumor as fact.

It's difficult to trace the litter box story back to its origins, but according to Patch O'Furr's Dogpatch Press, it may have originated with Bob, a Pittsburgh shock jock, who in 2008 blogged that a convention security guard reported that some furs "actually use litter boxes to make bathroom in," and that "the hotel has asked them not to this year because of the mess in the rooms."[282]

Fourteen years later, Bob mellowed out, criticizing the "unhinged" rumor on the air and giving the furs a thumbs-up: "Every year when we do a charity for Toys for Tots, we have a furry night when a bunch of furries come out, we have Anthrocon in Pittsburgh, which is one of the bigger conventions. . . . We absolutely love furries! . . . It's just a little taste of the magic of our city."[283]

The litter box rumor appeared to be dying out in the spring of 2022 when John Oliver dedicated a piece about a looney lady running for governor on a "stamp out furries" platform—which was exactly when a liberal internet prankster started a new hoax to see if anyone would fall for it.[284] The prankster, Tracing Woodgrains, and their friends created a few authentic looking worksheets, the kind given to elementary school kids working on class projects. One bogus sheet described the school's Culture Month as including a week devoted to "youth subcultures, from goths to furries," while a second invited kids to create their own fursona and choose whether it's male, female, or nonbinary. They sent it to Libs of TikTok, a notorious site peddling reactionary falsehoods, hoping they would fall for the bait—which they did, much to the chuckling amusement of its instigators. Once it was revealed as a hoax in an article by Tracing Woodgrains, right-wing firebrand (and self-described "acclaimed children's author") Matt Walsh declared the left to be such "degenerate psycho perverts" that he found the story completely plausible, even if it weren't true.[285]

Now if you'll excuse me, I need to use the fire hydrant.

15

MUSIC TO MY FURRY EARS (AND EYES)

By now a decades-old art form, the music video is always looking for new ways to grab people's eyeballs, to cut through the clutter with flashy, unique, or just plain bizarre visual treatments. The furry zeitgeist has been spreading into every corner of our collective consciousness, and it was inevitable that more than a few catchy music videos would go anthro. Here are a mere handful that happened to catch my eye, but many, *many* others are out there for your amusement.

FURRY LIKE A FOX

In 2013 the popular Norwegian comedy duo Ylvis, comprised of brothers Vegard and Bård Ylvisåker, came up with a jokey music video, never intended to be taken seriously, for their TV series. Little did they realize that the video, *The Fox (What Does the Fox Say?)*, would become an international hit, with well over one billion YouTube views.

According to Vegard, the idea for the video emerged while the duo was hanging around their office. In an interview posted on YouTube, Vegard shared that they were playing with the idea of using animal sounds for a novelty record when they noticed a stuffed toy fox in their office. He shared, "We just looked at that and we felt, 'Hmm, we don't know what sound the fox makes.'"[286]

The music video begins at an outdoor party where guests are wearing animal costumes and as they walk by Bård, he musically describes what sounds the animals they're dressed like make, singing, for example, "The elephant goes 'toot,' ducks say, 'quack,' and fish go 'blub.'" But when it comes to the *Vulpes vulpes*, he's at a loss. Suddenly wearing an open-faced fox suit, he sings the question, "But what does the fox say?" According to the fur-suited singer, the fox supposedly makes a variety of ululating noises (starting with "Ring-ding-ding-ding-dingeringeding" and working its way up to "Abay-ba-da bum-bum bay-do"), each more humorous and unlikely than the last.

Worldwide sibling celebrity followed in the surreal song's wake, with numerous TV appearances, a *Today* show performance in Rockefeller Center, and a children's picture book based on the lyrics. The brothers claimed they'd never heard of furry fandom, and personally I believe them.[287] Nonetheless, Halloween sales of fox costumes were up by 40 percent that year,[288] the Fox network couldn't resist using it to promote their shows, and even Morgan Freeman found himself reciting the lyrics on TV.[289] As creative people, it's almost as if Vegard and his brother Bård heard the furry sirens' call and answered back.

FROM FOXES TO WOLVES

There must be something about Norwegians and weird animal songs. In 2021, two masked performers, known individually by the pseudonyms Keith and Jim and collectively as the band Subwoolfer, came up with "Give That Wolf a Banana," a song encouraging a hungry *Canis lupus* to forsake consuming grandmothers in favor of munching on tropical fruit. In the music video, the suit-and-tie-wearing singers sport long pointy ears and muzzles full of jagged teeth over a yellow fabric completely covering their heads.[290]

The song begins with the plaintive "Oh-ooh-ooh-ooh-ooh-ooh" of a wolf howl before the singers compliment the animal's attributes ("I really like your teeth/that hairy coat of yours with nothing underneath") but then grow slightly concerned ("Is that saliva or blood dripping off your chin?"). The mellow opening gives way to a pulsing dance beat as we see the pair performing on a distant stage in front of a huge cheering audience. They're soon joined by a pack of bow-tie-and-suspender-wearing backup dancers. The song's key lyric is "and before that wolf eats my grandma, give that wolf a banana," a strategy Little Red Riding Hood should keep in mind.

The pair won Norway's Melodi Grand Prix 2022, a musical competition, and represented their country in international competition in 2022's Eurovision Song Contest. Speculation ran rampant as to the actual identities of Keith and Jim. Some postulated the pair were actually the members of Ylvis,[291] but on February 4, 2023 the duo revealed themselves as British boy band veteran Ben Adams and Norwegian musician Gaute Ormåsen.[292] The band's "official story" claims the pair began their career "four and a half billion years ago" on the moon (which would explain why a good part of the video is set there) and describes them as the most successful band in the galaxy.[293] (As of this writing, that assertion remains unconfirmed.)

ON TO BUNNIES

Robbie Williams was originally a member of the British rock group Take That, and in 1996 began what would become a successful career as a solo artist.[294] In 2009 he released the single "You Know Me." The song's music video begins with Robbie in a makeup chair, getting ready for a performance. Behind him is a woman wearing a rabbit-print top and munching on a carrot, who then tells Robbie that someone is going to be late. In response he puts on headphones, leans back, and closes his eyes. His nose twitches a bit as he dozes off. Soon after, the camera tracks through a tunnel of dirt and tree roots and finds Robbie dressed in tweeds and wearing an open-faced costume rabbit's head. His rabbit's burrow is quite the mess, with leftover carrot greens and a knocked-over bottle of carrot juice on a nearby table.

Rabbit Robbie sings of his lost love and stepping outside he discovers a postcard addressed to "Mr. Rabbit, Wonderland" bearing the message "Wish you were here—XX," with a photo of a tropical beach on its reverse side. (Evidently his love isn't so much lost as on a holiday in the tropics.)

Crouching down outside, Rabbit Robbie sees his reflection in a pond, but it's his human reflection. Cabbages and frogs then sing backup as he drifts off to sleep on a picnic blanket and "wakes up" in a dream within a dream. Now his exposed face is rabbit-white and sporting a pink-nosed bunny muzzle. This dream features six female dancers wearing shiny bunny ears and puffy cotton tails and giving him "come hither" looks over their shoulders. Even more pleasant is the bunny gal riding a giant carrot swing and another lounging sensually on an equally oversized carrot.

When Rabbit Robbie finishes the song, suddenly we're back in the makeup room, as flesh-faced Rabbit Robbie sits pensively inside the mirror. Human Robbie is nowhere to be seen. Perhaps he's pondering whether to return to the real world or stay inside the mirror with those bunny gals. I know which one I'd pick.

RUN FOR YOUR LIFE

If only for its name, the experimental rock band Animal Collective belongs here. Animal Collective's music is a conglomeration of styles, including psychedelia, freak folk, noise, and electronica—with a little fur mixed in. In their exceedingly weird, ultra-low budget video "Who Could Win a Rabbit," two of the group's members reenact Aesop's fable of the "Tortoise and the Hare," but on bicycle. The hare has a full body coat of shaggy fur, except for on his exposed face, and the tortoise sports an oversized shell that could shelter one or more of the Ninja Turtles inside. After the tortoise and hare's bikes crash, the bicycle race turns into a foot race, ending in the tortoise's traditional victory. What's decidedly untraditional is the tortoise feasting on the hare's body—in this race, second place can be hazardous to your health.

ORDER IN THE COURT (MEDIUM RARE, PLEASE)

Prosthetics have to be the coolest way of helping a human take on an anthropomorphic fursona. Made of silicone, latex, or other materials, once these "appliances" have been applied and painted to seamlessly blend with an actor's face, the effect is uncannily realistic.

While prosthetics are rarely used in music videos, Capital Cities's *Kangaroo Court* used the technique to create a world of anthropomorphic animal people. In the video, a young zebra tries to pass as a stallion to get into the exclusive "no zebras allowed" Kangaroo Court nightclub. Using a bottle of Graze Away hair dye he paints his white stripes black, which allows him to gain admission, and inside he catches the eye of the bulldog gangster's poodle girlfriend. Everything goes according to plan until they notice his striped zebra tail. Sentenced to death in an actual kangaroo court, the zebra, who is now wearing a vertically black-and-white striped prison uniform, is taken to a butcher shop, eviscerated in a blizzard of red confetti, and winds up a steak consumed by a lion.

The video's director described its story as being one of "transformation, alienation, and being judged."[295] Fortunately, trying to pass as a species other than your own isn't a crime in our world—otherwise every furry who dons a fursuit would be risking their life. So would the actor playing the bulldog, who said of his prosthetic canine face, "I don't even want to take it off. I'm going to go for a drive later and see what happens."[296]

ORWELL THAT ENDS WELL

Coldplay's video for their song "Trouble in Town" also employs prosthetics to create an all-animal world. While *Kangaroo Court* features a secretive nightclub with elegantly dressed anthros, Coldplay's anthros live on the mean streets and in the run-down neighborhoods of an indifferent city.

The video's debt to George Orwell's *Animal Farm* is evidenced by billboards that read, "All Animals Are Equal" and "But Some Are More Equal Than Others," as well as a homeless deer seen reading the book. Throughout the video the audience is given glimpses of a televised political debate in which all the candidates are pigs. The video's centerpiece is a confrontation between an aggressive, hostile police leopard and a hoodie-wearing fox hanging out by a grocery store, and uses audio from 2013 of an actual encounter between a white cop and a black man in Philadelphia. The fox makes a run for it and manages to elude the leopard, and is then shown huddling in fear in an apartment with several other anthros, while the porcine political debate descends into chaos as a brawl breaks out between the candidates. The video ends with a title card sharing that all proceeds from the video would be donated to an organization fighting false arrests and a children's nutrition program.

"Trouble in Town" isn't Coldplay's only foray into furry storytelling. In 2015 the group was motion-captured and CGI-transformed to appear like chimpanzees in the video for their song "Adventure of a Lifetime." In it they sing and swing their way through the jungle, ultimately finding their instruments and performing with them.

ALLEY'S WELL THAT ENDS WELL

Face painting is a quick, simple, and low cost way to channel a different species. It has worked for decades in every stage production of *Cats*. It was also used to great effect in Gloria Estefan's video for the song "Bad Boy," in which she dumps her human boyfriend in favor of a much better and sexier time hanging out in an alley with a bunch of jazzily dressed cool cats.

The video for "Bad Boy" is sprinkled with silly cartoon-style gags: a feline nightclub called the Meow Lounge, a cat enjoying a Kit Kat candy bar, another one ogling the *Playcat* magazine centerfold (of a real world kitten), a fishbone xylophone, and the goldfish Gloria drops into a grateful street musician's hat as a form of tip.

Just as Gloria and the coolest cat of the bunch are about to smooch, a two-legged police dog breaks up the party. This causes Gloria to leave the alley and rejoin her somewhat miffed human boyfriend who appears jealous, as he asks if she's seeing another guy. "Not exactly," she responds as they walk away, her (newly grown?) feline tail peeking out from under her dress.

SEXY BEAST

The cool cats in Paula Abdul's *Opposites Attract* video are cartoon ones, as she teams up with MC Skat Kat for some fancy footwork. Reminiscent of Gene Kelly's dance with Jerry Mouse in 1945's *Anchors Aweigh,* and risking cries of "bestiality," Paula and the animated animal obviously have a thing going, as shown by their dirty dancing and exchange of suggestive lines. The video ends with Paula and MC walking off, hand in paw.

Paula choreographed MC's moves to match her own, which were performed by a dancer later rotoscoped into feline form. The video, created by Disney animators in their off-hours, won the 1991 Grammy Award for Best Short Form Music Video.[297] The two reunited in MC's *Skat Strut* video of 1991, apparently proving there's no separating lovers—human, animated, or otherwise—when the chemistry between them is as strong as theirs.

MOBY'S BEAUTIFUL (BUT JEALOUSY ISN'T)

The musician Moby is a long-time vegan and an impassioned animal rights activist, which makes the video for his song "Beautiful" all the stranger. In it he is at a swingers' partner-swapping party that takes a tragic turn when a jealous husband shoots and kills his wife, the person getting it on with his wife, and finally himself. Maybe if he had watched Moby performing on the living room TV instead of stewing about his wife, things would have turned out differently.

The video's doomed husband and wife are rabbits, and the fellow getting it on with the wife is a moose. The performers are not wearing classy fursuits, but instead the kind of sad, baggy animal suits that are available to rent at your friendly neighborhood costume shop and feel as if a million people have worn them before you.

It's noteworthy that the video is about animals throwing a swingers' party, not human swingers wearing animal suits to spice up their evening (you know, like every furry with a fursuit does every chance they get). Also, an actual human wouldn't be harmed by a gag gun that shoots out a flag reading "BANG!" when fired, nor would the street be filled with fiber stuffing if they shot themself and others with it.

PAR-TAY . . . WITH THE FURRIES!

The indie band The Pain of Being Pure at Heart's video for their song "Higher than the Stars," features more fursuiters than you can shake a tail at.[298] This video marks the moment anthro-themed music videos went from "random creative concept" to "let's get furry!"

As in *The Wizard of Oz,* the video begins in black-and-white, and in it viewers watch as a kid with whiskers painted on his face hands a young woman a flyer for a party, which is somehow bright orange in this monochrome world. A black pawprint on the flyer is a harbinger of things to come.

Black-and-white footage of the band performing is intercut with the woman heading to the party. When she reaches her destination, a copy of the flyer is taped on a closed garage shutter, but the shutter rises to reveal—now in full color—a passel of fursuiters dancing away while the band performs. The woman's "What have I gotten myself into?" expression gradually gives way to a smile as she warms up to the silly scene in front of her.

The video alternates between the band performing while surrounded by (occasionally annoying) fursuiters, and the woman enjoying herself—particularly with a fox she seems to have taken a liking to. (Fun fact: according to WikiFur, "a revised ending shows the protagonist falling unconscious after partying and drinking with the fursuiters, only to wake up and find herself having become a fursuiter.")[299]

MY FURRY AGENDA

In the video for "Higher Than the Stars" the fursuiters' reveal is a surprise gag ("oh wow, it's a furry party!") and the video's payoff, but the gender-fluid singer and performance artist Dorian Electra included fursuiters in an entirely different manner in their video for the song "My Agenda."[300] In the "My Agenda" video, the fursuiters are simply there, existing and in the process mocking the "gay agenda" scare tactics of homophobic right-wingers through

Dorian's plot to turn everyone (including frogs, another right-wing rumor) gay by way of infused drinking water.[301]

In the video we are taken into a secret headquarters hidden inside a generic city's water tower, where Dorian, surrounded by rainbow suspenders-wearing bodyguard backup dancers, brags about their evil scheme. ("My agenda's gonna getcha.") The next moment, Dorian is in a Jeep and accompanied by their posse: four Super Soaker-toting fursuiters. But they're not fursuit-wearing furries here, they're Dorian's anthropomorphic hench-animals. At random moments they're freeze-frame-transformed into colorful manga-style illustrations, pulling them further into the video's fantasy and away from the reality of a person inside a suit.

One moment later, Dorian is shown as a flight attendant serving infused water to a plane full of anthro passengers who are freaking out. Another moment (and costume change) later, Dorian's riding a rainbow bomb, *Dr. Strangelove*-style, labeled "Love Wins" and "Pride Through Strength" into the heart of the city. One rainbow mushroom cloud later, a kaiju-sized and now gay Pepe the Frog (a right-wing mascot) is stomping through the city, knocking over buildings with carefree abandon, while the song's lyrics boil down to a repeated "homosexual." Take that, bigots!

While older music videos often used anthropomorphic themes or characters, thanks to Dorian Electra and The Pains of Being Pure at Heart casting actual fursuiters, the furry age of music videos has officially begun.

16

MAINSTREAM, HERE WE COME (MAYBE)

Will furry go mainstream—that is, eventually be accepted as just another subculture, a fun form of escape every bit as valid (or silly) as LARP'ers (live action role-playing gamers), cosplayers, and the fandoms that have grown around superheroes, sci-fi adventurers, wizards in training, and other pop culture perennials? (All of which, like our beloved fursuiters, involve dress-up to one degree or another.)

Do furs even want that to happen? Would this cause people who don't take furry fandom as "seriously," who weren't born with the furry gene, to join in, and if so do we want that? And most of all, do we want furry to be viewed as just another market, another demographic, to be catered to and monetized by entrepreneurs who see us as a furry money tree to be shaken for all it's worth? To answer the first question, probably. The more *CSI*-era misinformation about furry that fades into the background, the more comfortable the average person will feel to join in, the more word will spread, the more the furry community's profile will rise, and yes, the more the community will be seen as simply another piece of the pop culture patchwork that everyone, to one degree or another, takes part in. As to the second question: we may not have any voice in the matter, it may already be out of our paws. Numerous throwaway media references, both subtle and overt, and increasingly sympathetic, have raised our profile to the point where non-furs don't automatically bring up a particular TV series when hearing about our community.

Unfortunately, these references have also raised furries's profile to the point where certain people's eyes suddenly fill with cartoon dollar signs when they hear the "F" word. Take for instance, those rainbow-scarfing Skittles candy folks. At the end of 2021, after a chat with a furry on their Twitter feed (@BlueFolf: "Skittles are you a furry we need to know are you a furry?" @Skittles: "How do you know I'm not?"[302]), the company suggested furs create a fursona of "Cheryl," a fox and bunny hybrid they may have hoped to use as part of a marketing campaign, perhaps directed at the furry community.[303] If that was Skittles's goal, it didn't quite work out the way they intended. Furs, proud of their self-created, exploitation-resistant community, did not take kindly to a thirty-five billion dollar corporation's attempt to get some free art, especially when said company has been accused of buying cocoa from producers using child slave labor.[304]

While a handful of furs did indeed take a shot at rendering Cheryl, Boozy Badger, a well-known fur, had an idea for a different kind of contest and on Twitter offered "$5 to the person who draws the most outrageous NSFW image of a bag of Skittles wearing fox ears just getting completely railed by a strangely muscular horse-man."[305] Furry artists eagerly took Boozy up on his challenge and created a barrage of decidedly risqué art, none of which is suitable for reproduction here, and certainly not on a bag of candy. In addition, generous furs added to Boozy's five dollars, bringing the winning artist's prize to a respectable $475—and in an act of jaw-dropping generosity, a deep-pocketed fur promised ten thousand dollars to the charity of the winning artist's choice.

The winning artist, Zeiros Lion, delivered on Boozy's art challenge big time, fox-eared Skittles bag and all. And that ten thousand dollar prize? The artist explained, in a fittingly poetic coda to the story, "We ended up donating to a group called International Rights Advocates. They partner with smaller groups to handle fundraising. In this case, they're handling the money on behalf of Slave Free Chocolate, a group trying to end slave labor in the cocoa farming and harvesting field."[306]

In 2019 Converse had better luck with Furboliche, a Brazilian furry bowling club. The company supplied the members with sneakers to wear at their bowling event and photographed the occasion. (The furs were wearing fur heads, but not full fursuits, just street clothes and their new Converse shoes.) The company built a marketing campaign around the furry bowlers that included placing enormous photos of them in Converse's store windows. The story was posted on the furry news website Flayrah, and unleashed no small amount of impassioned commentary from readers.[307] Most were upset to the point of outrage over what they saw as furry culture being exploited to sell sneakers, arguing that the blatant commercialism cheapened the culture.

On the other hand, Sonious, the story's writer, referred to it as an example of "'co-creative marketing' . . . when two groups have a mutual desire to sell a product, and can utilize each other's resources to reach a wider audience."[308] For Converse, an opportunity to sell more sneakers was obvious, and for Furboliche, it was a way of expanding the Brazilian furry community and inviting more furs to go bowling with them. (As Sonious described it, "the Brazilian furries *got paid* to advertise their own event.") According to the article, Brasil FurFest announced a sponsorship by Converse for their next convention.

Crash Azarel, a Brazilian fur who was part of the event, gave words of support for the collaboration, stating: "A lot of people got mad because of the exposure it gave the fandom, but wanting us to be this little group nobody knows about is a little silly. The fandom is already very well known. There's good and bad exposure. What's wrong with showing fursuiters having fun?" Crash also pointed out that most of the criticism came from US and European furries, who live in countries where furry is well known and essentially financially independent, while the furry community in Brazil is small by comparison and local conventions might need the financial support a sponsor could provide.

It's certainly a slippery slope. The day may come when a convention beholden to an advertiser underwriting the event is told not to hold the event or not to invite a specific guest or else their funding will be pulled. Crash offered two solutions to such a conundrum: a. Simply refuse to compromise. If the company wants to sponsor the convention badly enough, let them come around, not the furs, or b. Have the large European and American furry communities who want Brazilian conventions to avoid sponsorships offer financial support so they don't need an advertiser's support.

FURRY PROMOTIONS

While the Brazilian bowling team accepted help from Converse to spread word of furry fandom in Brazil, elsewhere we may not need big companies or ad agencies to alert people. At the moment it seems *any* entertainment involving anthropomorphism of any sort is described as "furry," even when it has nothing to do with our community. Or, just as often, the media assumes if it's anthro, it must be furry, and then is surprised when furries don't sign onto it. (As case examples, recall the furry responses summed up in headlines like, "No, Furries Don't Want to Fuck The Masked Singer—Any of Them,"[309] "FYI, Even Furries Think The *Cats* Trailer Looks Bad,"[310] and "I'm a Furry. Netflix's *Sexy Beasts* Misses the Entire Point of Dressing Up Like an Animal."[311])

Not even Donald Trump Jr. is immune from misguided messaging on furry. His 2022 Easter message to the world was a photo of three heavily armed bunnies guarding Easter eggs with the caption "Come and Take It." The response was online mockery declaring Don Jr. a furry.[312]

On the other hand, we do have some well-known folks speaking up on our behalf, celebrities who aren't afraid to let their furry flag fly. Take comedian Margaret Cho, who poodled up for her *Masked Singer* performance, dropped in on a furry convention to admire the fursuiters,[313] and enthused in a Dogpatch Press interview, "From what I know, it's so cute, and I'm a big animal lover so it's just like having giant adorable animals around you with very human qualities."[314] Then there's performance artist and rock musician Andrew W. K., who discovered and embraced the furry community. The community in turn embraced him back with a slew of art of his wolf fursona Party Animal.[315]

Among other attention-generating events that brought an eye to furry fandom is the video created by Ruby Bruce Lee, a furry, and her father, Violent J of the hip-hop group Insane Clown Posse, which exposed the Chinese fursuit pirates who sold Ruby a crummy knockoff suit,[316] as well as furry-friendly singer Jello Biafra's Dogpatch Press interview, in which he chose the lamprey from the cover of his Lard album *The Power of Lard* as his fursona.[317] In the interview, Biafra also shares how on one occasion he merged his Incredibly Strange Dance Party event with San Francisco's legendary Frolic furry dance.

BIG SCREEN FURRIES

It's common at furry conventions to see furs sporting tails but not full fursuits. It's a sight that's becoming more common outside of conventions as well—in particular, at the movies.

In 2009 Sigourney Weaver explained why she took on the role of a blue-skinned, long eared and tailed alien in *Avatar*, saying, "You offer me ears and a tail, and I'll go anywhere."[318] Then there's the Spuckler farm boy in the 2008 *Simpsons* episode "Apocalypse Cow," who, jealous of the titular bovine's caudal appendage, says, "I wished I had a tail what with to swat away flies. Mine just hangs there."[318] But the tail breakthrough might be best viewable in Disney's 2022 film *Turning Red*. The film's protagonist, Meilin, is the recipient of a family curse that turns her into a gigantic red panda when anxious. Happily, her supportive friends are impressed with her new form, one of them even confessing, "I've always wanted a tail."[320] Contrary to what might have been expected, Mei's furry form makes her popular among the neighborhood kids, who begin emulating her by wearing red panda tails and ears—more future furries!

A few years ago, a mock motivational poster featuring the sultry mouse chanteuse from Disney's *The Great Mouse Detective* above the caption, "Disney: Turning kids into furries for over ninety years" was making the rounds.[321] That acknowledgement was updated not long ago by the humor website Cracked.com, with an article titled "4 Ways Disney Managed to Aggressively Raise a Generation of Furries."[322] This wasn't a snarky put-down of furs or Disney, but an enthusiastic endorsement of the studio's female (and quite a few male) furry heartthrobs, from *Chip 'n Dale: Rescue Rangers*'s fearless mouse Gadget Hackwrench to *Zootopia*'s bedroom-eyed fox Nick Wilde (with stops in between for non-Disney *Animaniacs*'s mink Minerva Mink and *The Secret of NIMH*'s studly rat Justin). Just as many Gen Zers crush on Nick Wilde, their predecessors had a thing for Disney's Robin Hood fox, whom they credit as activating their furry gene.

Speaking of Disney's *Robin Hood*, adults were not immune to his charms either; in 2015 BuzzFeed published "18 Times The Fox In 'Robin Hood' Was Weirdly Hot."[323] The author's selections included "When he leaned against a tree and you can tell that he'd have those hot ab muscles lines going towards his belt if he had his shirt off," "When he was so brave and fearless and you would've given anything to be the girl fox," and turning the passion dial up to "eleven," "[W]hen he took you to his cave/bed/lair on your wedding night and looked at you so with such intense lust, and you were like 'yes Robin, this is how I always imagined it. Take me now, you fox! Take me like I'm a bag of gold from the rich!'" (The word "furry" was never mentioned, by the way.)

FURRY NFTS

There's no longer any doubt about it, having a thing for attractive cartoon animals (without necessarily thinking of yourself as a furry) has become a thing. So have NFTs. My introduction to NFTs was the September 2021 *Rolling Stone* story titled "Furries Realllllly Hate Lindsay Lohan's Furry NFT."[323] At that point they'd been around since the mid-teens, but this was the first time they'd crossed my radar.

An NFT, I learned, is a non-fungible token. As any furry artist knows, a digital image can be endlessly reproduced and distributed, with the millionth copy indistinguishable from the original, so why would anyone want to bid on something that a laser printer could spit out by the hundreds? Well, you see, those copies are fungible: any one of them could be exchanged for an identical one of equal value. However if one had a unique, provable identity separating it from its infinite clones, it would be *non*-fungible: its guaranteed one-of-a-kindness imbuing it with whatever value an eager buyer might be willing to part with to own it. That unique, provable identity comes by way of an Ethereum blockchain, a digital signature connecting that image's particular iteration to its owner.

But to get back to Lohan, the pop star/actor authorized the auction of a canine likeness of herself to help promote the Canine Cartel, an outfit auctioning ten thousand digital NFT images of various anthropomorphic dogs. The responding furry outcry was passionate and immediate, much of it centered on canine Lohan's lack of visible ears that should have been peeking out of the top of her head, but even more of it generated over anger that furry imagery was being employed to make big bucks for certain folks.[325]

Even though Lohan never referred to the image as her fursona or described herself as a furry, everyone else did, including BuzzFeed,[326] the Onion's *AV Club*,[327] and Seattle's *The Stranger*.[328] And just like Lohan's non-fursona, the Canine Cartel's absolutely, totally, expressly non-furry premise could very easily be mistaken for one.

Many a furry creator has indulged in world-building, constructing an entire reality for their characters to inhabit, and the Canine Cartel seems to have done likewise. They're not just selling NFTs of their characters, they're selling a world their dogs rule. As their website explains:

> The cats used to run everything in this shithole land. A hound couldn't sell a spliff to a rat without turning up looking like a used ball of yarn. . . . Eventually, we were an army . . . ready to declare war with the cats. . . . Years of bloodshed went by until finally, every dog and cat in this hellhole met for the ultimate battle. . . . The war was won, the cats were gone, and The Canine Cartel took over. . . . What you'll find here is a crew of tight knit tabby-whacking mutts who know their way around an AK-47.

Friendly, eh? For whatever reason, profile pictures of anthropomorphic animals—definitely of the furry variety, even if they're never called such—are particularly popular NFT offerings. In addition to the mentioned canines, one can also speculate in the Bored Ape Yacht Club's NFTs like any other financial asset. Its ten thousand images were snapped up in their first twelve hours on the market.[329] The token itself doubles as your membership to a swamp club for apes, explains its website, whose landing page depicts a sleazy-looking waterfront dive bar. Entering the site takes you to its equally sleazy interior. (The glowing purple door at the back of the bar is the entrance to the "Bathroom, a communal graffiti/message board"; click on it to leave a message for a fellow ape or just some good old bathroom graffiti.)

As the site's home page explains, "Each Bored Ape is unique and programmatically generated from over 170 possible traits, including expression, headwear, clothing, and more. All apes are dope, but some are rarer than others."[330] (And thus more valuable, in theory at least, like the rare trading card that no matter how many packs you buy, never turns up.)

Truth be told, the Bored Apes are more chimp than ape-like in appearance. Additionally, while those 170 traits give each one a superficially different appearance, look long enough and you'll see those recurring traits show up in different combinations: grimacing or bored, slack-jawed expressions, a variety of eyeglasses and hats, striped shirts, tank tops, and bubblegum chewers ad infinitum. These NFT collections are created by a computer putting together a series of unique images based on one-time-only random combinations of traits.

The Lazy Lions is yet another anthro animal-themed NFT. Its landing page shows the felines' private island, replete with golf course, amusement park, numerous bars, an ongoing rave, a cluster of skyscrapers, and, for some reason, a rocket taking off from a mountaintop. A lighthouse beams out the message "Community is the project/The project is the community."[331]

Similar to the apes and canines, the Lazy Lions are, according to the website, "programmatically generated from over 160 possible traits, including clothing, mane, expression, and more." The website also boasts numerous benefits of being a Lazy Lion, such as monthly "ROARwards" and other goodies, as well as commercial ownership of your totally unique NFT. (People will surely want to buy a T-shirt of their particular lion!)

Pudgy Penguins, Weird Whales, Doge Pound dogs, CyberKongz, Cool Cats, SupDucks, Stoner Cats: there are numerous character-based NFTs out there waiting to relieve you of your hard-earned cash in exchange for promises of future wealth, but the proliferation of these cartoon character-type critters is quite intriguing to this furry. It's almost as if you're buying a fursona as well as investing in NFTs.

A feature of these offerings is an "exclusive" membership in a community of like-minded people. As the Lazy Lions site puts it, "When you join the Lazy Lions—by purchasing an NFT or just joining our Discord—you're instantly part of our community. A global community that empowers and supports each other on this exciting journey into Web 3.0. We're focused on building authentic connections as we delve into the metaverse together."[331]

A community based on anthropomorphic animals inviting you to be a part of something bigger than yourself: it's what we furs have created for ourselves and you're welcome to join us, free of charge. You don't have to buy a token, fungible or otherwise, you just have to be into it.

17

THE FURRY FUTURE

Over the next decade or two, the greymuzzles who birthed the furry community will gradually be leaving the scene, making more room for the next generation, which already dominates the furry community. According to the website Furscience, 75 percent of furries are twenty-five or younger.[333] (In the eyes of the Facebook group Greymuzzles, which is for older furs, anyone over *thirty* is a greymuzzle![334])

Furries are particularly widespread in America's technology sector. According to a *Business Insider* article:

> Furries are developing vaccines, building your favorite apps, and crashing Microsoft meetings. Some tech companies actively recruited at furry events as early as the late 1990s . . . the tech field, which has always prided itself on valuing those who "think different," has proven to be more willing to embrace furries than the world at large . . . . In turn, furries have come to play a major, in-

fluential role in the development of the tech industry over the last several decades. A long-running in-joke holds that if all the furries disappeared, Silicon Valley would simply cease to function.[335]

According to the article, furries inside the industry network with each other and often help fellow furs find jobs. The "big three" tech companies—Microsoft, Amazon, and Google—refused to comment for the article on furs possibly in their employ, but it's impossible for such behemoths to *not* be home to sizeable furry communities.

The *Business Insider* article mentioned and Input magazine profiled a furry who goes by the name Chise and is a scientist actively involved in the COVID-19 vaccine development. According to the Input article, "When she was a young girl growing up in the US, Chise had two big dreams: being a doctor and starring in a Disney movie."[336] Her wish for a career in the medical field came true, as she's now a senior scientist in vaccine research and development. Her second wish has yet to come true, but she discovered the next best thing in 2015 when a coworker told her about furry fandom. She's now a pine marten, a type of weasel, in a make-believe anthropomorphic animal universe. (The Input article is illustrated with two lab coat-wearing versions of Chise's fursona created by furry artists.)

Chise updates her Twitter followers on developments in COVID-19 research, very often with multiple postings in a single day filled with scientific jargon. For example:

Encouraging news! Moderna's Omicron bivalent booster vaccine candidate, mRNA-1273.214, demonstrated potent neutralizing titers against Omicron BA.4 and BA.5 in ALL participants REGARDLESS of prior infection! This IS the LEAD Fall 2022 booster candidate. Let's talk about that![337]

Chise's tweets also offer commonsense advice and information about dealing with COVID-19. For example:

To help clear up some confusion. If you test positive for SARS-COV-2 after being vaccinated and are experiencing mild symptoms or even no symptoms at all? Your vaccine worked. No, it did not fail. Very few vaccines (if any, for that matter) provide 100% sterilizing immunity.[338]

Chise's upbeat tweets sometimes bring her into conflict with other (presumably non-furry) COVID bloggers and their followers who don't share her optimistic perspective on the virus. The pine marten remains undeterred, however. As she shared in the Input article, "Being encouraged and feeling positive about data, especially when relating to the effectiveness of the vaccines and their application in the real world and helping this pandemic come to an end, should be celebrated. I don't think [my upbeat tone] should be disdained. If anything, I have to ask, Why would you not be optimistic about it?"

Among those who've taken issue with Chise is a German physicist who, according to the Input article, claimed she was hiding *something* behind her anonymity, and as a furry she couldn't possibly be a "real" scientist. But Chise isn't bothered by this. Like many in professional fields, she prefers to keep her furry and professional lives distinct, fearing an anti-vaccine activist might try to expose her furry identity to the world and discredit her professionally. As she shared with Input, "My job isn't really aware of my participation in the furry fandom. It's something I keep close to me."

FORMIDABLE FURS

There's no small number of furs who are at or near the top of their profession, and most of them, like Chise or a furry I know who is on the absolute cutting edge of advanced heart research, prefer to keep those two spheres of their lives far apart.

The truth is that furries are everywhere, even outer space. While a virtual reality ride will be the closest to space most of us will ever get, one furry has been there: Cameron Bess, a.k.a. MeepsKitten, was a passenger on Jeff Bezos's December 2021 NS-19 mission, which launched his Blue Origin private rocket ship flight. The entire voyage lasted less than eleven minutes, and only three of them were in zero gravity, but Meeps had escaped the Earth's atmosphere and gravity's relentless pull.

Jeff Bezos's astronauts were allowed to take a few personal items with them on the ride, and Meeps brought a glove from his fursuit; a pink, yellow, and blue pansexual flag; and a record by Porter Robinson, a musician popular in the gay community. Together the items reflect communities Meeps identifies with, and choosing these items was a sign of allegiance.

Meeps is fortunate to have a venture capitalist dad who was able to afford his son's (as well as his own) undisclosed space fare. (As the old expression goes, if you have to ask how much a yacht costs, you can't afford one.) And Meeps seems aware of this privilege and to feel a corresponding duty to give back. He spoke to this in a sophisticated YouTube video he created to share his story. In it we see him begin to suit up and groom the fur atop his suit's head, when he suddenly stops, turns to the camera, and says, "If you guys don't mind, I'm gonna do this video as myself—it's a little bit more personal." Soon after, he shares the fact that he's pansexual, then adds, "but my story does not represent the entirety of the LGBTQ+ community, and yes, I am a furry—but no, not all furries are like me."[339]

In his video, Meeps speaks directly to younger furs dealing with guilt or shame over being different. He tells them that he hopes they feel emboldened by knowing someone like them went to space, saying:

> There are probably a fair amount of you who don't feel like you're accepted for who you are . . . just because you're uniquely you. You may not feel like you have a place to shine because you feel like the world won't accept you. . . . I hope those of you who are afraid of who you are, maybe that's because you're queer or you're a part of the furry community, which is wildly misunderstood . . . I hope you can point at my mission and feel a little cooler about yourself.

Meeps also speaks in the video to the nature of differences within his communities and that he doesn't reflect all people that share his identifiers of queer or furry. And he's right, of course. No matter what our sexual orientation is, no matter what community we feel a part of, we're as different from each other as people in other communities are from their allies. Someone once said, we're all equal not because we're all the same, we're all equal because we're all different.

For another superb example of individuality, consider openly gay, nonbinary, black, and proud video game champion and fur Dominique "Sonic-Fox" McLean. A fierce, relentless, trash-talking competitor, McClean wears their tail to championship competitions. In a 2019 Twitter thread, the trash-talking in-your-face champion outed themself as nonbinary and talked about their attraction to traditionally feminine items, sharing:

> I'm gonna try on jewelry, Ima try piercings, etc etc, the whole nine yards! I wanna completely overhaul how I generally present myself to the world, and have this new attire that I think feels right. To really express the true -me-.[340]

FURRY AND PROUD

A Vice article describes the furry community as "a happy home for large numbers of nonheterosexual, transgender, genderqueer, and gender nonconforming people, welcoming many who feel stigmatized at home, school, and work. For many under-eighteen furries, the community provides a place where they 'fit in' for the first time—one where they're celebrated for their creative invented fursonas."[341] I think this hits the nail on the head, furry fandom provides an outlet to so many, and we each have our unique way of connecting with it.

While some people keep their professional identities and furry identities distinct, as a writer about the furry community, I long ago shed any desire (or ability) to keep my furriness apart from the rest of my life. If anything, the two have irretrievably merged and today I let my furry flag fly. One look at my anthropomorphism-drenched apartment décor would instantly reveal me as one of the dreaded "lifestylers" the long-gone Burned Furs objected to.

I sometimes feel like the all-purpose fur, as I'm interested in all the forms furry takes. I love the cartoons and cartoon characters that opened me up to a more joyful reality than the one I was born into. I love the inspiration furry has given me to pursue my own creativity, and the freedom to step into a fursuit and take a vacation from my human self. I confess that there are certain aspects of furry erotica I find enjoyable, while at the same time I feel a kinship and identification with the alligator, the "spirit animal" I imagine as the protector of the vulnerable child I once was.

It's my hope that as furry fandom continues to grow, more people will be able to find community and connection through furry. Imagine the peace of mind, creativity, and positive energy that could be unleashed if more of us are willing to dip a paw in.

AFTERWORD

As I write this, my country has taken a huge leap—fifty, sixty years—into the past. Reproductive freedom has been lost, contraception may be next. Gay marriage has also been targeted.

Gay and transgender people, basically anyone non-cisgender, are being called a menace to "normal" people, and hard-won rights of equality are under attack. Repulsive claims that gay people are "grooming" children for pedophilia, discredited decades ago, have resurfaced. Organized gangs have been harassing Pride events and threatening political opponents with death. Turning any group of people into "the other" is a guaranteed way of targeting them for harassment, abuse, or worse.

As this book and others have pointed out, the furry community is a safe, welcoming haven for young people—gay, transgender, nonbinary, and otherwise "differently identifying" teens and young adults who have been rejected by their peers or families for the "crime" of being true to themselves.

I have mocked peddlers of and believers in ludicrous "litter boxes for furries" rumors, but make no mistake: these preposterous accusations are a stealth attack on the young people I mentioned, and on the entire furry community. And it's no coincidence that these imaginary litter boxes are often described as located in all-gender restrooms. One reason I've written *Furry Planet* was to speak up on our behalf—to support anyone coming out of the "furry closet" with pride in our community and ourselves. I ask every fur reading this to consider doing likewise. Let the world know that your appreciation of and identification with imaginary, anthropomorphic animals is a basic and nurturing part of your identity. As a greymuzzle living in New York City, where people are appreciated for their differences, I know it's easy for me to advocate a kind of bravery I might not be capable of were I in your shoes, but look to your fellow furs for support and validation. You may be different, but you are not alone.

ACKNOWLEDGMENTS

The book you're holding, reading on your screen, or listening to on your phone would not exist without the help and support of the many people who generously shared their time and knowledge.

I'll start right off with Mark Merlino and Rod O'Riley, they of the Prancing Skiltaire, the "nexus of furrydom" ominously hinted at in that long-ago *Vanity Fair* article, and Steve Gallacci, without whose *Albedo Anthropomorphics* comics there might not be a furry fandom. I also owe thanks to Fred Patten's sister Sherry for sharing her reminiscences of the man who did so much for our community.

This book would have had no right to call itself *Furry Planet* without the help of so many furs around the world: China's Robert Lynn (the "blue fox"); the people at Japan Meeting of Furries (JMoF); Bernard Doove ("Chakat Goldfur") of Australia; Eurofurence's creators Tobias Kohler ("Unci Narynin") and Gerrit Heitsch ("Tes-Tui-H'ar"); Taffka, the Moscow unicorn; and Pawsry Hamktxchuzhni, head of Singapore's Global Furry TV. Thank you Britfur Tim Stoddard, for your generosity in letting me quote liberally from your forthcoming *Furtannia: The History of the Furry Fandom in the United Kingdom*.

Much appreciated is California State University at San Bernardino's Dr. Stuart Sumida, who knows his cartoon critters from the inside-out. Likewise to Jeff and his fellow *BoJack Horseman* fans who filled in the gaps in my knowledge of that messed-up equine's doings. A heartfelt bravo to the staff and resources of the Billy Rose Theatre Division at the New York Public Library for the Performing Arts, without whom it would've been impossible to uncover the facts about Hume Cronyn's long forgotten 1958 play, *The Man in the Dog Suit*.

Thanks to all the "remarkable furs" profiled in this book: Furscience's Sharon Roberts, France's Liassur and his mighty morphin' power filters, Warren Wolfy, my guide to the virtual world, and Coela Can't!, who taught me the difference between a primagen and a protogen.

I owe thanks to furry's master journalists, Patch O'Furr of Dogpatch Press and Flayrah's Laurence Parry ("GreenReaper"), for keeping the furry community up to date on issues affecting us. The inside scoop from Army vet Kanic on being a "milfur" was also an important addition to *Furry Planet*.

Conversing with mainstream authors like William Kotzwinkle (of *Doctor Rat*) and Kirsten Bakis (of *Lives of Monster Dogs*) was a treat, as was speaking with their furry counterparts Kyell Gold, Gre7g Luterman, and Mary E. Lowd. I am super indebted to Dr. David Benaron ("Spottacus Cheetah"), one of the most amazing furs I have ever met, for his time, and to YouTuber Odin Wolf for putting me in touch with Spotti.

Thanks also to Sweden's Margit Brundin for sharing the story of her heartfelt rabbit statuary, to Yago Partal of Barcelona for providing insight into his Creature Portraits photographs, to Dragoneer for his inside scoop on Fur Affinity, and especially to Anthony Ausgang for his appreciation of all things lowbrow and furry.

Much appreciation to my "furry after dark" friends—Virgose, TF Freak, Jack, and Jack Newhorse, who openly and honestly spoke of their NSFW furry kinks.

Now it's time to thank the people *not* in these pages who made this book possible. I'm referring of course to Julia Abramoff (who kept me on my toes and made this book a whole lot better) and Drew Anderla at Apollo Publishers, and my brilliant agent, Malaga Baldi, who introduced Julia and Drew to the wonders of furry.

NOTES

1. Members of our community have even been spotted in Antarctica!
2. Or as they're known in the furry community, "greymuzzles." It's all relative though; the Facebook Greymuzzles page considers anyone over *thirty* a greymuzzle.
3. Humans's love for their companion animals has created an annual *151 billion dollar* worldwide industry offering their four-legged friends everything from spas to pet therapists, birthday parties, luxury hotel stays, and so much more. (See https://www.grandviewresearch.com/industry-analysis/pet-care-market, 2021, retrieved February 2, 2023.) But those lucky critters are *actual* animals, not the imaginary or symbolic ones this book examines, and we won't spend more time on this. In other words, to quote an old sign still occasionally seen, "NO PETS ALLOWED."
4. "MFF 2022 Wrapup," Furfest.org, Midwest Furry Fandom, Inc., December 7, 2022, https://www.furfest.org/news/2022/12/7/2022-wrapup.
5. The story of Mark, Rod, and the birth of ConFurence can be found in my previous book. Joe Strike, *Furry Nation: The True Story of America's Most Misunderstood Subculture* (Jersey City: Cleis Press, 2017).
6. Tim Stoddard, *Furtannia: The History of the Furry Fandom in the United Kingdom* (Cathedral City, CA: Uncle Bear Publishing, 2023).
7. Many British furries consider Curtis as one of the founders, if not the "father" of UK furry fandom. (https://en.wikifur.com/wiki/Ian_Curtis, accessed February 7, 2023.)
8. Stoddard, *Furtannia*.
9. Stoddard, *Furtannia*, 121.
10. An animal-related charity is a standard feature of furry conventions.
11. Correspondence with Narynin and Tes-Tui-H'ar.
12. According to the original invitation: "Eurofurence will be held in Tes's house at Kaiser-Wilhelm-Koog (north-west of Hamburg, north of where the Elbe River flows into the North Sea). It is an old farmhouse with a barn and enough space around it. The next neighbors are far, so it doesn't matter if we make noise. The sea is not behind the house, but within walking distance. The landscape is flat, the most distinctive landmarks are some large wind turbines."
13. "Template:Convention resources/Eurofurence," Wikifur, last modified October 19, 2016, https://en.wikifur.com/wiki/Template:Convention_resources/Eurofurence#Eurofurence_17_.282011.29.
14. Correspondence with Taffka.
15. Including furs who enjoy the great outdoors. In the harsh old days of the Soviet Union, being sent to Siberia meant exile to a cold, forbidding, and remote region within Russia's borders and grueling work at a forced labor camp. Today, however, Siberia is home to SibFyr, where outdoorsy furs gather to camp out. As its website explains, "Siberia is not only frosts and mountains, it is also a good mood, a sea of positive and outdoor activities." "SibFyr (СибФыр)," vk.com, VK Holding, updated May 2, 2018, https://vk.com/sibfur.

16. "The commission at the RKN proposed to recognize radical feminism and child-free as extremism," TASS, September 29, 2021, https://tass.ru/obschestvo/12537875.
17. Local fursuiters in the United States and abroad regularly gather in a park or other public place to enjoy a stroll and each other's company.
18. Patch O'Furr, "Anti-LGBT Russian government morality activist visits and harasses fursuit walkers," Dogpatch Press, December 7, 2021, https://dogpatch.press/2021/12/07/anti-lgbt-russian/.
19. Ibid.
20. "GFTV NewsHub," Global Furry Television, March 2022, https://globalfurrytv.news.blog/.
21. Correspondence with Pawsry Hamktxchuzhni.
22. "Singapore," Freedom House, https://freedomhouse.org/country/singapore/freedom-world/2022.
23. Pawsry estimates there are likely three hundred-plus active furs in Singapore.
24. Wang Yiping and Zhang Mengyu, "Young Chinese Find a New Way to Explore Intimacy: Furry Fandom," Sixth Tone, December 9, 2021, https://www.sixthtone.com/news/1009163/young-chinese-find-a-new-way-to-explore-intimacy-furry-fandom.
25. Josh Ye, "The furries of Hong Kong - men and women who dress up as animals and say they feel more at home in their second skin," *South China Morning Post*, May 3, 2017, https://www.scmp.com/lifestyle/article/2091482/wanna-be-my-dog-meet-hong-kongs-fabulous-furries.
26. Ibid.
27. Wang Yiping and Zhang Mengyu, "Young Chinese Find a New Way to Explore Intimacy: Furry Fandom," Sixth Tone, December 9, 2021, https://www.sixthtone.com/news/1009163/young-chinese-find-a-new-way-to-explore-intimacy-furry-fandom.
28. Ye, "The furries of Hong Kong."
29. Ibid.
30. *Doujinshi* are self-published works, very often fan fiction reinterpretations of existing characters as well as original stories.
31. The Kemono Market, held twice a year, hosts hundreds of *doujinshi* creators, dealers, and other vendors.
32. Amateur press associations (known as "venture companies" in Japan) are groups of creators, generally artists who provide a limited number of copies of their work for collation into issues that are only distributed to those who contributed to it.
33. Otaku is a Japanese term for an anime- or manga-obsessed nerd.
34. *Tokusatsu* characters are created through practical effects, such as an actor in a Godzilla suit.
35. *Kaiju* are giant-sized monsters, like Godzilla.
36. *Kaijin* are distorted mutant or genetically engineered humanoid beings.
37. Cosplay is an abbreviation of "costume play," where fans of various animation or superhero characters create their own version of their hero's outfit and perform with like-minded friends in imagined adventures.
38. *Kawaii* means cute.
39. Furry Down Under (FurDU) chair Christine Bradshaw informs me that there are actually numerous "soda roos," kangaroo fursuiters whose coloring matches the packaging of various popular soft drinks, though, as she says, "They don't use the [sodas'] logo because that's copyright infringement."
40. Bernard Doove (a.k.a. Chakat Goldfur), email messages to author, June 11, 2022, June 19, 2022.

41. No relation to William Kotzwinkle's novel *Doctor Rat*, Hilton's Doc Rat is an MD (and rat) living in an anthropomorphic version of Australia. Hilton created the character in the 1990s and under the name "Jenner," he launched the *Doc Rat* web comic in 2006. I highly recommend it: https://www.docrat.com.au/.
42. An informal measurement of the degree to which an anthropomorphic animal represents a human being vs. the real-life critter it's derived from. Compared to Miss Kitty and BoJack, *The Lion King*'s characters—apart from their facial expressions and ability to speak—are otherwise highly naturalistic.
43. A favorite family anecdote: a friend was watching Disney's *The Great Mouse Detective* with an acquaintance. At one point Basil, the film's Sherlockian rodent, examines a bit of dirt through a microscope and declares: "This could only have come from where the sewer meets the Thames." The acquaintance objected: "That's ridiculous, there's no way he could figure that out from a little bit of dirt," to which my friend replied, "You bought the talking mouse?"
44. Rhythm & Hues was an award-winning visual effects and animation studio that declared bankruptcy in 2013 and closed in 2020.
45. The Moving Picture Company is a global visual effects company.
46. *The Simpsons*, Season 32, Episode 15, "Do Pizza Bots Dream of Electric Guitars." Directed by Mike B. Anderson and Jennifer Moeller, aired March 14, 2021 on Fox.
47. Madeleine Aggeler, "How Do Furries Feel About the New *Cats* Movie?" *The Cut*, July 23, 2019, https://www.thecut.com/2019/07/how-do-furries-feel-about-the-new-cats-movie.html.
48. Ryan Broderick, "FYI, Even Furries Think The "Cats" Trailer Looks Bad," BuzzFeed News, July 20, 2019, https://www.buzzfeednews.com/article/ryanhatesthis/do-furries-like-the-cats-trailer.
49. Madeleine Aggeler, "How Do Furries Feel About the New *Cats* Movie?" *The Cut*, July 23, 2019, https://www.thecut.com/2019/07/how-do-furries-feel-about-the-new-cats-movie.html.
50. Priscilla Frank, "'The Masked Singer' Is Great Content For Furries, Hellish Nightmare For Everyone Else," Huffpost.com , January 3, 2019, https://www.huffpost.com/entry/the-masked-singer-fox-reality-singing-competition_n_5c2ce5a9e4b0407e9087436b.
51. Rebecca Alter, "Is *The Masked Singer* Furry Crossover Culture? We Asked an Expert," *Vulture*, October 4, 2019, https://www.vulture.com/2019/10/the-masked-singer-furry-culture.html.
52. Joseph Longo, "No, Furries Don't Want to Fuck The Masked Singer (Any of Them)," *MEL Magazine*, accessed March 5, 2022, https://melmagazine.com/en-us/story/no-furries-dont-want-to-fuck-the-masked-singer-any-of-them.
53. *Sexy Beasts,* 2021, Season 2, Episode 1, "Mick the Dragon." Directed by Sam Campbell, Netflix.
54. Kemi Alemoru, "The fursuit of happiness: Furries on Netflix's *Sexy Beasts*," *The Face*, July 22, 2021, https://theface.com/culture/sexy-beasts-netflix-furries, accessed March 3, 2022.
55. Riley Black, "I'm a Furry. Netflix's *Sexy Beasts* Misses the Entire Point of Dressing Up Like an Animal," Slate, July 22, 2021, https://slate.com/human-interest/2021/07/furry-sexy-beasts-costumes-netflix-mistakes.html.

56. Jason Tabrys, "'Sexy Beasts' Is Coming Back To Nurture Your Growing Furry Fandom, And Here Are The Pictures To Prove It," Uproxx, September 22, 2021, https://uproxx.com/tv/sexy-beasts-coming-back-season-2/.
57. Sonia Saraiya, "The 10 Best TV Shows of the 2010s," *Vanity Fair*, November 26, 2019, https://www.vanityfair.com/hollywood/2019/11/best-tv-shows-decade-2010s.
58. Ben Travers and Hanh Nguyen, "The Best Animated Series of All Time," IndieWire, March 3, 2022, https://www.indiewire.com/feature/best-animated-series-all-time-cartoons-anime-tv-1202021835/5/.
59. Jen Chaney, "The Best Writing on TV Is on *BoJack Horseman*," Vulture, July 23, 2019, https://www.vulture.com/2019/07/bojack-horseman-vulture-tv-awards-best-writing.html.
60. Alex Giobbi, "*BoJack Horseman*: The Main Characters Highest and Lowest Points," Screenrant, April 23, 2020, https://screenrant.com/bojack-horseman-netflix-highest-lowest/.
61. "List of awards and nominations received by *BoJack Horseman*," https://en.wikipedia.org/wiki/List_of_awards_and_nominations_received_by_BoJack_Horseman, retrieved May 24, 2022.
62. "BoJack Horseman," IMDb, accessed October 2, 2022, https://www.imdb.com/title/tt3398228/?ref_=nv_sr_srsg_0.
63. Way too many to recount here, enough to fill an entire website. A tiny sampling wouldn't begin to do them justice; instead see Hattie Soykan, "29 of the Best Animal Puns You Might Have Missed on BoJack Horseman," BuzzFeed, September 4, 2017, https://www.buzzfeed.com/hattiesoykan/xx-of-the-best-animal-jokes-on-bojack-horseman; and Alexandra Plesa, "80 Incredible Animal Puns You Probably Missed on BoJack Horseman," Ranker, October 24, 2019, https://www.ranker.com/list/bojack-horseman-animal-puns/alexandra-plesa.
64. Stephen Rodrick, "The World According to BoJack Horseman," *The New York Times Magazine*, July 22, 2016, https://www.nytimes.com/2016/07/24/magazine/the-world-according-to-bojack-horseman.html.
65. Kyle Gehler, "BoJack Horseman: Why the Show's World Really Has Talking Animals," Screenrant, August 3, 2020, https://screenrant.com/bojack-horseman-world-talking-animals-reason-meaning.
66. Coralie Kraft, "Persons of Interest: The Artist Behind TV's Richly Emotional Cartoon Comedies," *The New Yorker*, August 15, 2021, https://www.newyorker.com/culture/persons-of-interest/the-artist-behind-tvs-richly-emotional-comedies.
67. Ibid.
68. After its initial Netflix season, the show was acquired by Cartoon Network and now appears on Adult Swim.
69. Stephen Rodrick, "The World According to BoJack Horseman," *The New York Times Magazine*, July 22, 2016, https://www.nytimes.com/2016/07/24/magazine/the-world-according-to-bojack-horseman.html.
70. Nor is it for furries in general.

71. Chris Randle, "Lisa Hanawalt: BoJack cartoonist gets personal in Hot Dog Taste Test," *The Guardian*, May 31, 2016, https://www.theguardian.com/books/2016/may/31/lisa-hanawalt-comics-bojack-horseman-hot-dog-taste-test-new-book.
72. The Bechdel Test, created by cartoonist Alison Bechdel and her friend Liz Wallace, first appeared in Bechdel's comic *Dykes to Watch Out For*. It asks the question, can two women in a movie have a conversation that's not centered on their relationships with men?
73. In the 1930s, the New York-based Fleischer Studios was a major competitor to Walt Disney. The studio's cartoons were noted for their often-surrealistic nature, where inanimate objects come to life and characters transform and mutate in bizarre ways.
74. Virginia Streva, "John Oliver desperately wants to buy rat-erotica painting by Pennsylvania artist," *Philly Voice*, March 30, 2020, https://www.phillyvoice.com/john-oliver-rat-erotica-pennsylvania-york-covid-19-coronavirus-trump-last-week-tonight/.
75. Virginia Streva, "John Oliver obtains sought-after rat-erotica painting by Pennsylvania artist," *Philly Voice*, April 13, 2020, https://www.phillyvoice.com/john-oliver-rat-erotica-painting-pennyslvania-york-artist-last-week-tonight-coronavirus-covid-19/.
76. *Last Week Tonight*, "Last Week Tonight's Masterpiece Gallery Tour," YouTube video, Running Time 2:16, Published August 25, 2021, https://www.youtube.com/watch?v=NvpKES_kcYg.
77. Devon Ivie, "John Oliver Is Taking Last Week Tonight's Mascot Budget 'to My Grave,'" *Vulture*, February 4, 2021, https://www.vulture.com/article/john-oliver-last-week-tonight-mascots-interview.html.
78. Ibid.
79. *The Late Show with Stephen Colbert*, Season 6, Episode 84, "John Oliver/Ingrid Andress." Directed by Jake Plunkett, aired February 9, 2021, on CBS. https://www.youtube.com/watch?v=bzT-ib8Yo4g&list=PLi-W8h-RIIA6ZIgRKbdzEkyWRs52JcXp-S&index=39.
80. In 2021, right-wing politicians and media outlets began spreading the rumor that schools were installing litter boxes in bathrooms for students who are furries and "identify as cats." (Isabella Grullón Paz, "Litter Boxes for Students Who Identify as Furries? Not So, Says School Official," *The New York Times*, January 23, 2022, https://www.nytimes.com/2022/01/23/us/politics/michigan-litter-box-school.html.) Although the rumor has been repeatedly debunked it continues to spread and is viewed by many as a stealth attack on gay or transgender students. (Kathie Obradovich, "Silly school litter box rumors front a darker agenda," *News From the States*, February 14, 2022, https://www.newsfromthestates.com/article/silly-school-litter-box-rumors-front-darker-agenda.) I discuss this rumor in greater detail in Chapter 14, "Is Everybody Happy? (Well, Not Quite)."
81. *Last Week Tonight*, "Rocks: Last Week Tonight with John Oliver (Web Exclusive)," YouTube Video, 17:22, May 29, 2022, https://www.youtube.com/watch?v=AEa3sK1iZxc.
82. Kandiss Taylor (@KandissTaylor), "The furry days are over when I'm governor," Twitter, March 23, 2022, 8:08 a.m., https://twitter.com/KandissTaylor/status/1506603753008472064?ref_src=twsrc%5Etfw.
83. For examples of Liassur's work see Instagram, @liassur29.

84. In "A Virtual Murder," while working on a script for a VR murder mystery, Jessica's curiosity over what lies behind a locked door in the game leads her to the killer of one of its designers. *Murder She Wrote*, Season 10, Episode 5, "A Virtual Murder." Directed by Lee Smith, aired October 31, 1993 on CBS.
85. While the ride itself is stationary, its seats move to match the VR environment the ride is supposedly traveling through.
86. Steven Levy, "Palmer Luckey Says Working With Weapons Isn't as Fun as VR," *Wired*, March 14, 2022, https://www.wired.com/story/palmer-luckey-drones-autonomous-weapons-ukraine/.
87. Matt Baume, "How Furries Are Making Virtual Reality Actually Worth Visiting," Input magazine, July 27, 2021, https://www.inverse.com/input/gaming/how-furries-are-making-virtual-reality-worth-visiting.
88. Ibid.
89. Adafruit is an open-source hardware company selling electronic components and equipment.
90. If you understand those terms you're probably building your own protogen right now.
91. Dogpatch Press, https://dogpatch.press.
92. Tina Jordan, "What Were People Reading in the Summer of 1972?" *The New York Times*, July 14, 2022, https://www.nytimes.com/2022/07/14/books/review/jonathan-livingston-seagull-richard-bach.html.
93. William Grimes, "Eleanor Friede, 87, Is Dead; Edited 1970 Fable 'Seagull,'" *The New York Times*, July 25, 2008, https://www.nytimes.com/2008/07/25/books/25friede.html.
94. "I've just taken on a novel about rabbits, one of them with extra-sensory perception," the publisher told a friend. "Do you think I'm mad?" Isabel Quigly, "Obituary: Rex Collings," *Independent*, June 8, 1996, http://www.independent.co.uk/news/people/obituary-rex-collings-1335987.html.
95. Matt Reimann, "Watership Down: An Improvised Classic and Bestseller," *Books Tell You Why* (blog), May 9, 2016, https://blog.bookstellyouwhy.com/watership-down-an-improvised-classic-and-bestseller.
96. "Watership Down," *AbeBooks*, AbeBooks Inc., accessed February 13, 2023, https://www.abebooks.com/servlet/BookDetailsPL?bi=31363097752&searchurl=x%3D43%26fe%3Don%26y%3D6%26bi%3D0%26ds%3D50%26bx%3Doff%26sortby%3D1%26tn%3DWatership%2BDown%26an%3DAdams%26recentlyadded%3Dall&cm_sp=snippet-_-srp1-_-image1.
97. Richard Adams, "Introduction," *Watership Down* (New York: Scribner, 1972, 2022), xvii.
98. Richard Adams, *The Plague Dogs: A Novel* (New York: Fawcett Crest, 1979), 458, 461.
99. *The Daily Show with Jon Stewart*, Season 15, Episode 141, "David Sedaris." Directed by Chuck O'Neil, aired November 4, 2010, on Comedy Central.
100. David Sedaris, "The Squirrel and the Chipmunk," *Squirrel Seeks Chipmunk: A Modern Beastiary* (New York: Little, Brown, and Company, 2010), 19.
101. *The Daily Show with Jon Stewart*, "David Sedaris."
102. William Kotzwinkle, "How 'The Bear Went Over the Mountain' Came to Be Written," January 13, 2015, accessed October 15, 2015, kotzwinkle.com.
103. William Kotzwinkle, *The Bear Went Over the Mountain: A Novel* (New York: Henry Holt and Company, Inc., 1996), 194.
104. In an interview Kotzwinkle mused that as a result of the novel's popularity, "I'm also starting to feel that I'm being changed by the bear." Ron Hogan, "William Kotzwinkle," Beatrice.com, 1996, http://www.beatrice.com/interviews/kotzwinkle.

105. William Kotzwinkle, *Doctor Rat* (New York: Marlowe & Company, 1971, 1976), 11.
106. William Kotzwinkle, email message to author, October 24, 2015.
107. Kotzwinkle, *Doctor Rat*, 7.
108. Ibid.
109. Ibid.
110. William Kotzwinkle, email message to author, October 24, 2015.
111. Kotzwinkle, *Doctor Rat,* 131.
112. Ibid., 102.
113. Ibid., 165-166, 177, 153.
114. Movie rights to *The Bear Went Over the Mountain* were optioned by the Jim Henson Company when the book was published, but a film was never produced.
115. William Kotzwinkle, *Herr Nightingale and the Satin Woman* (New York: Alfred A. Knopf, 1978), 16.
116. Kotzwinkle, *Herr Nightingale and the Satin Woman*, 22.
117. Kotzwinkle, *Herr Nightingale and the Satin Woman*, 49.
118. William Kotzwinkle, email message to author, October 24, 2015.
119. *The New York Observer*, February 17, 1997. (Photocopy from author's files.)
120. Kirsten Bakis, *Lives of the Monster Dogs* (New York: Warner Books, 1997), 76-78, 261-262.
121. M. G. Lord, "Unleashed on Manhattan," Review of *Lives of the Monster Dogs* by Kirsten Bakis, *The New York Times,* March 9, 1997, https://www.nytimes.com/1997/03/09/books/unleashed-on-manhattan.html.
122. Kirsten Bakis, email message to author, October 1, 2015.
123. "WedgeWorks ready to unleash 'Monster Dogs,'" *The Hollywood Reporter*, August 23, 2010, https://web.archive.org/web/20141029033352/ http://www.themovieinsider.com/m7861/4/lives-of-the-monster-dogs/.
124. Stefan Kanfer, "Krazy: George Herriman brought brilliant farce and artistic whimsy to the funny pages," *City Journal*, Winter 2013, https://www.city-journal.org/html/krazy-13540.html.
125. Most notably, *Calvin & Hobbes*'s Bill Watterson (See Colin Marshall, "George Herriman's Krazy Kat, Praised as the Greatest Comic Strip of All Time, Gets Digitized as Early Installments Enter the Public Domain," *Open Culture*, July 15, 2019, https://www.openculture.com/2019/07/krazy-kat-now-digitized-put-online.html), and *Peanuts*'s Charles M. Schulz (See Dan Taylor, "Museum exhibit celebrates cartoonists who inspired Charles Schulz," *The Press Democrat*, April 6, 2022, https://www.pressdemocrat.com/article/entertainment/celebrating-cartoonists-who-inspired-charles-schulz/).
126. Jay Kantor, *Krazy Kat: A Novel in Five Panels* (New York: Alfred A. Knopf, 1988), 33, 22.
127. Gojiro is a variation on Godzilla's original Japanese name Gojira. Mark Jacobson, *Gojiro* (New York: Grove Press, 1997).
128. Laurel Maury, "Lethem Updates Cult Classic 'Omega' Comic Series," Review of *Omega: The Unknown* by Jonathan Lethem, Karl Rusnak, Farel Dalrymple, and Paul Hornschemeier, *NPR*, January 8, 2009, https://www.npr.org/2009/01/08/99088514/lethem-updates-cult-classic-omega-comic-series.
129. Jonathan Lethem, "Novelist Jonathan Lethem on Bob Dylan's 'Mad-Scientist Audacity,'" *Rolling Stone*, December 9, 2016, https://www.rollingstone.com/music/music-features/novelist-jonathan-lethem-on-bob-dylans-mad-scientist-audacity-105901.
130. James Verini, "The Talking Heads Song that Explains Talking Heads," *The New Yorker*, June 14, 2012, https://www.newyorker.com/culture/culture-desk/the-talking-heads-song-that-explains-talking-heads.

131. Jonathan Lethem, "'They Live': Jonathan Lethem explains a cult classic," *Salon*, November 6, 2010, https://www.salon.com/2010/11/06/lethem_slide_show/.
132. Lethem's fascination with comic books and superheroes is reflected in the title of his semi-autobiographical novel *The Fortress of Solitude* (New York: Doubleday, 2003) and his short story "Super Goat Man," which was published by *The New Yorker* in the April 5, 2004 issue (https://www.newyorker.com/magazine/2019/12/30/super-goat-man).
133. The jacket copy for the 2003 paperback edition of *Gun, with Occasional Music* (New York, Houghton Mifflin Harcourt: 2003) describes the book this way: "Gumshoe Conrad Metcalf has problems—there's a rabbit in his waiting room and a trigger-happy kangaroo on his tail. Near-future Oakland is a brave new world where evolved animals are members of society, the police monitor citizens by their karma levels, and mind-numbing drugs such as Forgettol and Acceptol are all the rage."
134. Lethem, *Gun, with Occasional Music*, 8.
135. Lethem, *Gun, with Occasional Music*, 48-49, 222.
136. Jonathan Lethem, "The Dystopianist, Thinking of His Rival, Is Interrupted by a Knock on the Door," *Men and Cartoons* (New York: Doubleday, 2004), 117-118.
137. David Duchovny, *Holy Cow: A Novel*, (New York: Farrar, Straus and Giroux, 2015), 4.
138. According to one definition, "postmodern texts frequently use a stylistic device called pastiche . . . [i]t is about copying the style of other texts and putting these styles together in a playful, ironic way while disregarding the traditional rules for style and genre." "Postmodernism: Fragmentation and pastiche," *Prime Study Guides*, Prime Study Guides ApS, accessed February 22, 2023, https://primestudyguides.com/postmodernism/fragmentation-and-pastiche.
139. "The hammerspace phenomenon is basically the ability for anime characters to be able to pull objects out of thin air, without any evidence of having said objects anywhere on their person." American cartoon characters such as Bugs Bunny have utilized hammerspace since the 1940s." Frank Sanchez, "Lesson 4 - Hidden Objects: The Hammerspace Phenomenon," AnimeInfo.org, accessed February 22, 2023, https://web.archive.org/web/20061009180922/http://www.animeinfo.org/animeu/phys101-l4.html.
140. Duchovny, *Holy Cow*, "Acknowledgments."
141. Duchovny, *Holy Cow*, 58.
142. Richard Adams, *The Plague Dogs: A Novel* (New York: Fawcett Crest, 1979), 469.
143. Duchovny, *Holy Cow*, 149.
144. Humphrey Carpenter, *J. R. R. Tolkien: A Biography* (New York: HarperCollins, 1977), https://interestingliterature.com/2014/11/five-fascinating-facts-about-c-s-lewis/.
145. Natasha Hinde, "The Dinosaur Dress-Up Trend Is Spreading. Here's How It Started," Huffington Post, March 16, 2021, https://www.huffingtonpost.co.uk/entry/dinosaurs-of-plymouth_uk_604b9887c5b-6cf72d095ff0a.
146. "Ickenham Dinosaurs," Facebook Group, https://www.facebook.com/groups/1411673242511933/.
147. Barnaby Kellaway, Thomas George, "Man calls police on mum and friends dressed as dinosaurs in local park," *Manchester Evening News*, April 8, 2021, https://www.manchestereveningnews.co.uk/news/greater-manchester-news/mum-who-dressed-dinosaur-suit-20347647.
148. Natasha Hinde, "The Dinosaur Dress-Up Trend Is Spreading. Here's How It Started," Huffington Post, March 16, 2021, https://www.huffingtonpost.co.uk/entry/dinosaurs-of-plymouth_uk_604b9887c5b-6cf72d095ff0a.

149. Christian Allaire, "First Thanksgiving, Now Christmas: The Ross Family Officially Wins Holiday Style," *Vogue*, December 28, 2018, https://www.vogue.com/article/diana-tracee-ellis-ross-family-holiday-style.
150. Strike, *Furry Nation*.
151. Quartz Husky (@QuartzHusky), "Hey y'all, I've seen some of the bootleg Quartz suits around on Tik Tok and social media. If you got scammed & now have the suit its cool. Continue to enjoy your suit! If you want more uniqueness, change a few features and make your own character! Either way, I'm not offended," Twitter, August 1, 2020, 1:10 p.m., https://twitter.com/QuartzHusky/status/1289609347916423168?cxt=HHwWgICnmdG3zuUjAAAA.
152. Odin Wolf, "The MOST EXPENSIVE Furry Fursuits Ever!" YouTube Video, 16:52, January 31, 2020, https://www.youtube.com/watch?v=wba3tyrE--Q.
153. The following year, the in-demand and very high-end (and without a fancy website) Czech Republic-based suit builder Zuri Studios auctioned the number-one spot in their waiting list of future clients; it went for fifty thousand dollars. Patch O'Furr, "$50,000 FURSUIT: crypto-fueled bidding smashes auction record at The Dealers Den," Dogpatch Press, June 4, 2021, https://dogpatch.press/2021/06/04/50000-fursuit-record-dealers-den.
154. Spottacus Cheetah, email message to author, November 16, 2021.
155. Will Greenwald, "Your Smartwatch's Heart Rate Monitor Was Developed by a Furry," *PC Magazine,* June 4, 2022, https://www.pcmag.com/news/your-smartwatchs-heart-rate-monitor-was-developed-by-a-furry.
156. Spottacus Cheetah, Zoom interview with the author, April 13, 2022.
157. Further Confusion is a San Francisco-area convention, usually held in San Jose, California, in January.
158. Mary Mallory, "Hollywood Heights: George Ali, World's Greatest Animal Impersonator," *Los Angeles Daily Mirror* (Blog), November 24, 2014, https://ladailymirror.com/2014/11/24/mary-mallory-hollywood-heights-george-ali-worlds-greatest-animal-impersonator/.
159. Ibid.
160. The description of Ali's Nana head is reminiscent of ones worn by human spectators at a canine theatrical piece described in Kirsten Bakis's *Lives of the Monster Dogs* (New York: Farrar, Straus and Giroux, 1997) as "disturbingly realistic canine heads, with ears and mouths that moved awkwardly . . . operated by hidden strings and pulleys."
161. Anita Hamilton, "Oz Film Co. & 'Creature' Actor Fred Woodward," *50+ World*, Senior City Inc., January 19, 2020, https://50plusworld.com/oz-film-co-creature-actor-fred-woodward.
162. Victoria and Albert Museum, "The Story of Pantomime," accessed February 23, 2023, https://www.vam.ac.uk/articles/the-story-of-pantomime.
163. Museum summary of Photograph by Otto Van Bosch, "Charles Laurie Jnr," Victoria and Albert Museum, record created May 10, 2021, https://collections.vam.ac.uk/item/O1617598/charles-lauri-jnr-photograph-van-bosch-otto/.
164. Victoria and Albert Museum, "The Story of Pantomime."
165. "Albert Felino," *Footlight Notes* (blog), June 14, 2013, https://footlightnotes.wordpress.com/tag/animal-impersonator.
166. Fred Patten, "Theatrical Panto-animals, Part 3: History book reviews." Review of *Conquest: Story of a Theatre Family*, by Frances Fleetwood, Dogpatch Press, September 1, 2015, https://dogpatch.press/2015/09/01/panto-animals-part-3/.

167. *Arthur Hill: The Original Cowardly Lion*, Travelanche, August 4, 2019, accessed February 23, 2023 https://travsd.wordpress.com/2019/08/14/arthur-hill-the-original-cowardly-lion/.
168. *Reel Classics*, "The Wizard of Oz: The Nikko Controversy," November 8, 1998, accessed February 23, 2023, http://www.reelclassics.com/Musicals/Wizoz/wizoz-nikko.htm.
169. *Monty Python's Flying Circus*, Season 3, Episode 4, "Blood, Devastation, Death, War and Horror/Pantomime Horses." Directed by Ian MacNaughton, aired November 9,1972, on BBC.
170. Facebook, The London Pantomime Horse Race, https://www.facebook.com/pantohorserace.org.
171. A truncated audio version of the segment can be heard at https://www.youtube.com/watch?v=RZx9YBhZrZA.
172. Albert Beich and William H. Wright, *The Man in the Dog Suit: A Comedy in Three Acts from a Novel by Edwin Corle*, (New York: Dramatists Play Service, 1959).
173. Edwin Corle, *Three Ways to Mecca* (New York: Duell, Sloan and Pearce, 1947).
174. Albert Beich, the play's coauthor, scripted TV episodes (*The Flying Nun, The Perils of Pauline*) and movie comedies (*The Lieutenant Wore Skirts, The Bride Goes Wild*). A movie called *The Man in the Dog Suit* would have been a natural fit for his talents; a stage play, evidently not as much.
175. Hume Cronyn, *A Terrible Liar: A Memoir* (New York: William Morrow & Company, 1991).
176. Furrball is a small blue cat and like the rest of the *Tiny Toon* cast members is a youthful stand-in for a classic *Looney Tunes* character; Furrball is an ersatz Sylvester.
177. The Rainbow Awards are a mainstream awards competition for outstanding LGBT fiction and nonfiction.
178. *BoJack Horseman* creator Raphael Bob-Waksberg made the identical point when discussing his anthropomorphic protagonist.
179. No relation to the 1960s underground cartoonist of the same name. This Griffin, among his other work, created the long-running, multiple-Ursa Major Awards–winning web comic *Housepets*.
180. The Ursa Major Award, the Furry Writers' Guild's Cóyotl Award, and the Leo Literary Award.
181. A sculptor who specializes in fabulous works featuring bejeweled human heads on taxidermed animal bodies asked that their interview not be included in this book when they learned its title included the word "furry."
182. Kasmin Gallery, "Barry Flanagan: Kasmin Sculpture Garden," https://www.kasmingallery.com/exhibition/flanagan-kasmin-sculpture-garden/viewingroom.
183. Roberta Smith, "Barry Flanagan, British Sculptor of Sly Works, Dies at 68," Obituary, *The New York Times*, September 10, 2009, https://www.nytimes.com/2009/09/11/arts/design/11flanagan.html.
184. Paul Levy, "Barry Flanagan: Sculptor known for his distinctive giant bronzes," Obituary, *Independent*, September 4, 2009, https://www.independent.co.uk/news/obituaries/barry-flanagan-sculptor-known-for-his-distinctive-giant-bronzes-1781433.html?r=91183.
185. Jonathan Jones, "Barry Flanagan review – a hare-brained scheme that wasted three decades," *The Guardian*, March 5, 2020, https://www.theguardian.com/artanddesign/2020/mar/05/barry-flanagan-review-waddington-custot-london.
186. Amid Amidi, "The End of the Creator-Driven Era in TV Animation," *Cartoon Brew*, October 19, 2010, https://www.cartoonbrew.com/ideas-commentary/the-end-of-the-creator-driven-era-29614.html.
187. Ibid.
188. Brandon T. Snider, *The Elements of Harmony: Friendship is Magic* (New York: Little, Brown and Company, 2013), 77.

189. JH Wiki: *My Little Pony: Friendship is Magic fandom*: History/Origins (2010–2012), https://the-jh-movie-collection-official.fandom.com/wiki/My_Little_Pony:_Friendship_is_Magic_fandom#Origins_(2010%E2%80%9312), accessed February 25, 2023.
190. Brony Music Archive, "Brony Music Archive – Deleted Music Collection," Tumblr, February 18, 2015, https://bronymusicarchive.tumblr.com/.
191. Deleted Pony Songs, "Picture Perfect Pony Official Music Video Animation," YouTube Video, 3:04, March 29, 2014, https://www.youtube.com/watch?v=UIIuzXjEBLA.
192. For the most part Hasbro turned a blind eye to fan creations, but one animator's work matched the show's visual style, directorial techniques, character voices, and musical production numbers so closely that he was rewarded with a "cease and desist" letter from Hasbro's lawyers. thecianinator, "PONY.MOV movie," YouTube Video, 42:14, March 11, 2014, https://www.youtube.com/watch?v=6q8qrtUMCYY.
193. MoonShadeOsu, "[Archive] Ponies Royale – PMV by Feedsy," YouTube Video, 3:16, December 22, 2013, https://www.youtube.com/watch?v=j6uOTsksIFU.
194. "Mixermike622," *My Little Pony: Animation is Magic Wiki*, *Fandom*, created February 27, 2015, https://mlp-animation.fandom.com/wiki/Mixermike622.
195. *My Little Pony: Friendship Is Magic*, Season 5, Episode 13, "Do Princesses Dream of Magic Sheep?" Directed by Jim Miller and Jayson Thiessen, aired July 11, 2015, on Discovery Family. The episode's title is a pun on the Philip K. Dick sci-fi novel *Do Androids Dream of Electric Sheep?*, the basis for the movie *Blade Runner*.
196. Latin for "nightmare."
197. "'My Little Pony: Friendship Is Magic' Episode List," IMDB, Accessed May 24, 2023, https://www.imdb.com/title/tt1751105/episodes/?ref_=tt_ov_epl.
198. @foalpapers "The Giant My Little Pony Convention & Event Spreadsheet of Doom," Google Sheet, last updated November 9, 2022, accessed February 25, 2023, https://docs.google.com/spreadsheets/d/1smBLl_b-QL-SrsiM-O9EMkXaXHHSTe2HwngGUh5G-B3Xg/edit#gid=0.
199. In *Star Trek: The Next Generation*, de Lancie portrayed Q, a cosmic mischief maker and as a result was cast as Discord, a character inspired by his *Star Trek* role.
200. Two years later Discovery Kids premiered a new iteration of the franchise, creating even more episodes.
201. "The mythical minotaur—part man, part bull—was Picasso's alter ego in the 1930s and part of a broader exploration of Classicism that persisted in his work for many years. The minotaur was also emblematic for Surrealists, who saw it as the personification of forbidden desires. For Picasso it expressed complex emotions at a time of personal turmoil. The minotaur symbolized lasciviousness, violence, guilt, and despair." Gallery label for *Minotaur Ravishing a Female Centaur (Minotaure amoureux d'une femme-centaure)*, state III, from the *Vollard Suite (Suite Vollard)*, 1933, published 1939 by Pablo Picasso. In exhibition *Picasso: Variations and Themes*, at the Museum of Modern Art, New York, March 28–September 30, 2010, https://www.moma.org/collection/works/64803.
202. "Chagall's sense of identification with goats is a well-known aspect of his art." Simon Abrahams, "Chagall as an Animal (20th Century)," *Every Painter Paints Himself* (blog), September 8, 2011, https://www.everypainterpaintshimself.com/article/chagall_as_an_animal_early_20th_century.

203. Yago Partal, Creature Portraits, accessed March 19, 2023, https://www.yagopartal.com/collections/yago-partal-for-creatures-united.
204. *TimeOut London* used Partal's portrait of a pigeon dressed like a maître d' on the cover of their "Cheap Eats" issue, likely due to the birds' diet of bird seed and breadcrumbs. The magazine also created a series of posters advertising their publication using Partal's creations speculating on the kind of "people" who might read its magazine: is a bug-eyed Sunda slow loris a "film fanatic?" Perhaps it's the animal's wide-eyed look. Is a ring-tailed lemur in disheveled clothing a "party animal?" Well, they do live in groups with as many as thirty members grooming one another. (https://www.nationalgeographic.com/animals/mammals/facts/ring-tailed-lemur, accessed February 27, 2023.)
205. Daniel Rolnik, "Anthony Ausgang Interview," *Fecal Face*, January 7, 2011, http://www.fecalface.com/SF/features-main-menu-102/2650-anthony-ausgang-interview.
206. Although *Hi-Fructose* (hifructose.com) describes itself as a magazine covering "New Contemporary Art," Wikipedia redirects searches for it to their "Lowbrow (Art Movement)" page. Several years ago I picked up a copy of *Hi-Fructose*. Out of its 121 pages of articles and ads, seventeen artists' work included anthropomorphic characters. That same issue of *Hi-Fructose* featured "ironic riffs" on Charlie Brown, Ronald McDonald, Casper the Friendly Ghost, and Chiclets chewing gum
207. Rolnik, "Anthony Ausgang Interview."
208. Kirsten Anderson, "Anthony Ausgang's MGMT album art," Interview with Anthony Ausgang for *Boing Boing*, February 17, 2010, https://boingboing.net/2010/02/17/anthony-ausgangs-mgm.html.
209. Although DeviantArt is a general art site and not specifically a furry one, there's no shortage of furry art to be found there.
210. The company's first public appearance was at Anthrocon 2008. In 2012 the convention banned the sale of adult items.
211. A social media platform hosting numerous servers devoted to various topics.
212. Marina Abramović, *The Artist is Present*, Performance, Museum of Modern Art, 2010, https://www.moma.org/learn/moma_learning/marina-abramovic-marina-abramovic-the-artist-is-present-2010.
213. "Hermann Nitsch," Artist page, *Artnet Magazine,* accessed February 28, 2023, https://www.artnet.com/artists/hermann-nitsch.
214. R. Corbett, "Philip Roth Tells Artist to Stop the Show," *Artnet Magazine*, April 3, 2012, http://www.artnet.com/magazineus/news/artnetnews/philip-roth-bryan-zanisnik.asp.
215. "About," Humanimal Entertainment (website), accessed June 22, 2022, https://www.humanimal.london/about.
216. "Home," Jason Wolfman Martin (website), accessed March 14, 2023, jasonwolfman.com.
217. "Power Animal System," Facebook page, accessed March 14, 2023, https://www.facebook.com/poweranimalsystems.
218. Morgan Y. Evans, "Interview: Jason Martin's Witchy Wolf Grrrl Power & Power Animal System," *New Noise* magazine, August 19, 2016, https://newnoisemagazine.com/interviews/interview-jason-martin-power-animal-system/.
219. Martin's website features a variety of his solo pieces, performing in drag, high heels, and various wigs over his power animal face while playing guitar or dancing.

220. See: *FREE!LOVE!TOOL!BOX!*, Exhibition, Yerba Buena Center for the Arts, October 12, 2012–January 27, 2013 (e-flux.com/announcements/33616/nayland-blake/); *Hare Attitudes*, Exhibition, Contemporary Arts Museum Houston, January 12, 1996–February 25, 1996 (camh.org/event/nayland-blake-hare-attitudes/); and several pieces held by the Whitney Museum of American art including *Negative Bunny*, Video, color, sound, 30 min. looped, 1994 and *The Little One*, Sculpture, porcelain, nylon, and silk, 1994 (whitney.org/artists/4014).
221. Elisa Wouk Almino, "Meet Nayland Blake's 'Fursona' at the New Museum," *Hyperallergic*, October 3, 2017, https://hyperallergic.com/403596/nayland-blake-gnomen-performance-new-museum/.
222. Christopher Knight, "Review: Nayland Blake turns bunnies and shoes into meditations on sex, power and prejudice," Exhibition review of "No Wrong Holes: Thirty Years of Nayland Blake" at the Institute of Contemporary Art, Los Angeles, *Los Angeles Times*, November 30, 2019, https://www.latimes.com/entertainment-arts/story/2019-11-30/nayland-blake-ica-la.
223. ARTnews (@artnews), "Nayland Blake has long used bunnies in their work as a metaphor to examine stereotypes around black and queer communities…" Instagram post, January 18, 2020, https://www.instagram.com/p/B7dq1S0DhO8/.
224. Nayland Blake, *Birthday Present*, Stuffed toys, 1993. See *Artnet*, https://www.artnet.com/artists/nayland-blake/birthday-present-nGTNxkee-Ma0Yt-CuiAsFg2.
225. "Art Meta Official," Facebook, https://www.facebook.com/artmetaofficial.
226. Carolina A. Miranda, "L.A. Artist toys with race and queerness, plus a bunny suit," *Los Angeles Times*, September 30, 2019, https://www.latimes.com/entertainment-arts/story/2019-09-30/artist-nayland-blake-race-queer-life-gingerbread.
227. "Nayland Blake," National Black Justice Coalition, February 5, 2018, https://beenhere.org/2018/02/05/nayland-blake/.
228. "No Wrong Holes: Thirty Years of Nayland Blake," Exhibition, Institute of Contemporary Art, Los Angeles, October 16, 2020 – January 3, 2021, https://www.theicala.org/en/exhibitions/67-no-wrong-holes-br-thirty-years-of-nayland-blake.
229. Lora Morinis, "Nayland Blake," Hammer Museum, Los Angeles, Accessed March 1, 2023, https://hammer.ucla.edu/take-it-or-leave-it/artists/nayland-blake.
230. Jonathan Alexander, "Getting Hard with Nayland Blake: On the Artist's Recent Retrospective in Los Angeles," Review of "No Wrong Holes" exhibition, Institute of Contemporary Art, Los Angeles, *LA Review of Books*, March 7, 2020, https://lareviewofbooks.org/article/getting-hard-with-nayland-blake-on-the-artists-recent-retrospective-in-los-angeles/.
231. Coco Romack, "An Artist's Personal Museum in Brooklyn," *T: The New York Times Style Magazine*, October 14, 2019, https://www.nytimes.com/2019/10/14/t-magazine/nayland-blake.html.
232. Nayland Blake, *Heavenly Bunny Suit*, Nylon with metal armature, 1994. Final sales price per Matthew Marks Gallery. See https://www.artsy.net/artwork/nayland-blake-heavenly-bunny-suit.

233. Coates videotaped people mimicking slowed-down recordings of bird cries, then sped up the recordings to match the original bird cries; the sped-up videos became part of a multi-screen video installation. *Dawn Chorus*, 14 or 7 channel video installation, 18 min. loop, 2007, https://www.marcuscoates.co.uk/projects/68-dawn-chorus.

234. Coates arranged for seven naturalists for each of seven naturalists to take on the role birds and talk about their lives as that species. *Conference for the Birds*, National Trust and Mapping Art in the Heritage Experience, Newcastle University, 2019, https://www.marcuscoates.co.uk/projects/172-conference-for-the-birds.

235. A multi-artist show exploring the human-animal relationship. *The Human* Zoo, Exhibition, The Hatton Gallery, Newcastle, U.K., June 27, 2003 – August 23, 2003, http://1995-2015.undo.net/it/mostra/14984.

236. Rosemarie McGoldrick (Curator), *The Animal Gaze*, Multi-Artist Exhibition, Plymouth City Museum and Art Gallery, February 12, 2009–March 22, 2009, https://mirrorplymouth.com/whats-on/the-animal-gaze.

237. Marcus Coates, *Dawn Chorus*, 14 or 7 channel video installation, 18 min. loop, 2007, https://www.marcuscoates.co.uk/projects/68-dawn-chorus.

238. Marcus Coates, *Journey to the Lower World*, 2 channel video installation, Walker Art Gallery, Liverpool, UK, 2004, https://www.liverpoolmuseums.org.uk/artifact/journey-lower-world.

239. Ibid.

240. Marcus Coates, *Stoat*, Single channel digital video, 3 minutes, Workplace Gallery, London, UK, 1999, https://www.workplacegallery.co.uk/artists/9-marcus-coates/works/132/.

241. Marcus Coates, *Goshawk (Self-portrait)*, Silver gelatin print, 1999, https://www.marcuscoates.co.uk/projects/31-goshawk-self-portrait.

242. Marcus Coates, *Finfolk*, Digital Video, 2003, https://www.marcuscoates.co.uk/projects/46-finfolk.

243. Selkies are mythical beings capable of shedding their human skin to become seals.

244. Marcus Coates, *Conference for the Birds*, National Trust and Mapping Art in the Heritage Experience, Newcastle University, 2019, https://www.marcuscoates.co.uk/projects/172-conference-for-the-birds.

245. Portions of this work are included in a video profile of Coates by the British Council Arts. "In Conversation: Marcus Coates," YouTube video, 6:36, January 17, 2014, https://www.youtube.com/watch?v=LErNGrBC-Bw.

246. In Charles Foster's *Being a Beast: Adventures Across the Species Divide* (New York: Metropolitan Books/Henry Holt and Company, 2016), the author attempted to literally live as an animal: sleeping in a burrow, eating worms, trying to catch a fish with his teeth while swimming like an otter, etc.

247. "Marcus Coates," *Frieze*, June 6, 2007, https://www.frieze.com/article/marcus-coates.

248. Rob Roth, *Craig's Dream*, Performance. http://www.rob-roth.com/portfolio/craigs-dream/#main.

249. Rob Roth, *Click + Drag*, Performance, 1996. https://www.rob-roth.com/portfolio/click-drag/#main.

250. William Van Meter, "Remembering Web 1.0's Click + Drag Subculture," The Cut, April 24, 2015, https://www.thecut.com/2015/04/remembering-web-10s-click-drag-subculture.html.

251. Genesis P-Orridge was an androgynous musician, performance artist, and founder of the rock group Throbbing Gristle.

252. Mark Hudson, "Return of the teatime terror," *The Telegraph*, March 30, 2002, https://www.telegraph.co.uk/culture/tvandradio/3575363/Return-of-the-teatime-terror.html.

253. John Guy Collick, "The Singing Ringing Tree," *John Guy Collick* (Blog), April 30, 2013, http://johnguycollick.com/the-singing-ringing-tree/.
254. Tate, "Mark Wallinger | Turner Prize Winner 2007 | TateShots," YouTube Video, 3:43, August 7, 2008, https://www.youtube.com/watch?v=kTWP3T5GJmo.
255. British bookmakers actually place odds on which submission will win the prestigious competition, which comes with a £25,000 award. The idea of the general American public doing likewise—betting money on the possible winner of a fine arts competition—is beyond imagination.
256. Waldemar Januszczak, "There will be no miracles here," *The Sunday Times*, October 28, 2007, https://www.thetimes.co.uk/article/there-will-be-no-miracles-here-ll2cxgz8mxw.
257. Adrian Searle, "Opinion: Wallinger deserved to win the Turner prize," *The Guardian*, December 3, 2007, https://www.theguardian.com/artanddesign/artblog/2007/dec/04/icantthinkofabetterwinne.
258. Dalya Alberge, "Bear faced cheek wins the Turner (and a Michelangelo compliment)," *The Times*, December 4, 2007, https://www.thetimes.co.uk/article/bear-faced-cheek-wins-the-turner-and-a-michelangelo-compliment-9j9kwwsrx6p.
259. Charlotte Higgins, "Bear man walks away with Turner Prize," *The Guardian*, December 3, 2007, https://www.theguardian.com/artanddesign/2007/dec/03/art.turnerprize20071.
260. Chris Wiegand, "Reviews roundup: Turner prize 2007," *The Guardian*, December 4, 2007, https://www.theguardian.com/artanddesign/2007/dec/04/turnerprize2007.turnerprize"Research Findings: 10.3 Bullying," Furscience (website), accessed May 30, 2023, https://furscience.com/research-findings/disclosure-stigma-bullying/10-3-bullying/.
261. "Research Findings: 10.3 Bullying," Furscience (website), accessed May 30, 2023, https://furscience.com/research-findings/disclosure-stigma-bullying/10-3-bullying/.
262. Elle Hunt, "Milo Yiannopoulos book deal cancelled after outrage over child abuse comments," *The Guardian*, February 21, 2017, https://www.theguardian.com/books/2017/feb/21/milo-yiannopoulos-book-deal-cancelled-outrage-child-abuse-comments.
263. Kari Paul and Jim Waterson, "Facebook bans Alex Jones, Milo Yiannopoulos and other far-right figures," *The Guardian*, May 2, 2019, https://www.theguardian.com/technology/2019/may/02/facebook-ban-alex-jones-milo-yiannopoulos.
264. Shamim Adam, "Conservative Commentator Milo Yiannopoulos Not Allowed in Australia After New Zealand Mosque Shooting Comments," *Time*, March 16, 2019, https://time.com/5552976/milo-yiannopoulos-banned-australia/.
265. Jared Holt, "Furry Convention Shows Milo Yiannopoulos the Door," *Right Wing Watch*, September 16, 2019, https://www.rightwingwatch.org/post/milo-adopts-fursona-but-furries-say-no-thanks/.
266. Jack Crosbie, "Milo Yiannopoulos Tries to Break Into the World of Furries, Is Brutally Rejected," *Splinter News*, September 16, 2019, https://splinternews.com/desperately-broke-milo-yiannopoulos-tries-to-break-into-1838148262?utm_medium=sharefromsite&utm_source=splinter_twitter&utm_campaign=top.
267. Furry Raiders (@Furry_Raiders), "The Furry Fandom will always be a open and free place to express yourself. We're happy to welcome Milo Yiannopoulos to the Furry Fandom and the Furry Raiders. #theycantbanusall," Twitter, September 15, 2019, 3:47 p.m., https://twitter.com/Furry_Raiders/status/1173322482033389568.

268. "Furry Raiders Armbands," *Furry Raiders* online shop, accessed March 2, 2023, https://furryraiders.org/products/furry-raiders-armbands.
269. Eric Killela, "Does the Furry Community Have a Nazi Problem?," *Rolling Stone*, April 14, 2017, https://www.rollingstone.com/culture/culture-features/does-the-furry-community-have-a-nazi-problem-194282/.
270. Starfoxacefox, Comment on YouTube video "Hitler Speeches with Accurate English Subtitles," January 13, 2014.
271. "Mission Statement," *Furry Raiders* (website), accessed March 2, 2023, https://furryraiders.org/pages/about-us.
272. Ibid.
273. Kelly Weill, "Neo-Nazis Are Tearing the Furry World Apart," *The Daily Beast*, May 5, 2017, https://www.thedailybeast.com/neo-nazis-are-tearing-apart-the-furry-world.
274. Denver did not have to go long without a furry convention. In 2018 "DenFur" replaced RMFC, attracting close to twenty-one hundred attendees to its premiere iteration.
275. Kameron Dunn, "What's Going On With Those Furry Nazis?," Slate, November 18, 2021, https://slate.com/human-interest/2021/11/nazi-furries-deradicalization-efforts.html.
276. Free Fur All, https://awooassociation.net/.
277. Patch O'Furr, "2 Uncool – a furry celebrity's disgrace is a test of fandom tolerance," Dogpatch Press, March 20, 2017, https://dogpatch.press/2017/03/20/disgrace-of-a-furry-celebrity/.
278. Free Fur All, AWOO Association, Application, https://awooassociation.org/application/notice.
279. Ibid.
280. Estimates of attendance at Free Fur All's inaugural July 2022 convention ranged from a meager eighty to a less than overwhelming two hundred and seven. (See Kelsey Weekman, "Furries Are Speaking Out Against Attendees of a Convention with Ties to the Far Right," BuzzFeed News, August 5, 2022, https://www.buzzfeednews.com/article/kelseyweekman/furry-free-fur-all-convention-backlash; Acton Rand Shafer, "A Little Furcon That Said No," *Acton's Hermitage* (Blog), September 1, 2022, https://www.asinglelion.com/actonhe/?tag=free-fur-all-2022.) Apparently Free Fur All's 2023 convention will not be for "all;" its *Top Gun*-themed website ("Free Fur All/Be My Wingman") boasts they "established an elite convention for the top 1 percent of anthro fans, and to insure that the handful of men and women who attended were the best anthros in the world." https://awooassociation.net/freefurall, accessed March 2, 2023.
281. Sky News Australia, "Students at elite Brisbane school have 'jumped' onto the 'new furries trend,'" YouTube Video, 2:12, March 20, 2022, https://www.youtube.com/watch?v=AzsJc1_NiJ4.
282. Patch O'Furr, "Origins of an urban legend: 'litter boxes for furries' joke gets revived for moral panic," Dogpatch Press, January 31, 2022, https://dogpatch.press/2022/01/31/urban-legend-litter-boxes/.
283. Ibid.
284. Tracing Woodgrains, "How I Convinced Libs of TikTok to Publish a False Story," *Blocked and Reported*, April 29, 2022, https://www.blockedandreported.org/p/how-i-convinced-libs-of-tiktok-to.

285. Matt Walsh (@MattWalshBlog), "The left are such degenerate psycho perverts that the story was completely plausible and nothing about it rang false at all. Not exactly something to gloat about if you're on the left," Twitter, April 26, 2022, 8:14 p.m., https://twitter.com/MattWalshBlog/status/1519107606014537732?s=20&t=t1nAqf-7wa431ecbBMVbR9A.

286. BK007, "Ylvis talks about their cult hit The Fox – London interview," YouTube Video, 4:12, November 20, 2013, https://www.youtube.com/watch?v=G1rOX4xblAQ.

287. Amanda Walgrove, "Vegard Ylvisåker from Ylvis Reveals the Story Behind 'The Fox' YouTube Sensation," *What's Trending*, September 8, 2013, https://whatstrending.com/6344-vegard-ylvisaker-from-ylvis-reveals-the-story-be/.

288. "'What Does the Fox Say?' FOX COSTUMES EXPLODE . . . Thanks to Viral Video," *TMZ*, EHM Productions, Inc., October 18, 2013, https://www.tmz.com/2013/10/18/what-does-the-fox-say-costumes-halloween-viral-video/.

289. Screen Junkies, "Morgan Freeman Reads The Fox by Ylvis," YouTube Video, October 24, 2013, 4:35, https://youtu.be/jXSYybCVxVM?t=51.

290. Subwoolfer, "Subwoolfer – Give That Wolf A Banana (Official Music Video)," YouTube Video, January 10, 2022, 2:52, https://www.youtube.com/watch?v=sDvXhZtcp0w.

291. Renske Ten Veen, "Norway: Are Ylvis behind Subwoolfer's Melodi Grand Prix 2022 entry?" wiwibloggs, January 10, 2022, https://wiwibloggs.com/2022/01/10/norway-are-ylvis-behind-subwoolfers-melodi-grand-prix-2022-entry/.

292. Elizabeth Aubrey, "The true identity of Norway's 2022 Eurovision entry Subwoolfer has been revealed," *NME*, February 4, 2023, https://www.nme.com/news/music/the-true-identity-of-norways-2022-eurovision-entry-subwoolfer-has-been-revealed-3392202.

293. Corinne Cumming, "Norway: Subwoolfer complete a mission millions of years in the making," *Eurovision.tv*, European Broadcasting Union, May 5, 2022, https://eurovision.tv/story/subwoolfer-norway-22.

294. "Timeline: 1996–1998," Robbie Williams Official Website, accessed March 2, 2023, https://robbiewilliams.com/pages/timeline.

295. Capital Cities, "Capital Cities – Kangaroo Court (Behind the Scenes)," YouTube Video, September 5, 2013, 5:22, https://youtu.be/tY3B82MOM3A?t=182.

296. Ibid.

297. OldSchool80s, "Flashback Video: 'Opposites Attract' by Paula Abdul," 80sxchange.com (blog), RBG Creative LLC., April 19, 2021, https://www.80sxchange.com/post/flashback-video-opposites-attract-by-paula-abdul.

298. Slumberland Records, "The Paints of Being Pure At Heart – 'Higher Than The Stars,'" YouTube Video, May 13, 2010, 3:48, https://www.youtube.com/watch?v=I4yhyNgr0jo.

299. "Higher Than the Stars," wikifur.com, November 24, 2015, https://en.wikifur.com/wiki/Higher_Than_The_Stars.

300. Dorian Electra, "Dorian Electra – My Agenda (Official Video)," November 4, 2021, 2:52, https://www.youtube.com/watch?v=lq9P-JsS3-EY.

301. Hannah Boast, "Theorizing the Gay Frog," *Environmental Humanities*, 14 No. 3, (November 2022): 661–679, doi. https://doi.org/10.1215/22011919-9962959.

302. "@BlueFolf" has since deleted his original tweet that began the discussion. Skittles (@Skittles), "Skittles fursona art contest?" Twitter, December 7, 2021, 10:07 p.m., https://twitter.com/Skittles/status/1468416924132511746?lang=en.
303. Allie Capps, "Skittles may have bitten off more than it can chew after inspiring furry art contest," *We Got This Covered*, December 10, 2021, https://wegotthiscovered.com/news/skittles-may-have-bitten-off-more-than-it-can-chew-after-inspiring-furry-art-contest/.
304. Oliver Balch, "Mars, Nestlé and Hershey to face child slavery lawsuit in US," *The Guardian*, February 12, 2021, https://www.theguardian.com/global-development/2021/feb/12/mars-nestle-and-hershey-to-face-landmark-child-slavery-lawsuit-in-us.
305. Col. Boozy Badger (@BoozyBadger) December 8, 2021, https://twitter.com/BoozyBadger/status/1468699381281001472.
306. Zeiros Lion (@ZeirosLion), Twitter message to author, May 27, 2022.
307. Sonioius (Tantroo McNally), "Shoe ad drops - gets furries to 'converse' about marketing and fandom," *Flayrah*, July 20, 2019, https://www.flayrah.com/7669/shoe-ad-drops-gets-furries-converse-about-marketing-and-fandom.
308. Ibid.
309. Joseph Longo, "No, Furries Don't Want to Fuck The Masked Singer (Any of Them)," *MEL Magazine*, accessed March 5, 2022, https://melmagazine.com/en-us/story/no-furries-dont-want-to-fuck-the-masked-singer-any-of-them.
310. Broderick, "FYI, Even Furries Think The "Cats" Trailer Looks Bad."
311. Riley Black, "I'm a Furry. Netflix's *Sexy Beasts* Misses the Entire Point of Dressing Up Like an Animal," Slate, July 22, 2021, https://slate.com/human-interest/2021/07/furry-sexy-beasts-costumes-netflix-mistakes.html.
312. Donald Trump Jr., (@donaldjtrumpjr) "#easter," Instagram post, April 17, 2022, https://www.instagram.com/p/Ccdr2FwlerO/?utm_source=ig_embed&ig_rid=-91d1a616-b5e1-40b9-93b4-d552ea4adf07.
313. Monstersoftalk, "Monsters of Talk: Margaret Cho at the Furries Convention," YouTube Video, September 9, 2013, 5:42, https://www.youtube.com/watch?v=kKC_TCDRFkY.
314. Patch O'Furr, "Margaret Cho barks about furries, pride, and costuming on *The Masked Singer*," Interview with Margaret Cho, Dogpatch Press, January 30, 2019, https://dogpatch.press/2019/01/30/margaret-cho-masked-singer.
315. auri (@woah_its_auri), "remember when andrew wk was a furry?" Twitter, July 15, 2018, 9:22 a.m., https://twitter.com/woah_its_auri/status/1018485891453636609.
316. Psychopathic Records, "Snakebusters Episode 1," YouTube Video, July 9, 2018, 4:32, https://www.youtube.com/watch?v=HNS-BIMLs96M.
317. Patch O'Furr, "Jello Biafra's Incredibly Strange Interview and dance party with furries: San Francisco, 12/1/18," Interview with Jello Biafra, Dogpatch Press, November 12, 2018, https://dogpatch.press/2018/11/12/jello-biafra-dance-party-furries/.
318. *The Daily Show*, Season 14, Episode 159, "Sigourney Weaver." Directed by Chuck O'Neil, aired December 14, 2009, on Comedy Central.
319. *The Simpsons*, Season 19, Episode 17, "Apocalypse Cow." Directed by Mike B. Anderson, Mark Kirkland, and Nancy Kruse, aired April 27, 2008, on Fox.
320. *Turning Red*, directed by Domee Shi (Disney, 2022), 1 hr, 40 min.
321. The "inspirational" poster, whose original artist and source is unknown, depicts Miss Kitty shaking her caboose.

322. Zanandi Botes, "4 Ways Disney Managed To Aggressively Raise A Generation Of Furries," *Cracked,* Literally Media Ltd., May 21, 2022, https://www.cracked.com/article_33996_4-ways-disney-managed-to-aggressively-raise-a-generation-of-furries.html.

323. Katie Notopoulos, "18 Times The Fox in 'Robin Hood' Was Weirdly Hot," BuzzFeed, May 4, 2015, https://www.buzzfeed.com/katienotopoulos/the-fox-in-robin-hood-is-hot-af-tbqh.

324. E. J. Dickson, "Furries Reallllllly Hate Lindsay Lohan's Furry NFT," *Rolling Stone*, September 30, 2021, https://www.rollingstone.com/culture/culture-news/lindsay-lohan-furry-nft-1235298/.

325. Edward Ongweso Jr., "NFT Collector Sells People's Fursonas for $100K In Right-Click Mindset War," Vice, November 18, 2021, https://www.vice.com/en/article/pkpbay/nft-collector-sells-peoples-fursonas-for-dollar100k-in-right-click-mindset-war.

326. Megan Liscomb, "Lindsay Lohan's Fursona and 12 More Weird and Wild Celebrity NFT Projects from 2021," BuzzFeed, December 20, 2021, https://www.buzzfeed.com/meganeliscomb/celebrity-nfts-2021.

327. Tatiana Tenreyro, "The furries aren't here for Lindsay Lohan's fursona NFT," *AV Club*, October 1, 2021, https://www.avclub.com/the-furries-arent-here-for-lindsay-lohans-fursona-nft-1847782531.

328. Matt Baume, "Psychology Professor Explains Why Furries Are So Unhappy about Lindsay Lohan's Fursona," *The Stranger*, Index Newspapers LLC, October 7, 2021, https://www.thestranger.com/slog/2021/10/07/61753550/heres-the-science-behind-why-furries-hate-lindsay-lohans-furry-nft.

329. Daniel Van Boom, "Bored Ape Yacht Club NFTs Explained," *CNET*, August 11, 2022, https://www.cnet.com/culture/internet/bored-ape-yacht-club-nfts-explained/.

330. "Welcome to the Bored Ape Yacht Club," Bored Ape Yacht Club, accessed March 3, 2023, https://boredapeyachtclub.com/#/home.

331. "Welcome to Lazy Lions Private Island," Lazy Lions, accessed March 3, 2023, https://www.lazylionsnft.com/.

332. Ibid.

333. "What's a Furry?" Furscience (website), accessed March 3, 2023, https://furscience.com/whats-a-furry/.

334. "Greymuzzles (30 and older furs only)," Facebook Group page, created February 24, 2012, https://www.facebook.com/groups/242876589134127.

335. Kylie Robison, "Furries are developing vaccines, building your favorite apps, and crashing Microsoft meetings. The inside story of how one of the web's oldest communities became a force to be reckoned with in the tech industry," *Business Insider*, March 11, 2022, https://www.businessinsider.com/furry-fandom-big-tech-software-developers-2022-3.

336. Chris Stokel-Walker, "This furry scientist won't let Twitter's COVID pessimists kill her vibe," Input magazine, June 2, 2021, https://www.inputmag.com/features/furry-scientist-vaccines-chise-covid-19-twitter-controversy.

337. Chise (@sailorrooscout), "Encouraging news! Moderna's Omicron bivalent booster vaccine candidate, mRNA-1273.214, demonstrated potent neutralizing titers against Omicron BA.4 and BA.5 in ALL participants REGARDLESS of prior infection! This IS the LEAD Fall 2022 booster candidate. Let's talk about that!" Twitter, June 22, 2022, 11:05 a.m., https://twitter.com/sailorrooscout/status/1539625566353195008, posted June 21, 2022.

338. Chise (@sailorrooscout), "To help clear up some confusion. If you test positive for SARS-COV-2 after being vaccinated and are experiencing mild symptoms or even no symptoms at all? Your vaccine worked. No, it did not fail. Very few vaccines (if any, for that matter) provide 100% sterilizing immunity," Twitter, May 13, 2022, 11:00 a.m., https://twitter.com/sailorrooscout/status/1525128877462507524.

339. MeepsKitten, "I'm Going to Space (Not Clickbait)," YouTube Video, November 23, 2021, 9:17, https://www.youtube.com/watch?v=10qQeCCe3xw.

340. SonicFox @ Vancouver (@SonicFox), "I'm gonna try on jewelry, Ima try piercings, etc etc, the whole nine yards! I wanna completely overhaul how I generally present myself to the world, and have this new attire that I think feels right. To really express the true -me-. Tldr im finna get some drip," Twitter, September 3, 2019, 11:48 a.m., https://twitter.com/SonicFox/status/1168913597369593856.

341. Kerry Neville, "How the Furry Community Became a Safe Space for Youth," Vice, August 3, 2017, https://www.vice.com/en/article/bjmq9d/how-the-furry-community-became-a-safe-space-for-youth.

Cover of the first issue of *Albedo Anthropomorphics*, the first furry comic book, 1983. Courtesy of Steve Gallacci.

Poster for a furry party in England. Courtesy of Merlino/O'Riley.

Program cover for ConFurence Zero, the first furry convention, 1989. Courtesy of Merlino/O'Riley.

Art for the second AussieCon Art Show. Courtesy of Craig Hilton.

Promotional image for the 2018 Super Furry Fusion conference in Shanghai. Courtesy of Shanghai Tanmoe Culture Co., Ltd.

Group photo from China's 2022 Once Upon a Fur Con. Courtesy of OUFC.

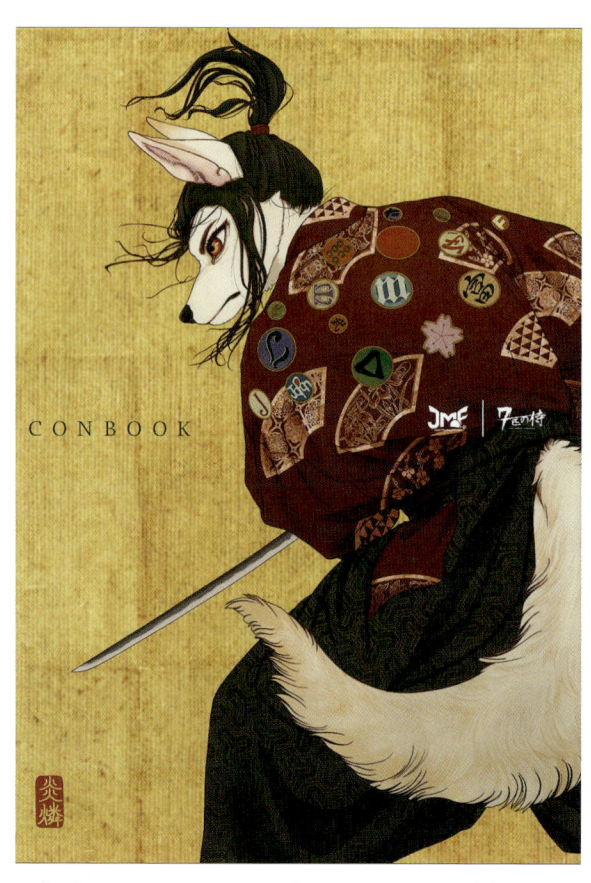

Conference book cover for the 2022 Japan Meeting of Furries. Courtesy of the JMoF Executive Committee.

Art for the 2015 Rusfurence. Courtesy of Dmitry Prokhorov.

Warren Wolfy in a fursuit and as an avatar. Courtesy of Warren Wolfy.

An image transformed by Liassur's filter. Courtesy of Liassur.

Spottacus Cheetah in a custom fursuit. Courtesy of Spottacus Cheetah.

Spottacus Cheetah in a custom fursuit. Courtesy of Spottacus Cheetah.

The author wearing part of his fursuit. Courtesy of the author.

Photograph by Oliver Coombes of the author as his fursona, Komos.
Photograph courtesy of Oliver Coombes and the author.

"Scene from the New Classic Burlesque of 'The Birds of Aristophanes,' at the Haymarket Theatre" by Robinson Planche. This illustration first appeared in the *Illustrated London News* in 1846.

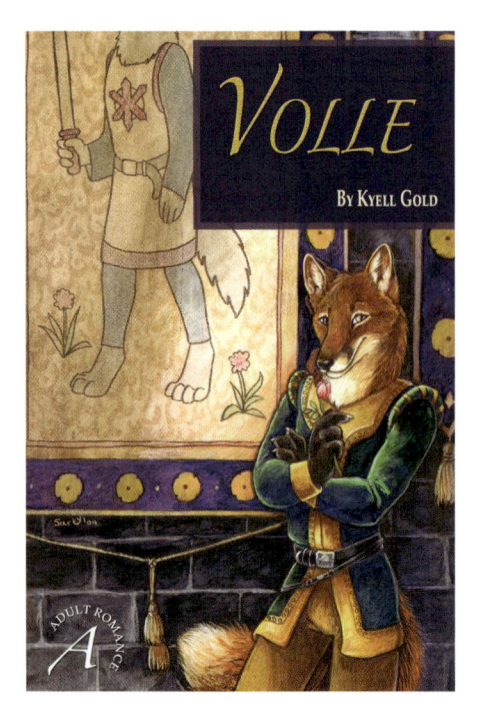

Cover art by Sara Miles for Kyell Gold's furry novel *Volle*. Courtesy of Sofawolf Press and Kyell Gold.

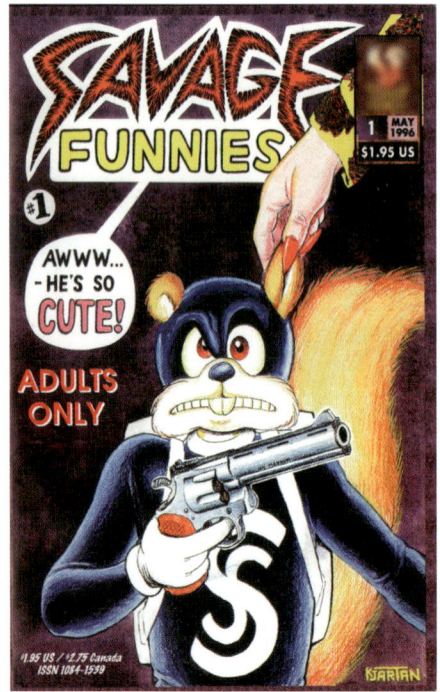

Cover art for a 1996 issue of *Savage Funnies* by Kjartan Arnorsson (Karno). Courtesy of Kjartan Arnorsson.

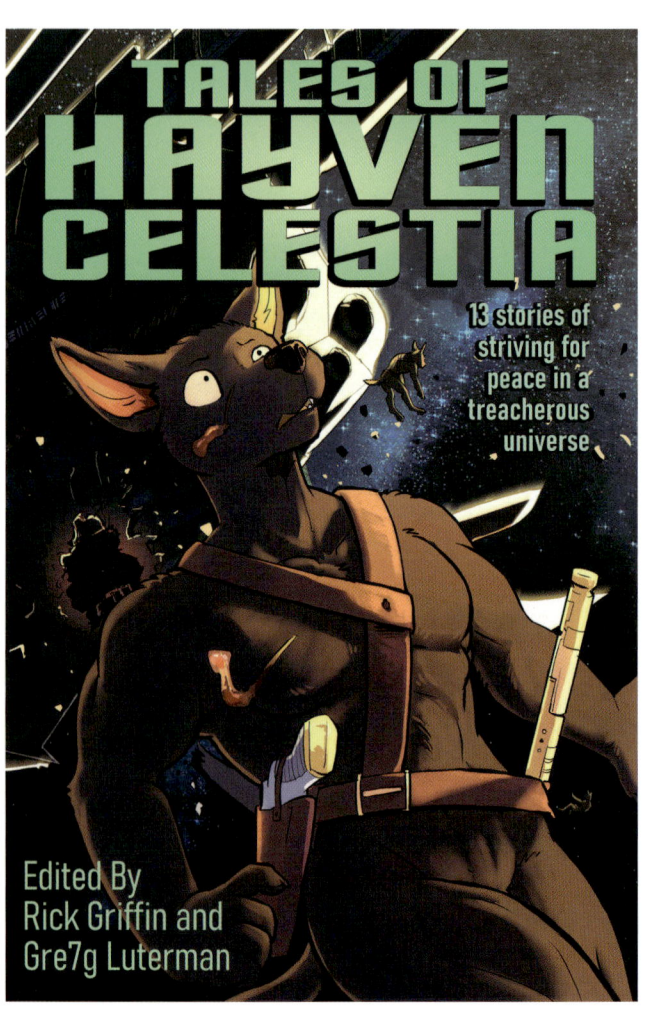

Cover art for *Tales of Hayven Celestia* edited by Rick Griffin and Gre7g Luterman. Courtesy of Gre7g Luterman.

Why did the dinosaurs cross the road? The Dinosaurs and Friends of Plymouth (UK). Courtesy of Dawn Lapthorn.

Photograph by Andreas Paulsson of Margit Brudnin's 2018 ceramic sculpture "Sit Beside Me." Courtesy of Andreas Paulsson.

Photograph by Andreas Paulsson of Margit Brundin's 2019 ceramic sculpture "Silent Conversation." Courtesy of Andreas Paulsson.

Sophie Ryder's "Girl with Knees Up" galvanized wire sculpture, 2020. ©MMXXIII Sophie Ryder – All Rights Reserved, www.sophieryder.com.

Dr. Pickelle's "Ash the Dragoness." Courtesy of Dr. Pickelle.

Artwork by Dr. Pickelle. Courtesy of Dr. Pickelle.

Anthony Ausgang's "Get Up and Go!" painting, 2010. Courtesy of Anthony Ausgang.

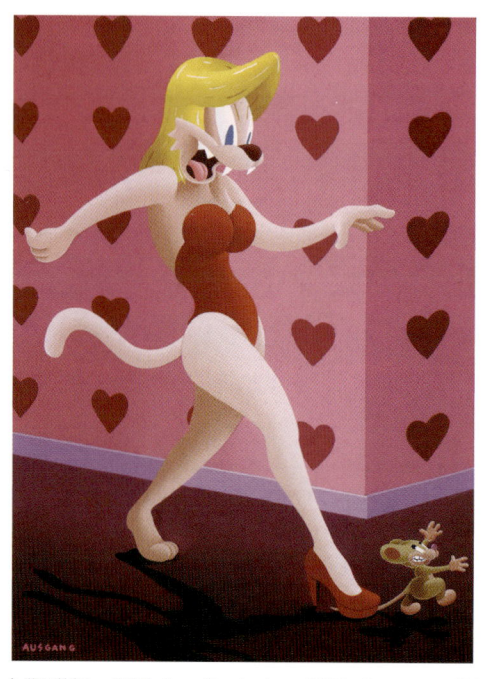

Anthony Ausgang's "Kill 'Em With Love" painting, 2003. Courtesy of Anthony Ausgang.

Stigmata's illustration "Fitness Goals." Courtesy of Stigmata.

Left: Heather Bruton's "Legendaries Tigress" artwork. Courtesy of Heather Bruton.
Right: "Power Animal System," multimedia performance project by artist Jason Martin. Courtesy of Jason Martin.

Photograph of Rob Roth's performance art character Craig. Courtesy of Rob Roth.